# Raspberry Pi for Secret Agents

*Third Edition*

**Turn your Raspberry Pi into a secret agent toolbox with this set of exciting projects**

**Matthew Poole**

**[PACKT]** open source*
PUBLISHING    community experience distilled

BIRMINGHAM - MUMBAI

# Raspberry Pi for Secret Agents

*Third Edition*

First published: April 2013

Second edition: January 2015

Third edition: July 2016

Production reference: 1210716

Published by Packt Publishing Ltd.
Livery Place
35 Livery Street
Birmingham
B3 2PB, UK.
ISBN 978-1-78646-354-8

www.packtpub.com

Cover image by Connecting Objects (`connectingobjects.com`)

# Credits

**Author**

Matthew Poole

**Reviewer**

Jon Witts

**Commissioning Editor**

Kartikey Pandey

**Acquisition Editor**

Tushar Gupta

**Content Development Editor**

Trusha Shriyan

**Technical Editor**

Rupali R. Shrawane

**Copy Editor**

Safis Editing

**Project Coordinator**

Kinjal Bari

**Proofreader**

Safis Editing

**Indexer**

Tejal Daruwale Soni

**Production Coordinator**

Arvindkumar Gupta

# About the Author

**Matthew Poole** is a systems engineer based near Southampton on the south coast of England, with over 20 years of industry experience. After graduating in electronics and communications engineering, he went on to train as and become an air traffic engineer for Civil Aviation Authority, UK, working on microprocessor-based control and communications systems.

Later, he became a software architect and mobile technology specialist, working for several consultancies and global organizations in both hands-on architecture and product-management roles .

He is now a partner at Connecting Objects, a boutique systems consultancy focusing on the design of Bluetooth and other wireless-based IoT systems, taking ideas from concept to prototype. He is also the Director of Technology for Mobile Onboard, a leading UK-based transport technology company specializing in bus connectivity and mobile ticketing systems.

He is also the author of *Building a Home Security System with Raspberry Pi, Packt Publishing.*

You can find his blog at http://cubiksoundz.com and LinkedIn profile at https://www
.linkedin.com/in/cubik, or you can reach him on Twitter at @cubiksoundz.

# About the Reviewer

**Jon Witts** has been working within the IT industry since 2002 and specifically within educational IT since 2004. He was introduced to Linux back in 2001 through his collaboration with two German artists who were visiting the arts organization he was then working with. Having studied Fine Arts and Educational Technology, and having sought to innovate with open and accessible digital technologies within his creative practice, Jon is happiest when deconstructing technology and finding its limits.

Jon has embedded within his school the use of Raspberry Pi computers, as an integral part of the delivery of the school's Computer Science curriculum, as well as to run various school clubs and projects. Jon is a Raspberry Pi Certified Educator and also helps to organize and run the Hull Raspberry Jam events.

*I would like to thank my wife, Sally, and our three daughters for putting up with all the cables and components around the house, not least for being so tolerant of the need to dodge the robots racing round the kitchen floor!*

# www.PacktPub.com

For support files and downloads related to your book, please visit www.PacktPub.com.

Did you know that Packt offers eBook versions of every book published, with PDF and ePub files available? You can upgrade to the eBook version at www.PacktPub.com and as a print book customer, you are entitled to a discount on the eBook copy. Get in touch with us at service@packtpub.com for more details.

At www.PacktPub.com, you can also read a collection of free technical articles, sign up for a range of free newsletters and receive exclusive discounts and offers on Packt books and eBooks.

https://www2.packtpub.com/books/subscription/packtlib

Do you need instant solutions to your IT questions? PacktLib is Packt's online digital book library. Here, you can search, access, and read Packt's entire library of books.

## Why subscribe?

- Fully searchable across every book published by Packt
- Copy and paste, print, and bookmark content
- On demand and accessible via a web browser

## Free access for Packt account holders

If you have an account with Packt at www.PacktPub.com, you can use this to access PacktLib today and view 9 entirely free books. Simply use your login credentials for immediate access.

# Table of Contents

# Preface

The Raspberry Pi was developed with the intention of promoting basic computer science in schools, but the Pi also represents a welcome return to simple, fun, and open computing.

Using gadgets for purposes other than the intended ones, especially for mischief and pranks, has always been an important part of adopting a new technology and making it your own.

With a £25 Raspberry Pi computer and a few common USB gadgets, anyone can afford to become a secret agent.

This third edition by Matthew Poole takes the previous edition's projects and brings them up to date to now support the new Raspberry Pi Zero, Raspberry Pi Version 3, and the Raspbian Jessie operating system.

There is also a new chapter that looks at ways to connect sensors and gadgets to our Pi to protect ourselves against other would-be secret agents.

## What this book covers

Chapter 1, *Getting Up to No Good*, looks at all of the different models of the Raspberry Pi available, and then takes you through the initial setup, preparing it for sneaky headless operations over the network.

Chapter 2, *Audio Antics*, teaches you how to eavesdrop on conversations with a Pi Zero-based wearable voice recorder, or play pranks on friends by broadcasting your own distorted voice from a distance using the Bluetooth audio.

Chapter 3, *Webcam and Video Wizardry*, shows you how to set up a webcam video feed with built-in motion detection that can be used to detect intruders, or to stage a playback scare by automatically switching on a TV.

Chapter 4, *Wi-Fi Pranks – Exploring Your Network*, teaches you how to capture, manipulate, and spy on the traffic that flows through your network.

Chapter 5, *Taking Your Pi Off-Road*, shows you how to encrypt your Pi and send it away on missions while keeping in touch with it via smartphone, GPS, and Twitter updates. You'll also learn how to turn your Pi into a cellular 4G-connected router while staying anonymous on the Internet.

Chapter 6, *Detecting and Protecting Against Your Enemies*, looks at ways to detect infiltrations and protect ourselves against other would-be spies, by plugging sensors and other gadgets into our Raspberry Pi, alerting us when people stray into our territories.

# What you need for this book

The following hardware is recommended for maximum enjoyment:

- The Raspberry Pi computer (Version 2/Version 3, and Pi Zero)
- An SD card (4 GB minimum, class 10 recommended)
- A PC/laptop running Windows, Linux, or Mac OS X with an internal or external SD card reader
- A Pi Zero connector kit
- A USB microphone / sound card (projects verified with Formosa AS301 Tube Delight and pluggable USB audio adapter.
- A USB Bluetooth adapter (projects verified with Cambridge Silicon Radio dongles) or Pi 3 onboard Bluetooth
- A Bluetooth headset and/or speaker
- Official Raspberry Pi Camera module
- A camera module or USB webcam (projects verified with Logitech C270)
- A USB Wi-Fi adapter (projects verified with Farnell element14 Wi-Pi dongle)
- A USB 3G/4G modem (projects verified with Huawei E3372 HiLink modem)
- A USB GPS receiver (projects verified with U-blox7)
- A lithium polymer battery pack (projects verified with RS Components USB Power Banks and iMuto X4)
- Waveshare Laser Sensor module
- LED matrix display (project verified with the Ciesco Pi-Lite board)
- Passive IR motion sensor (projects verified with Parallax 555-28027)
- USB to 3.3V TTL serial/UART converter
- An Android phone or iPhone (projects verified with Samsung Galaxy S7 Edge and iPhone 4S)

All software mentioned in this book is free of charge and can be downloaded from the Internet.

# Who this book is for

This book is for all the mischievous Raspberry Pi owners who would like to see their computer transformed into a neat spy gadget to be used in a series of practical pranks and projects. No previous skills are required to follow the book, and if you're completely new to Linux, you'll pick up most of the basics along the way.

# Conventions

In this book, you will find a number of text styles that distinguish between different kinds of information. Here are some examples of these styles and an explanation of their meaning.

Code words in text, database table names, folder names, filenames, file extensions, pathnames, dummy URLs, user input, and Twitter handles are shown as follows: "The cat command is commonly used to output the contents of text files, and /proc/asound is a directory."

A block of code is set as follows:

```
#!/bin/bash
sudo echo 17 > /sys/class/gpio/export
sudo echo in > /sys/class/gpio/gpio17/direction

# loop forever
while true
do
  # read the beam state
  BEAM=$(sudo cat /sys/class/gpio/gpio17/value)
```

Any command-line input or output is written as follows:

```
pi@raspberrypi ~ $ cat /proc/asound/cards
```

**New terms** and **important words** are shown in bold. Words that you see on the screen, for example, in menus or dialog boxes, appear in the text like this: "Just right-click on the image file and select **Send to**, then click on **Compressed (zipped)** folder."

Warnings or important notes appear in a box like this.

Tips and tricks appear like this.

# Reader feedback

Feedback from our readers is always welcome. Let us know what you think about this book—what you liked or disliked. Reader feedback is important for us as it helps us develop titles that you will really get the most out of.

To send us general feedback, simply e-mail feedback@packtpub.com, and mention the book's title in the subject of your message.

If there is a topic that you have expertise in and you are interested in either writing or contributing to a book, see our author guide at www.packtpub.com/authors.

# Customer support

Now that you are the proud owner of a Packt book, we have a number of things to help you to get the most from your purchase.

## Downloading the example code

You can download the example code files for this book from your account at http://www.packtpub.com. If you purchased this book elsewhere, you can visit http://www.packtpub.com/support and register to have the files e-mailed directly to you.

You can download the code files by following these steps:

1. Log in or register to our website using your e-mail address and password.
2. Hover the mouse pointer on the **SUPPORT** tab at the top.
3. Click on **Code Downloads & Errata**.
4. Enter the name of the book in the **Search** box.
5. Select the book for which you're looking to download the code files.
6. Choose from the drop-down menu where you purchased this book from.
7. Click on **Code Download**.

Once the file is downloaded, please make sure that you unzip or extract the folder using the latest version of:

- WinRAR / 7-Zip for Windows
- Zipeg / iZip / UnRarX for Mac
- 7-Zip / PeaZip for Linux

The code bundle for the book is also hosted on GitHub at `https://github.com/PacktPublishing/Raspberry-Pi-for-Secret-Agents-Third-Edition`. We also have other code bundles from our rich catalog of books and videos available at `https://github.com/PacktPublishing/`. Check them out!

# Downloading the color images of this book

We also provide you with a PDF file that has color images of the screenshots/diagrams used in this book. The color images will help you better understand the changes in the output. You can download this file from `http://www.packtpub.com/sites/default/files/downloads/RaspberryPiforSecretAgentsThirdEdition_ColorImages.pdf`.

# Errata

Although we have taken every care to ensure the accuracy of our content, mistakes do happen. If you find a mistake in one of our books-maybe a mistake in the text or the code-we would be grateful if you could report this to us. By doing so, you can save other readers from frustration and help us improve subsequent versions of this book. If you find any errata, please report them by visiting http://www.packtpub.com/submit-errata, selecting your book, clicking on the **Errata Submission Form** link, and entering the details of your errata. Once your errata are verified, your submission will be accepted and the errata will be uploaded to our website or added to any list of existing errata under the Errata section of that title.

To view the previously submitted errata, go to https://www.packtpub.com/books/content/support and enter the name of the book in the search field. The required information will appear under the **Errata** section.

# Piracy

Piracy of copyrighted material on the Internet is an ongoing problem across all media. At Packt, we take the protection of our copyright and licenses very seriously. If you come across any illegal copies of our works in any form on the Internet, please provide us with the location address or website name immediately so that we can pursue a remedy.

Please contact us at copyright@packtpub.com with a link to the suspected pirated material.

We appreciate your help in protecting our authors and our ability to bring you valuable content.

# Questions

If you have a problem with any aspect of this book, you can contact us at questions@packtpub.com, and we will do our best to address the problem.

# 1
# Getting up to No Good

Welcome, fellow pranksters and mischief-makers, to the beginning of your journey toward a stealthier lifestyle. Naturally, you're anxious to get started with the cool stuff, so we'll only devote this first chapter to the basic steps you'll need to get your **Raspberry Pi** up and running.

In this chapter, we will look at the following topics:

- Exploring the different versions of Raspberry Pi available
- Preparing the SD card with the latest Raspbian Jessie operating system
- Learning how to remotely access the Raspberry Pi over the home network
- Updating our operating system with the latest packages
- Backing up our SD card to avert disaster

## A brief history lesson on the Pi

The Raspberry Pi is a credit-card-sized computer created by the non-profit Raspberry Pi Foundation in the UK. It all started when a chap named Eben Upton got together with his colleagues at the University of Cambridge's computer laboratory to discuss how they could bring back the kind of simple programming and experimentation that was widespread among kids in the 1980s on home computers such as the BBC Micro, ZX Spectrum, and Commodore 64. Eben is now CEO of the Raspberry Pi Foundation as well as being a technical architect at Broadcom (the company that makes the main chip for the Raspberry Pi).

After several years of tinkering, the Foundation came up with two designs for the Raspberry Pi. The £25 Model B was released first, around February 2012, originally with 256 MB of RAM. A second revision, with 512 MB of RAM, was announced in October 2012, and the £15 Model A went on sale the following year, in February 2013.

In July 2014, with over 3 million Pis sold worldwide, the Foundation unveiled the Raspberry Pi Model B+, a £25 board revision incorporating numerous improvements requested by the ever-growing Pi community.

As the Pi community grows from strength-to-strength, in February 2015 the Foundation released the Raspberry Pi 2: 6 times faster than the Model B/B+ with its upgraded ARM processor, and 1 GB of RAM.

In November 2015, the Foundation rocked the community with the launch of the **Raspberry Pi Zero**—an amazing feat of engineering—being a fully functional PC the size of a small luggage tag (65 mm x 30 mm) that could easily be lost down the back of a sofa. What's more amazing is the price—just £4—and they were giving these things away on the front of magazines. This device is truly a secret agent's delight.

The latest part of this story is that as I write the third edition of this book, the Foundation have just released the **Raspberry Pi 3**—even more awesome than the Pi 2, with a faster processor and now with onboard Wi-Fi and Bluetooth—which means no more dongles for many wireless projects:

Say hello to the super-tiny Pi Zero – a game changer for mischief-makers everywhere...

So, which Pi is good for the spy?

As you've just discovered, there have been several versions of the mini-PC board released since 2012 and most of them are still available to purchase now. I'll go through each of the versions released with their respective features; however, for our secret agent projects we will be focusing on the Raspberry Pi 2, 3, and Zero boards, as they are the most recent and most useful for spies like us.

# Raspberry Pi Model A

The baby of the family is the **Model A**, and was released as a lower cost version of the Model B (discussed next). Its main differences from the **Model B** is that it features just 256 MB of memory and has no Ethernet port, so if you want to connect this board to a network, you are limited to using a USB Wi-Fi dongle or a USB-to-Ethernet adapter:

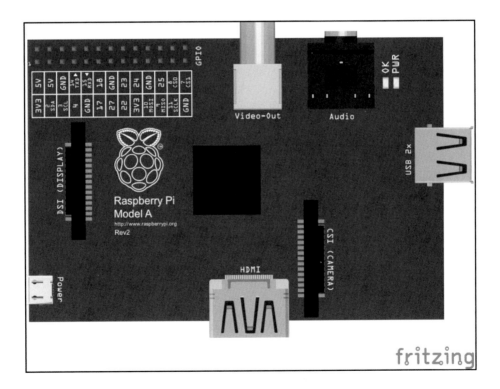

Overhead view of the original Raspberry Pi Model A board

# Raspberry Pi Model B

This was the first version of the Raspberry Pi to be released, with an updated revision coming later that improved the power system and USB port protection. It features 512 MB of memory and has an Ethernet port for connecting to your network. This was the most common version used at the time, as having the **Ethernet port** is incredibly useful, especially for getting up and running quickly in order to set up and configure your Pi without the need for a keyboard and monitor to always be available:

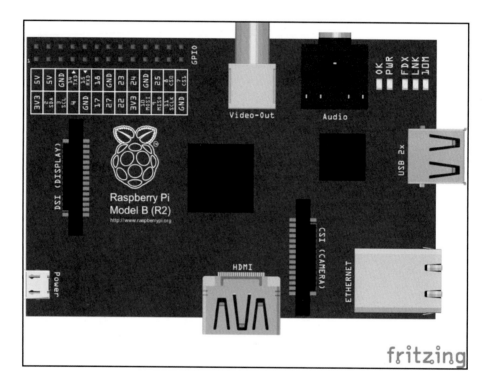

Overhead view of the original Raspberry Pi Model B board

# Raspberry Pi Model B+

In 2014, the Raspberry Pi Foundation released a new version of the board, the **Model B+**, which had fundamental changes compared to the previous version. The most fundamental changes are the board layout, form factor and mounting points—much to the dismay of the many enclosure and accessory manufacturers out there.

The main electronic changes to this board are the addition of two more USB ports, which can deliver more power to peripherals, an expanded GPIO interface, and the removal of the **composite video port**, which is now consolidated into the **audio jack**. It also now uses a **microSD card** with a better card slot:

Raspberry Pi Model B+ features more USB ports and a 40-pin GPIO connector

A lower cost **model A+** was also subsequently released that had only 1 USB port and no Ethernet port:

The smaller Raspberry Pi A+ featuring just one USB connector and no Ethernet port

# Raspberry Pi Model 2

In February 2015, a more powerful Raspberry Pi was released—the **Raspberry Pi Model 2**. It's similar to the Model B+ in terms of form-factor and interfaces, but is now reportedly 6 times faster than the Model B/B+, with its upgraded ARM processor, and 1 GB of memory.

At the same low cost of less than £30, it's a fantastic little board and is a great power-house for embedded systems:

Raspberry Pi 2 Model B – looks just like a Version 1 Model B+ but has more a powerful CPU and more RAM

Fortunately, the Raspberry Pi has now standardized its layout and mounting points so that add-ons will fit all of the different models:

Raspberry Pi 2 Model B connector layout

# Raspberry Pi Zero

November 2015 saw the launch of **the Raspberry Pi Zero**—a complete PC board that could be bought for just £4 and at the minute size of just 65mm x 30mm. The Foundation's aim was to take a Raspberry Pi Model A and make it as small and as cheap as possible. They even gave it away free on the front of *The MagPi* magazine when it was launched.

*"We all need access to tools. Cost should never be a barrier."*

*-Eben Upton*

Up to now, the Raspberry Pi was always licensed to, and manufactured by, the likes of **RS Components** and **Farnell element14**, who have the financial might to ramp up production.

However, with the Zero, this is a *go-it-alone* project, with the Foundation funding and handling the manufacturing process themselves. As a result, even at the time of writing, demand has way outstripped supply, and Zeros are currently pretty difficult to get your hands on—no thanks to the many profiteers out there buying them for £4 in quantities and then trying to sell them online for a massive profit.

The Foundation are addressing this with plans to massively ramp-up production in Q2 of 2016, so hopefully by the time you read this, they will be in plentiful supply.

With its low cost and tiny form-factor, the Raspberry Pi Zero is going to be very useful in our stealthy and mischievous antics:

The very small Raspberry Pi Zero featuring micro-HDMI and micro-USB connectors and noticeable absence of a physical connector on the GPIO port

# Raspberry Pi 3

As I write (February 2016), the Foundation has just launched their next update of the Pi—the **Raspberry Pi 3**—and just in time, as not only is it more powerful, with a 64-bit ARMv8 processor, it also includes **Wi-Fi** and **Bluetooth** connectivity on the board, without requiring any additional dongles to be connected to the USB ports. They are also easier to get your hands on at this time compared to the Pi Zero.

This could be a game-changer for our sneaky activities, as it means we can build more discreet secret agent tools and devices. Incidentally, the Raspberry Pi 3 is available at the same benchmark cost of less than £30 from the main distributors, RS and Farnell element14:

The new Raspberry Pi 3–looks like the previous model but now with Wi-Fi and Bluetooth 4.1 on-board

As you have seen, in its short lifetime the Raspberry Pi already has several models available, each of which suits different application needs. To help us choose, the following table provides a comparison between the various models:

| | Model B+ | Model 2 | Model 3 | Zero |
|---|---|---|---|---|
| **Processor** | Broadcom BCM2835 SoC featuring ARM1176 32-bit dual-core CPU | Broadcom BCM2836Soc featuring ARMv7 32-bit quad-core CPU | Broadcom BCM2837 SoC featuring ARMv8 64-bit quad-core CPU | Broadcom BCM2835 SoC featuring ARM1176 32-bit dual-core CPU |
| **GPU** | VideoCore IV | | | |
| **Clock** | 700MHz | 900MHz | 1.2GHz | 1GHz |
| **Memory** | 512 MB | 1 GB | 1 GB | 512 MB |
| **USB Ports** | 4 | 4 | 4 | 1 (Micro-USB) |
| **Ethernet** | Yes | Yes | Yes | No |
| **Wi-Fi** | No | No | Yes | No |
| **Bluetooth** | No | No | Yes | No |
| **GPIO Pins** | 40 | 40 | 40 | 40 (unpop.) |
| **Storage** | MicroSD card | MicroSD card | MicroSD card | MicroSD card |

# So, which Pi for us spies?

In this latest edition of this book, we're going to focus on the current Raspberry Pi version 2 and new version 3 models, as well as the Raspberry Pi Zero for those projects that might require a computer board that's somewhat more discreet. Each of these versions has different features and advantages, so we'll chose the right version for the job for each of our secret agent tools.

The Raspberry Pi Foundation site has more detailed information about each model here: ht tps://www.raspberrypi.org/products/.

# Where to buy a Pi

The main distributors for the Raspberry Pi 2 and 3 are RS Components and Farnell element14, but you may need a trade account to buy from them. Alternatively, there are other vendors on the Internet that sell them, including CPC and Maplin Electronics, as well as a plethora of independent sellers on Amazon and eBay.

The Raspberry Pi Zero is currently manufactured by the Raspberry Pi Foundation and is distributed through their official partners:

- The Pi Hut: http://thepihut.com/products/raspberry-pi-zero
- Pimoroni: https://shop.pimoroni.com/products/raspberry-pi-zero
- Adafruit: https://www.adafruit.com/products/2885

# The ins and outs of the Raspberry Pi

At the heart of the Pi is the **Broadcom System on a Chip (SOC)**—think of it as all the common hardware components of a PC baked into a small piece of silicon. Different versions of the Pi have different types of Broadcom chip, as outlined in the model comparison table above, but they are each based on an **ARM processor**, with the Pi Model 3 having the most powerful ARM processor.

For graphics, the Pi sports a Broadcom VideoCore IV GPU, which is quite powerful for such a tiny device and is capable of full HD video playback through the HDMI connector built in to every Pi.

The following figure shows the Raspberry Pi Version 3 board layout and connectors:

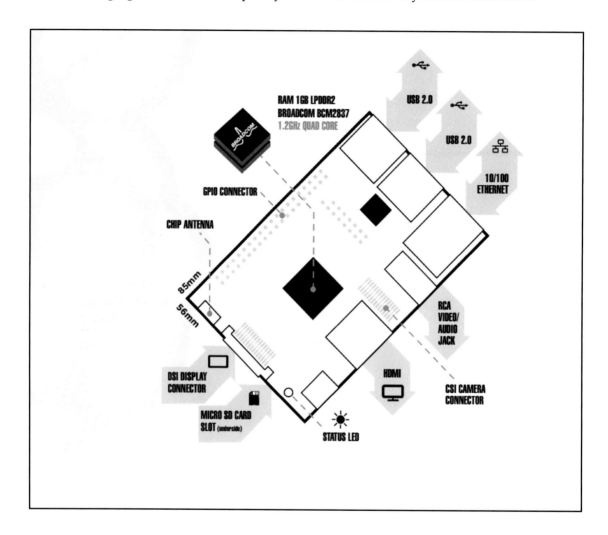

Raspberry Pi Version 3 layout taken from the RS Components product data sheet

# GPIO headers

At the edge of the board, we find the **GeneralPurpose Input/Output (GPIO)** pins, which as the name implies, can be used for any kind of general tinkering and to interface with other pieces of hardware.

# Audio/Video jack

The 3.5 mm four-pole jack socket is for the audio output, and on later models also contains the composite video output that was originally connected to an RCA socket. We can use that to connect the Pi to one of those old television sets using an RCA connector cable. You can also get audio out of the Pi through the HDMI connector.

# Status LEDs

**Status LEDs** are used to tell us what the Pi is up to at the moment. They have the following meanings:

- The green light labelled **ACT** will blink whenever the Pi is accessing data from the SD card
- The red light labelled **PWR** should stay solid as long as the Pi has sufficient power

# USB

The USB 2.0 ports allow us to connect keyboards, mice, and most importantly for us, Wi-Fi dongles, microphones, video cameras, and GPS receivers. We can also expand the number of USB ports available with the help of a self-powered USB hub.

# Ethernet port

The **Ethernet port** allows us to connect the Pi to a network at a maximum speed of 100 Mbit/s. This will most commonly be a home router or a switch, but it can also be connected directly to a PC or a laptop. A **Category 5 twisted-pair cable** is used for wired network connections.

# CSI camera connector

The **Camera Serial Interface (CSI)** is where the official Raspberry Pi camera module connects to, using a flexible flat cable.

# Display Serial Interface

The **DisplaySerial Interface** (**DSI**) is for connecting TFT or LCD display panels using a flexible flat cable and connects to the **Mobile Industry Processor Interface** (**MIPI**) inside the Broadcom chip, which feeds graphics data directly to the display panel.

# HDMI

The **High-Definition Multimedia Interface** (**HDMI**) connector is used to connect the Pi to a modern TV or monitor. The cable can carry high-resolution video up to 1920 x 1200 pixels, and digital sound. It also supports a feature called **Consumer Electronics Control** (**CEC**), which allows us to use the Pi as a remote control for many common television sets.

# Power

The power input on the Raspberry Pi is a **5V (DC) Micro-USB Type B** jack. A power supply with a standard USB to micro-USB cable, such as a common cell phone charger, is then connected to feed the Pi.

Take a look at the output printed on your power adapter. The voltage should be between 5V to 5.25V and the amperage provided should be at least 1A.

The most frequently reported issues from Raspberry Pi users are without a doubt those caused by insufficient power supplies and power-hungry USB devices. Should you experience random reboots, or that your Ethernet port or attached USB device suddenly stops working, it's likely that your Pi is not getting enough stable power. Another indication of the Pi not getting enough power is if you see a *rainbow* icon in the top right-hand of the monitor.

The official 2A power supply sold by the Foundation is highly recommended—especially for the Raspberry Pi Version 3 (1A = 1000mA).

You can help your Pi by moving your devices to a self-powered USB hub (a hub that has its own power supply).

Also note that the Pi is very sensitive to devices being inserted or removed while it's running, and powering your Pi from another computer's USB port usually doesn't work well.

# MicroSD card

The **microSDcard** is where all our data lives, and the Pi will not start without one inserted into the slot. All models since the Model B+ use the tiny microSD cards, whereas earlier models used standard sized SD cards. The Pi 3 no longer has a push-to-release mechanism because so many people were accidentally ejecting their SD cards! You simply slide the card out now to remove it.

SD cards come with a wide variety of data storage capabilities. A card with a minimum of 4 GB of storage space is recommended for the projects in this book. The SD cards also carry a class number that indicates the read/write speed of the card—the higher the better.

## Preparing the SD card

The Raspberry Pi only boots from an SD card, and cannot boot from an external drive or USB stick (well that's not strictly true, but is outside the scope of this book).

It's recommended that you use a **Class 10** SD card for performance, but a Class 6 card will be fine for the projects in this book. You'll need to have a minimum card size of 4 GB.

Now we have our Raspberry Pi board and SD card to hand, we need to prepare the SD card so we can start creating some mischief. We're going to use the standard Raspbian operating system, as there really is no reason to use any other distribution, and it's the de facto operating system for the Raspberry Pi.

# Download the Raspbian image

You'll need to grab the latest **Raspbian OS** image from the Raspberry Pi site at `https://ww w.raspberrypi.org/downloads/`.

Download the Raspbian OS ZIP file containing the image to your PC.

At the time of writing the latest version was `2016-05-27-raspbian-jessie.zip`.

Once downloaded, unzip the file and you'll have the file `2016-05-27-raspian-jessie.img`.

The next thing to do is burn this image to your SD card.

# Using Microsoft Windows

On a Windows PC, the best way to burn the image to your SD card is to use the **Win32 Disk Imager** utility. This can be downloaded from `https://sourceforge.net/projects/win32diskimager/`.

The current version at the time of writing is 0.9.5.

It doesn't have an installer, and launches directly from the EXE file.

Now it's time to create your SD card image:

1. Insert your SD card into the PC and launch **Win32 Disk Imager**.
2. Select SD card device drive letter (make sure it's right!).
3. Choose the Raspbian image file you've just downloaded.
4. Click the **Write** button to create the SD card image:

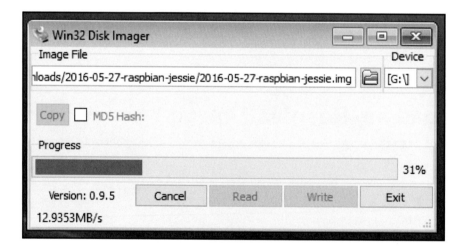

# Using Linux

On a Linux PC you'll need to use the `fdisk` and `dd` utilities to burn the image to your SD card.

Carry out the following steps to create your SD card image:

1. Extract the `2016-05-27-raspbian-jessie.img` to your `Home` folder.
2. Type the following command to check which drives you have before you insert your SD card, so that you can compare the difference in a moment to ensure you are selecting the right drive:

```
$ sudo fdisk -l
```

4. Now insert your SD card into the PC.
5. If you're not already in a shell terminal window, open one (*Ctrl + Alt + T*).
6. Type the following commands in the shell terminal:

```
$ sudo fdisk -l
```

In the list, check that your SD card appears as a drive device (for example, `/dev/sdb`). It's crucial you ensure you use the right device in the next step. We'll assume that your device is `/dev/sdb`.

To burn the image to the SD card, type the following command:

```
$ sudo dd if=2016-05-27-raspbian-jessie.img of=/dev/sdb
```

Hit *Enter* and go and make a cup of tea or coffee as this will take a while. You'll know when it's finished when the command (`$`) prompt re-appears.

When the command prompt does re-appear, type the following command:

```
$ sudo sync
```

Once that command has finished, you can remove the SD card from the PC.

# Boot up your Pi

You're now ready to boot up your Raspberry Pi. Pop in your newly burned SD card and plug the power in the Pi.

Assuming you have a monitor attached to your Pi, you should see your system booting up nicely. Although you could wait for it to boot up and connect via a terminal session (we'll look at that later), I recommend that you connect a monitor to it, at least in the first instance, just to make sure everything is working correctly.

In the new **Jessie** version of Raspbian you'll boot straight into a desktop GUI, which is a major change from previous versions. Previously, you'd be taken to the `raspi-config` utility the first time the system is run, where you'd set up your Pi, and importantly, expand the filesystem to use the entire space available on your SD card:

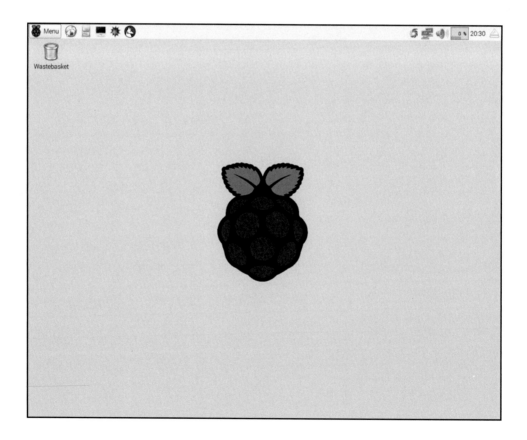

Debian Jessie boots into the GUI by default

# Expand the filesystem

When you first create your Raspbian SD card you'll only be left with about 200 MB of space in the filesystem, regardless of the size of your SD card. This is not much use, so we want to expand the filesystem so it uses all of the available space on the card.

Fortunately, this is very easy now on the Raspberry Pi, as this function is available in the **Raspberry Pi Configuration** tool on the desktop.

To access the new configuration tool, go to **Menu** and select **Preferences | RaspberryPi Configuration**:

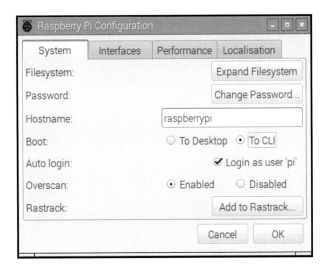

The new Raspberry Pi Configuration tool in Jessie

# Goodbye GUI

Most of our work is going to be done in the command-line interface (CLI); therefore, before we reboot the system in a minute, change the **Boot** option **To CLI** as shown above, so you'll boot into the command line going forward.

Anyway, now we click the **Expand Filesystem** button, and in a couple of seconds you'll see a confirmation message. The filesystem will be expanded when the system next reboots.

# Using the raspi-config utility

If you have an older version of Raspbian, or you're not using the desktop GUI, then you'll need to use the `raspi-config` utility (which is still better than the old days when we had to do this manually in the shell). The first time you boot up you'll be taken straight to the `raspi-config` utility:

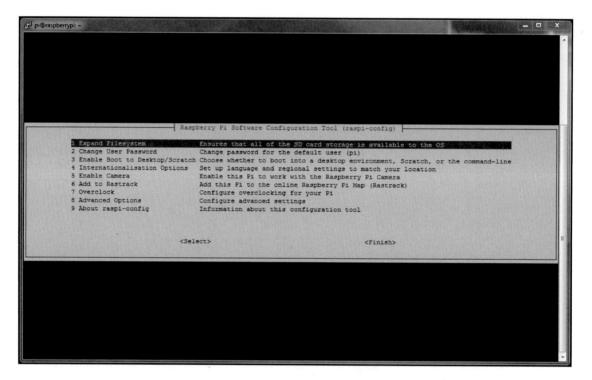

The first option is the **Expand Filesystem** option—select this and you'll see various commands scrolling up the screen. Once it's finished, you'll see the following message:

**Root partition has been resized.**

**The filesystem will be enlarged upon the next reboot.**

Click **OK**. Select **Finish** on the configuration screen and reboot your Pi when prompted.

After your Pi reboots with its fuller filesystem, you'll be taken straight to the shell prompt, where you can log in with the default user and password:

        **Login: pi**
        **Password: raspberry**

# Setting up your Pi

When you boot into the shell and you have the Ethernet connected, hopefully, the Pi will have connected to your home network and will have acquired an IP address from your router. If this is the case, then you should see the **IP address** that has been issued just before the login prompt:

As you can see from my screenshot, it's given me the IP address `192.168.0.118`. This is good, because I can now access the Pi remotely using a secure shell (SSH) client to connect to it from the comfort of my laptop. This is particularly useful when my Pi is in the study and I want to sit on my sofa in front of the TV but still work on it, which I often do when I can't be bothered to go to my study.

To do this on Windows, download **PuTTY**—a utility that allows you to connect to shell terminals remotely over the network (see below if you're on Linux). You can download it from `http://www.putty.org`.

Install and launch PuTTY and you're ready to connect to your Pi remotely from the comfort of your sofa:

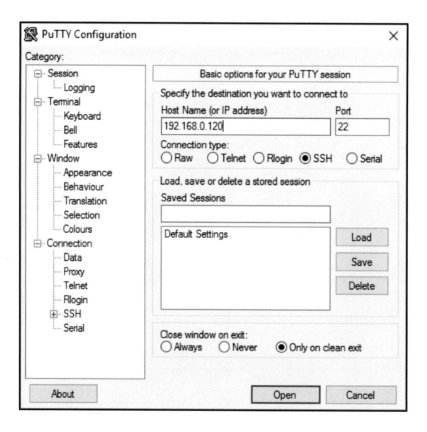

Type the **IP address** of the Raspberry Pi into the **Host Name** box and click **Open**, and you'll be connected to your Pi in a remote terminal window. Once you've logged in, you can now do pretty much everything on you Pi as if you were sat in front of it:

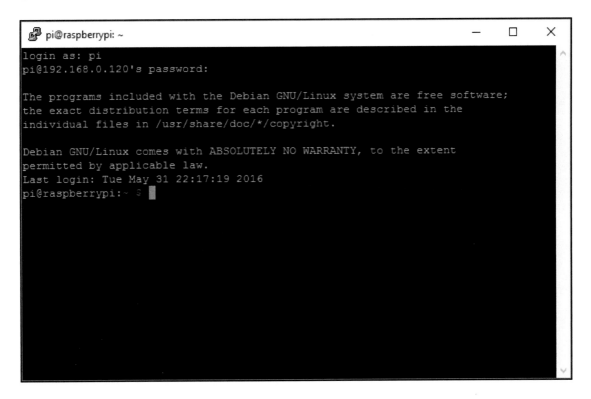

We'll assume from now on that most of the work we do will be through a remote shell session, unless otherwise highlighted.

If you want to use the command line to launch the Raspberry Pi remote shell, for example, from another Linux system, you use the following command from your terminal window (assuming your Pi has the IP address 192.168.0.120 in this case):

```
$ ssh pi@192.168.0.120
```

You'll then be prompted for the Pi's password and taken into a shell session:

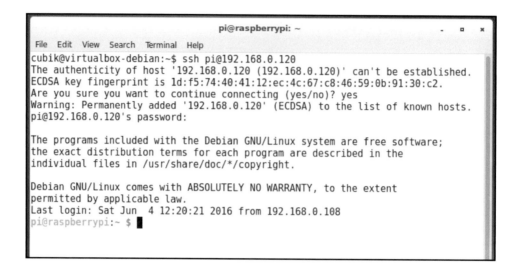

```
                          pi@raspberrypi: ~                    _  ▫  ✕

  File  Edit  View  Search  Terminal  Help
cubik@virtualbox-debian:~$ ssh pi@192.168.0.120
The authenticity of host '192.168.0.120 (192.168.0.120)' can't be established.
ECDSA key fingerprint is 1d:f5:74:40:41:12:ec:4c:67:c8:46:59:0b:91:30:c2.
Are you sure you want to continue connecting (yes/no)? yes
Warning: Permanently added '192.168.0.120' (ECDSA) to the list of known hosts.
pi@192.168.0.120's password:

The programs included with the Debian GNU/Linux system are free software;
the exact distribution terms for each program are described in the
individual files in /usr/share/doc/*/copyright.

Debian GNU/Linux comes with ABSOLUTELY NO WARRANTY, to the extent
permitted by applicable law.
Last login: Sat Jun  4 12:20:21 2016 from 192.168.0.108
pi@raspberrypi:~ $ ▮
```

Pi shell session launched from a Debian desktop terminal window

# The importance of a sneaky headless setup

You might be wondering why we bother with SSH and typing stuff in the command line at all when Raspbian comes with a perfectly nice graphical desktop environment and a whole repository of GUI applications. Well, the first reason is that we need all the CPU power we can get out of the Pi for our projects. With the current graphics drivers for X (the graphics system), the desktop eats up too much of the Pi's resources and the CPU is more concerned with redrawing fancy windows than with running our mischievous applications.

The second reason is that of stealth and secrecy. Usually, we want to be able to hide our Pi with as few wires as possible running to and from it. Obviously, a Pi hidden in a room becomes a lot more visible if someone trips over a connected monitor or keyboard. This is why we make sure all our pranks can be controlled and triggered from a remote location.

# Keeping your system up to date

A community effort, such as Raspbian and the Debian distribution on which it is based, is constantly being worked on and improved by hundreds of developers every day. All of them are trying hard to make the Pi run as smoothly as possible, support as many different peripherals as possible, and to squish any discovered software bugs.

All those improvements come to you in the form of package and firmware updates, and something that you should get into the habit of doing is updating the operating system regularly, and even though you may have the latest image installed, it's very likely that there are updated packages that can be installed. To update your OS, enter the following command:

```
$ sudo apt-get update
```

(This fetches information about which packages have been updated.)

Then enter the following command:

```
$ sudo apt-get upgrade
```

(This proceeds to install the updated packages. Select **Yes** when prompted for installation. It will also upgrade the Pi to the latest firmware from the Raspberry Pi Foundation's GitHub repository—an online source code management service.)

This all may take a while depending on the number of updates required.

# Backing up your SD card

It happens to everyone at one point or another—you've put hours into perfecting your Raspbian installation, setting up applications, and hacking away at clever code, when out of nowhere your cat/dog/next-of-kin swoops down on your keyboard and triggers the self-destruct mechanism from the *Erasing the Pi should it fall into the wrong hands* section in `Chapter 5`, *Taking Your Pi Off-Road*.

Not to worry, Agent, backing up an SD card is quite simple as long as you've got the required disk space to store it.

# Complete SD card backup in Windows

We'll be making a complete mirror image of your SD card. The data will be stored in a single file that will be the same size as that of your SD card. To do this, we'll use the Win32 Disk Imager application we installed earlier on to create our SD card image:

1. Power off your Pi safely by running the following command and wait for the green activity LED to stop flickering:

   ```
   $ sudo shutdown -h now
   ```

2. Move the SD card to your computer's card reader.
3. Start the **Win32 Disk Imager** application on your PC.
4. Ensure that the correct volume of your SD card is shown under **Device**.
5. Click on the folder icon and navigate to the folder where you'd like to store the image.
6. Enter a good file name for your image and click on **Open**. The standard file extension for image files is .img.
7. Finally, after verifying that the full **Image File** path looks good, click on **Read**:

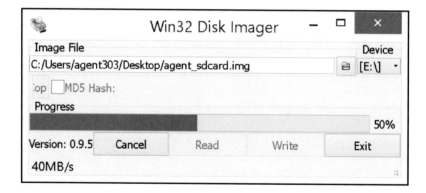

Once your image backup has completed successfully, you can compress it to save quite a bit of disk space. Just right-click on the image file and select **Send to**, then click on **Compressed (zipped)** folder.

# Complete SD card backup in MAC OS X

We'll be making a complete mirror image of your SD card. The data will be stored in a single compressed file, which should result in a smaller size than that of your SD card. The steps to be followed for a data backup are as follows:

1. Power off your Pi safely by running the following command and wait for the green activity LED to stop flickering:

   ```
   $ sudo shutdown -h now
   ```

2. Move the SD card to your computer's card reader.
3. Open up a terminal (located in /Applications/Utilities on the Mac).
4. Type diskutillist to obtain a readout of all connected storage devices.
5. To correctly identify your SD card, we're looking for a disk that has at least one Windows and one Linux entry under **TYPE** (there will be two of each type if we installed Raspbian through **NOOBS**).
6. Take note of that disk's first **IDENTIFIER** field (**disk1** in the screenshot).
7. As a security precaution, we will first unmount the SD card so that no applications running in the background can change data as we make our backup. Use the following command, but replace [disk] with the **IDENTIFIER** field of your SD card:

   ```
   $ diskutil unmountdisk [disk]
   ```

8. Now we'll do a complete copy of the SD card and store it in a file called agent_sdcard.img.gz on your desktop. Type the following command, but replace [disk] with the **IDENTIFIER** field of your SD card (note the letter *r* in front of *disk*):

   ```
   $ sudo dd if=/dev/r[disk] bs=4m | gzip > ~/Desktop/agent_sdcard.img.gz
   ```

9. You might be asked to input your user password so that `sudo` is allowed to start. The backup process doesn't produce much output as it runs, but a status report can be produced by pressing *Ctrl + T* in the `Terminal` window:

```
agentbook:~ agent$ diskutil list
/dev/disk0
   #:                       TYPE NAME              SIZE       IDENTIFIER
   0:      GUID_partition_scheme                  *121.3 GB   disk0
   1:                        EFI EFI              209.7 MB    disk0s1
   2:                  Apple_HFS MacHD            120.5 GB    disk0s2
   3:                 Apple_Boot Recovery HD      650.0 MB    disk0s3
/dev/disk1
   #:                       TYPE NAME              SIZE       IDENTIFIER
   0:     FDisk_partition_scheme                  *15.9 GB    disk1
   1:             Windows_FAT_16 RECOVERY         1.5 GB      disk1s1
   2:                      Linux                  33.6 MB     disk1s3
   3:             Windows_FAT_32 BOOT             62.9 MB     disk1s5
   4:                      Linux                  14.3 GB     disk1s6
agentbook:~ agent$ diskutil unmountdisk disk1
Unmount of all volumes on disk1 was successful
agentbook:~ agent$ sudo dd if=/dev/rdisk1 bs=4m | gzip > ~/Desktop/agent_sdcard.img.gz
Password:
3798+1 records in
3798+1 records out
15931539456 bytes transferred in 894.658617 secs (17807395 bytes/sec)
```

Backing up an SD card in Mac OS X

To restore your SD card from a backup image, repeat the previous steps, but use this command instead at step 7:

```
$ gzip -dc ~/Desktop/agent_sdcard.img.gz | sudo dd of=/dev/r[disk] bs=4m
```

If you type the wrong disk you could potentially overwrite your Mac's internal hard drive without any warning. Do triple-check!

# Complete SD card backup in Linux

We'll be making a complete mirror image of your SD card. The data will be stored in a single compressed file, which should result in a smaller size than that of your SD card:

1. Power off your Pi safely by running the following command, and wait for the green activity LED to stop flickering:

```
$ sudo shutdown -h now
```

2. Move the SD card to your computer's card reader.

3. Open up a terminal session *(Ctrl + Alt + T)*.

4. Type `sudo lsblk -f` to obtain a readout of all connected storage devices.

5. To correctly identify your SD card, we're looking for a disk that has at least one `vfat` and one `ext4` entry under `FSTYPE` (there will be two of each type if we installed Raspbian through NOOBS).

6. Take note of that disk's `NAME` (sdb in the screenshot).

7. If any of the partitions under your disk's `NAME` have a `MOUNTPOINT` listed, you should unmount it first. Use the following command, but replace `[mountpoint]` with the mountpoint of your partition:

```
$ sudo umount [mountpoint]
```

8. Now we'll do a complete copy of the SD card and store it in a file called `agent_sdcard.img.gz` in your `home` directory. Type the following command, but replace `[disk]` with the `NAME` of your SD card:

```
$ sudo dd if=/dev/[disk] bs=4M | gzip > ~/agent_sdcard.img.gz
```

9. The backup process doesn't produce much output as it runs, but a status report can be produced by typing `sudopkill-USR1dd` in another `terminal` console:

```
$ sudo lsblk -f
NAME    FSTYPE LABEL     UUID                                   MOUNTPOINT
sda
├─sda1 btrfs   EeeHD     736b2bb6-906d-42b0-bba8-c4c37106aa95 /
└─sda2 swap    swap      f05d0121-2073-4073-bc59-8a7414bd91bd [SWAP]
sdb
├─sdb1 vfat    RECOVERY  D083-9842
├─sdb2
├─sdb3 ext4    SETTINGS  4f7087b8-01d0-4a6d-bc09-ec298e6673d6
├─sdb5 vfat    BOOT      012F-16E2
└─sdb6 ext4    root      883f6b84-d74e-411d-9c55-14c0eaf6d28f
$ sudo dd if=/dev/sdb bs=4M | gzip > ~/agent_sdcard.img.gz
3798+1 records in
3798+1 records out
15931539456 bytes (16 GB) copied, 2782.84 s, 5.7 MB/s
```

Backing up an SD card in Linux

To restore your SD card from a backup image, repeat the previous steps, but use this command instead at step 7:

```
$ gzip -dc ~/agent_sdcard.img.gz | sudo dd of=/dev/[disk] bs=4M
```

If you type the wrong disk you could potentially overwrite your computer's internal hard drive without any warning. Do triple-check!

# Summary

In this chapter, we took a look at the versions of the Raspberry Pi that are now available, looked at their different parts, and learned a bit about how the Pi came to be.

We also learned about the importance of a good power supply and how a powered USB hub can help alleviate some of the power drain caused by hungry USB peripherals.

We then took our Raspberry Pi out of its box and gave it an operating system in order to prepare it for being the centerpiece of our secret agent toolkit, by installing Raspbian onto our SD card before popping it into the card slot.

Raspbian was booted and configured and the filesystem was expanded using the GUI-based or the `raspi-config` configuration utility. We also learned a few helpful Linux commands and how to set up remote connections from SSH clients over the network.

Finally, we learned how to keep Raspbian up to date and how to create a complete backup image of our precious SD card.

In the upcoming chapter, we'll be connecting sound gadgets to the Pi and getting our feet wet in the big pond of spy techniques.

# 2
# Audio Antics

Greetings! Glad to see that you have powered through the initial setup and can join us for our first day of spy class. In this chapter, we'll be exploring the auditory domain and all the fun things humans and machines can do with sound waves. In particular we will:

- Take a detailed look at Linux's sound architecture
- Look at how to connect and configure audio gadgets to our Pi, and select which audio output to use
- Connect a microphone, record audio using our Pi, and build a wearable voice recorder using a Pi Zero
- Use Bluetooth to send and receive audio wirelessly
- Learn about the SoX utility to manipulate audio files
- Configure a Voice-over IP network so we can call our fellow agents
- Use voice commands to control our Pi

## Configuring your audio gadgets

Before you go jamming all your microphones and noisemakers into the Pi, let's take a minute to get to know the underlying sound system and the audio capabilities of the Raspberry Pi board itself.

## Sound variations

Across the range of Raspberry Pi versions, there are significant differences in how we can get sound out of our Pi. The earlier models featured a standard 3.5 mm stereo output, while from the Model B+ onwards, the output is a 3.5 mm four-pole jack, which is also shared with the composite video out.

However, on the Pi Zero there is no dedicated audio output port, in order to keep the board as small and as low-cost as possible, but you can get sound from the audio channels on the HDMI connection, as with all versions.

There are no native audio input capabilities on the Raspberry Pi, so if we want to put sound into the Raspberry Pi for processing and recording, we will need to connect an external audio device to one of the USB ports.

# Introducing the ALSA sound system

The **Advanced Linux Sound Architecture (ALSA)** is the underlying framework responsible for making all the sound stuff work on the Pi. ALSA provides kernel drivers for the Pi itself and for most USB gadgets that produce or record sound. The framework also includes code to help programmers make audio applications, and a couple of command-line utilities that will prove very useful to us.

In ALSA lingo, each audio device on your system is a card, a word inherited from the days when most computers had a dedicated sound card. This means that any USB device you connect that makes or records sound is a card as far as ALSA is concerned-be it a microphone, headset, or webcam.

Type in the following command to view a list of all connected audio devices that ALSA knows about:

```
pi@raspberrypi ~ $ cat /proc/asound/cards
```

The cat command is commonly used to output the contents of text files, and /proc/asound is a directory (or folder in the Windows world), in which ALSA provides detailed status information about the sound system. On the Pi 3, you should see the following output for the previous command:

```
pi@raspberrypi:~ $ cat /proc/asound/cards
 0 [ALSA           ]: bcm2835 - bcm2835 ALSA
```

As you can see, presently there's only one card-number zero, the audio core of the Pi itself. When we plug in a new sound device, it'll be assigned the next available card number, starting at one. Type in the following command to list the contents of the asound directory:

```
pi@raspberrypi ~ $ ls -l /proc/asound
```

The black/white names are files that you can output with `cat`. The blue ones are directories, and the cyan ones are **symbolic links**, or **symlinks**, which just point to other files or directories. You might be puzzled by the `total 0` output. Usually it'll tell you the number of files in the directory, but because `/proc/asound` is a special information-only directory where the file sizes are zero, it appears empty to the `ls` command:

```
pi@raspberrypi: ~                                    —    □    ✕

pi@raspberrypi:~ $ ls -l /proc/asound
total 0
lrwxrwxrwx 1 root  root 5 Mar 27 12:14 ALSA -> card0
dr-xr-xr-x 4 root  root 0 Mar 27 12:14 card0
-r--r--r-- 1 root  root 0 Mar 27 12:14 cards
-r--r--r-- 1 root  root 0 Mar 27 12:14 devices
-r--r--r-- 1 root  root 0 Mar 27 12:14 modules
dr-xr-xr-x 2 root  root 0 Mar 27 12:14 oss
-r--r--r-- 1 root  root 0 Mar 27 12:14 pcm
dr-xr-xr-x 2 root  root 0 Mar 27 12:14 seq
-r--r--r-- 1 root  root 0 Mar 27 12:14 timers
-r--r--r-- 1 root  root 0 Mar 27 12:14 version
pi@raspberrypi:~ $
```

Directory listing of /proc/asound

# Controlling the volume

It's time to make some noise! Let's start up **AlsaMixer** to make sure the volume is loud enough for us to hear anything, using the following command:

```
pi@raspberrypi ~ $ alsamixer
```

You'll be presented with a colorful console application that allows you to tweak volume levels and other sound system parameters:

AlsaMixer showing default volume of Raspberry Pi audio core

Let's have a look at the mixer application from the top:

1.  The `Card: bcm2835 ALSA` and `Chip: Broadcom Mixer` lines tell us that we are indeed viewing the volume level of the Pi itself and not some plugged-in audio device.
2.  The `Item: PCM [dB gain: -20.00]` line tells us two things; one is that the current focus of our keyboard input is the **PCM** control (just another word for digital audio interface in ALSA lingo), and the next one is that the current gain of the output signal is at `-20.00` decibels (basically just a measure of the audio volume).
3.  Use your arrow up and down keys to increase or decrease the volume meter and notice how that also changes the dB gain. For a first audio test, you want to set the dB gain to be somewhere around zero. That's equal to 86 percent of the full meter (the percentage is the number printed just below the meter).
4.  When you're happy with the volume level, press the *Esc* key to quit AlsaMixer.

Watch out for muted devices!

If you find yourself looking at a black, empty volume meter with **MM** at the base and `[dB gain: mute]` on the `Item:` line, you've encountered a device that has been muted-completely silenced. Simply press the *M* key to unmute the device and make your changes to the volume level.

# Switching between HDMI and analog audio output

As you may recall, the Raspberry Pi has two possible audio outputs (with the exception of the Pi Zero). We can either send sound to our monitor or TV through the HDMI cable, or we can send it out of the 3.5 mm analog audio jack to a plugged-in pair of headphones or speakers.

Use the `raspi-config` utility to change this setting (Advanced Option A9) with:

```
pi@raspberrypi ~ $ sudo raspi-config
```

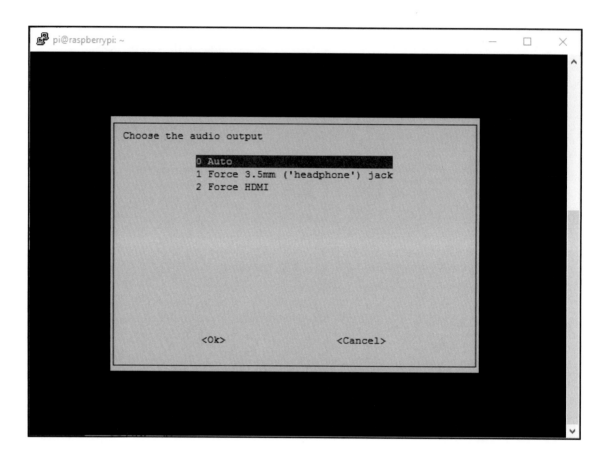

Changing the audio output using raspi-config

You can also use the `amixer` command to flip a virtual switch that determines the path of the audio output in the following two ways:

- `amixer cset numid=3 1`: This sets the audio out to the 3.5 mm analog jack
- `amixer cset numid=3 2`: This sets the audio out to the HDMI cable

Running these commands will return an output something like this:

```
numid=3,iface=MIXER,name='PCM Playback Route'
; type=INTEGER,access=rw------,values=1,min=0,max=2,step=0   : values=1
```

This is confirmation in the interface that you have made changes, plus also hints on what other values it will accept-in this case between and 2.

## Testing the speakers

Now that you've decided where to send the sound, type in the following command to test your speakers:

```
pi@raspberrypi ~ $ speaker-test -c2 -t wav
```

With a bit of luck, you should hear a woman's voice say *Front Left* in your left-hand side speaker and *Front Right* in your right-hand speaker. These words will be repeated until you overcome the urge to start marching and press *Ctrl + C* to quit the speaker-test application.

## Preparing to record

As mentioned previously, in order to get sound into the Raspberry Pi we need to plug in an external device such as a USB microphone, headset, or webcam. In my setup, I have a rather small and aesthetically pleasing USB sound card I bought from Maplin Electronics (maplin.co.uk, order code A03NC) which gives me 3.5 mm mic-in and audio-out jacks. It also glows blue, which makes me very happy:

The Formosa AS301 Tube Delight sound card works with the Raspberry Pi

Before inserting your device, you will want to power down your Pi, as hot-plugging gadgets into a Pi has been known to cause reboots, but also it might not install the new hardware until you have done so.

We can check whether ALSA has detected our new audio device and added it to the list of cards using the following command:

```
pi@raspberrypi ~ $ cat /proc/asound/cards
```

In the following screenshot, my Tube Delight device was attached and assigned card number one:

```
pi@raspberrypi: ~                                               —    □    ×
pi@raspberrypi:~ $ cat /proc/asound/cards
 0 [ALSA          ]: bcm2835 - bcm2835 ALSA
                     bcm2835 ALSA
 1 [Adapter       ]: USB-Audio - USB Audio Adapter
                     Formosa21 Inc. USB Audio Adapter at usb-3f980000.usb-1.4,
full speed
pi@raspberrypi:~ $
```

List of detected ALSA cards showing a new addition

If you want a device that's a little subtler, then you can't go far wrong with a Plugable USB audio adapter. This device is probably more suitable for plugging into a Pi Zero. On the downside, it doesn't glow blue:

Plugable USB audio adapter is quite a bit smaller than the Tube Delight but doesn't glow blue

With this device plugged into the Pi, you should see the following screen when listing the detected ALSA cards:

```
pi@raspberrypi: ~                                          —   □   ×
pi@raspberrypi:~ $ cat /proc/asound/cards
 0 [ALSA           ]: bcm2835 - bcm2835 ALSA
                      bcm2835 ALSA
 1 [Device         ]: USB-Audio - USB Audio Device
                      C-Media Electronics Inc. USB Audio Device at usb-3
f980000.usb-1.5, full speed
pi@raspberrypi:~ $ 
```

If your gadget doesn't show up in the cards list, it could be that no drivers were found and loaded for your device, and your best bet is to search the Raspberry Pi forums for hints on your gadget at http://www.raspberrypi.org/forums/.

Next, we'll have a look at the new device in alsamixer using the following command:

```
pi@raspberrypi ~ $ alsamixer -c1
```

The `-c1` argument tells `alsamixer` to show the controls for card number one, but you can easily switch between cards using the *F6* or *S* keys.

Note that if you have connected just a USB microphone with no audio output port, then you may be presented with a message saying something like **This sound device does not have playback controls**, which is obviously true in this case.

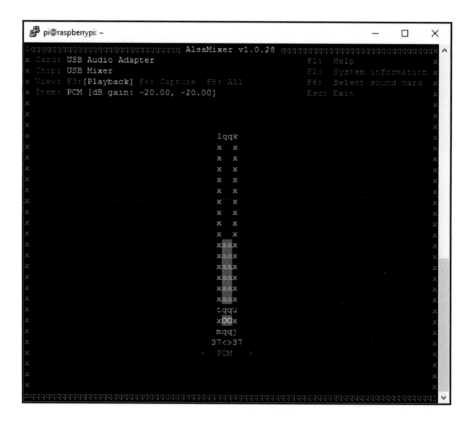

AlsaMixer showing default volume of newly added card

Now, let's have a closer look at the other views available:

- *F1* or *H*: This displays a help page with a comprehensive list of all the keyboard shortcuts
- *F2* or */*: This displays a dialog that allows you to view the information files in `/proc/asound`
- *F3* or *Tab:* This displays the **Playback** meters and controls view

- *F4 or Tab:* This displays the **Capture** (recording) meters and controls view
- *F5 or Tab:* This displays a combined **Playback** and **Capture** view

If you're accessing the AlsaMixer using an SSH terminal window (as I am), then you may not be able to use the function keys to select the view. In which case, use the *Tab* key to switch views.

Since we're about to record some sound, we'll want to focus on the **Capture** view.

It's fairly common for the microphone of your audio gadget to be inactive and unable to record by default until you enable it to capture! Find your **Capture** control, usually labeled **Mic**, toggle it on using the spacebar so that it displays the word **CAPTURE**, and adjust the recording volume using the arrow keys. Press *Esc* when done:

AlsaMixer showing a toggled on capture device

Note that it's possible for a cheap webcam to have no visible meters or controls. It may still be able to record sound; you just won't be able to adjust the recording volume manually.

# Testing the microphone

To aid us in the recording and playback of sound files, we'll install the absolutely invaluable **Sound eXchange (SoX)** application-the Swiss Army knife of sound processing. SoX is a command-line utility that can play, record, and convert pretty much any audio format found on planet Earth.

Type in the following command to install SoX and an add-on that deals with

MP3 files:

```
pi@raspberrypi ~ $ sudo apt-get install sox libsox-fmt-mp3
```

When prompted, press *Y* and *Enter* to continue with the installation.

Notice how easy it is to download and install new software packages from the Internet with the `apt-get` command. You can also search for packages using the command `apt-cache search [text to search for]`. Now type in the following command to start what we call a **monitoring loop**:

```
pi@raspberrypi ~ $ sox -t alsa plughw:1 -d
```

If everything is working right, you should be able to speak into the microphone connected to the external sound card and hear yourself from the monitor or desktop speakers plugged into the Pi, with a very slight delay:

SoX in a monitoring loop

Let's break down exactly what's happening here:

The `sox` command accepts an input file and an output file, in that order, together with a myriad of optional parameters. In this case, `-t alsa plughw:1` is the input file and `-d` is the output file.

`-t alsa plughw:1` means ALSA card number one and `-d` means default ALSA card, which is the Raspberry Pi sound core.

The status line that is continuously updated while `sox` is running provides many helpful pieces of information, starting from the left-hand side:

- Percentage completed of recording or playback (unknown in our monitoring loop)
- Elapsed time of recording or playback
- Remaining time of recording or playback (also unknown in a monitoring loop)
- Number of samples written to the output file
- Spiffy stereo peak-level meters that will help you calibrate the input volume of your microphone and will indicate with a *!* character if clipping occurs

When you've grown tired of hearing your own voice, press *Ctrl + C* to quit the monitoring loop.

# Clipping, feedback distortion, and improving sound quality

Here are three tips to make your recordings sound better:

- Clipping occurs when the microphone signal is amplified beyond its capability. Try lowering the capture volume in `alsamixer` or moving a little further away from the microphone.
- A feedback loop happens when your microphone gets too close to the speakers that are playing the recorded sound from that microphone. This loop of amplification will distort the sound and may produce a very unpleasant squeal (unless your name is Jimmy Hendrix). The easiest way to mitigate feedback is to listen through a pair of headphones instead of through the speakers.

- If you're getting a lot of crackling and popping from your microphone, there's a trick that might help improve the sound quality. What it does is limit the USB bus speed to 12 Mbps. Just keep in mind that this might affect your other USB devices for the worse, so consider reverting the change when you're done with audio projects. Type in the following command to open up a text editor where you'll make a simple adjustment to a configuration file:

```
pi@raspberrypi ~ $ sudo nano /boot/cmdline.txt
```

At the beginning of the line, add the `dwc_otg.speed=1` string and put a space after it to separate it from the next string, `dwc_otg.lpm_enable=0`. Now press *Ctrl + X* to exit and select **y** when prompted to save the modified buffer, then press the *Enter* key to confirm the filename to write to. Reboot your Pi and try recording again to see whether the audio quality has improved.

# Recording conversations for later retrieval

So we have our audio gear all configured and ready to record-let's get sneaky with it!

Picture the following scenario: you know that something fishy is about to go down and you'd like to record whatever sound that fishy thing makes. Your first challenge will be to hide the Pi out of sight with as few cables running to it as possible. Unless you're working with a battery, the Pi will have to be hidden somewhere within a few meters of a power outlet.

Next, you'll want to connect your USB microphone and keep it hidden, yet uncovered if possible, to avoid a muffled recording. Unless you expect the action to take place right in front of the microphone, you should set the capture signal to the max with `alsamixer` for the microphone to be able to pick up as much of the room as possible.

Now, all we need to worry about is how to trigger the recording.

# Writing to a WAV file

The **Waveform Audio File (WAV)** is the most common file format used for recording audio:

- To save a recording to a file named `myrec.wav` on the SD card, type in the following command:

  ```
  pi@raspberrypi ~ $ sox -t alsa plughw:1 myrec.wav
  ```

  To stop the recording, press *Ctrl + C*.

- Play back the recording using the following command:

  ```
  pi@raspberrypi ~ $ sox myrec.wav -d
  ```

- If your USB gadget happens to have a speaker output, or is a headset, you could listen to the recording in the headphones with the following command:

  ```
  pi@raspberrypi ~ $ sox myrec.wav -t alsa plughw:1
  ```

# Writing to an MP3 or OGG file

So far we've been storing our audio as uncompressed WAV files. This is fine for shorter recordings, but it'll eat up the free space on your SD card rather quickly if you want to record several hours of audio data. One hour of uncompressed 16-bit, 48 kHz, stereo sound will take up about 660 MB of space.

What we want to do is compress the audio data by encoding the sound to MP3 or OGG format. This will drastically reduce the file size, while keeping the audio sounding almost identical to the human ear.

Type in the following command to install the LAME encoder (for MP3) and the Vorbis encoder (for OGG):

```
pi@raspberrypi ~ $ sudo apt-get install lame vorbis-tools
```

To encode `myrec.wav` to `myrec.mp3`, use the following command:

```
pi@raspberrypi ~ $ lame myrec.wav
```

To encode `myrec.wav` to `myrec.ogg`, use the following command:

```
pi@raspberrypi ~ $ oggenc myrec.wav
```

Once you have your MP3 or OGG file, you can, of course, delete the original uncompressed `myrec.wav` file to save space using the `rm` command:

```
pi@raspberrypi ~ $ rm myrec.wav
```

But wouldn't it be convenient if we could just record straight to an MP3 or OGG file? Thanks to the ingenious pipeline feature of our operating system, this is easy with the following command:

```
pi@raspberrypi ~ $ sox -t alsa plughw:1 -t wav - | lame - myrec.mp3
```

The line does look a bit cryptic, so let me explain what's going on. The `|` character that separates the two commands is called a pipeline, or pipe. It allows us to chain the standard output stream from one application into the standard input stream of another application. So in this example, we tell `sox` not to write the recording to a file on the SD card, but instead pass on the data to `lame`, which in turn encodes the sound as soon as it comes in and stores it in a file named `myrec.mp3`. The lone `-` characters represent the standard input and standard output streams respectively. We also specify the `-t wav` argument, which provides `lame` with useful information about the incoming audio data.

For OGG output, we have to use a slightly different command:

```
pi@raspberrypi ~ $ sox -t alsa plughw:1 -t wav - | oggenc - -o myrec.ogg
```

You can then playback these formats with `sox` just like any other file:

```
pi@raspberrypi ~ $ sox myrec.mp3 -d
```

 **MP3 technology patents**: In some countries, there are legal uncertainties around the distribution of MP3 encoder and player binaries. This is a problem, not just for the developers of free audio software, but it affects you too as an end user and you'll often have to obtain the binaries in question from alternative sources.

# Creating command shortcuts with aliases

You're likely getting tired of typing those never-ending `sox` commands by now. Fortunately, there's a feature built into the bash shell named `alias` that allows us to create convenient shortcuts for commands we'd like to avoid typing over and over again. Shortcuts are created as follows:

Type in the following command to create an alias named `record` that will start a `sox` recording and output to an MP3 file that you'll specify when you use the shortcut:

```
pi@raspberrypi ~ $ alias record='sox -t alsa plughw:1 -t wav - | lame -'
```

Now all you have to do to start recording to the `newrec.mp3` file is type in the following:

```
pi@raspberrypi ~ $ record newrec.mp3
```

To view a list of all currently defined aliases, use the following command:

```
pi@raspberrypi ~ $ alias
```

As you can see, there are four default aliases added already by Raspbian. Should you wish to modify your alias, just create it again with the `alias` command and provide a new definition, or use the `unalias` command to remove it altogether.

Now there's only one problem with your nifty shortcut-it will disappear as soon as you reboot the Pi. To make it permanent, we will add it to a file named `.bash_aliases` in your home directory. The initial dot in the filename makes the file **hidden** from the normal `ls` file listing; you'll have to use `ls -a` to see it. This file will then be read every time you log in and your alias is recreated.

Start the `nano` text editor and edit the `.bash_aliases` file using the following command:

```
pi@raspberrypi ~ $ nano ~/.bash_aliases
```

The ~ character here is a shorter way of saying `/home/pi`-your home directory path.

Add your `alias` commands, one per line, then press *Ctrl + X* to exit and select **y** when prompted to save the modified buffer, then press the Enter key to confirm the filename to write to.

In order for your alias commands to take effect, you will need to log off and log back in again:

```
GNU nano 2.2.6          File: /home/pi/.bash_aliases

alias record='sox -t alsa plughw:1 -t wav - | lame -'




^G Get Help   ^O WriteOut   ^R Read File  ^Y Prev Page  ^K Cut Text   ^C Cur Pos
^X Exit       ^J Justify    ^W Where Is   ^V Next Page  ^U UnCut Text ^T To Spell
```

# Keep your recordings running safely with tmux

So you're logged in to the Pi over Wi-Fi and have started the recording. Just as things start to get interesting, there's a dip in the network connectivity and your SSH connection drops. Later, you retrieve the Pi only to discover that the recording stopped when your SSH session got cut.

Meet **tmux**, a terminal multiplexer or virtual console application that makes it possible to run commands in a protected session from which you can detach, on purpose or by accident, and then attach to again without interrupting the applications running inside the session.

Let's install it using the following command:

```
pi@raspberrypi ~ $ sudo apt-get install tmux
```

Now we're going to start a new tmux session using the following command:

```
pi@raspberrypi ~ $ tmux
```

Notice the green status line across the bottom of the screen. It tells us that we are inside the first session **[0]** and we're looking at the first window **0:** running the `bash` command-our login shell.

To demonstrate the basic capabilities of `tmux`, let's get a recording going using that handy alias we defined previously:

```
pi@raspberrypi ~ $ record bgrec.mp3
```

Now, with the recording running, press *Ctrl + B* followed by *C* to create a new window.

We are now looking at the second window **1:** running a new, separate bash login shell. Also notice on the status line how the currently active window is indicated by the * character.

We can switch between these windows by pressing *Ctrl + B*, followed by *N* for the next window:

```
 pi@raspberrypi: ~                                         —   □   ×
top - 19:21:25 up  3:41,  3 users,  load average: 0.31, 0.22, 0.12
Tasks: 122 total,   3 running, 119 sleeping,   0 stopped,   0 zombie
%Cpu(s):  7.6 us,  1.1 sy,  0.0 ni, 91.1 id,  0.0 wa,  0.0 hi,  0.2 si,  0.0 st
KiB Mem:    948012 total,    327632 used,    620380 free,     27624 buffers
KiB Swap:   102396 total,         0 used,    102396 free,    205128 cached Mem

  PID USER      PR  NI    VIRT    RES    SHR S  %CPU %MEM     TIME+ COMMAND
19577 pi        20   0    4616   2988   1832 R  28.0  0.3   0:34.79 lame
19063 root      20   0       0      0      0 S   5.6  0.0   1:02.13 kworker/0:0
19565 pi        20   0    5296   2780   2360 S   1.0  0.3   0:00.91 tmux
19576 pi        20   0    9620   4196   3624 S   0.7  0.4   0:00.86 sox
  596 root      20   0  111600  32556  18308 S   0.3  3.4   0:04.89 Xorg
 1296 root      20   0       0      0      0 S   0.3  0.0   0:00.28 kworker/3:0
19591 pi        20   0    5112   2528   2152 R   0.3  0.3   0:00.33 top
    1 root      20   0   22832   3916   2736 S   0.0  0.4   0:06.12 systemd
    2 root      20   0       0      0      0 S   0.0  0.0   0:00.00 kthreadd
    3 root      20   0       0      0      0 S   0.0  0.0   0:00.56 ksoftirqd/0
    5 root       0 -20       0      0      0 S   0.0  0.0   0:00.00 kworker/0:0H
    7 root      20   0       0      0      0 R   0.0  0.0   0:01.90 rcu_sched
    8 root      20   0       0      0      0 S   0.0  0.0   0:00.00 rcu_bh
    9 root      rt   0       0      0      0 S   0.0  0.0   0:00.01 migration/0
   10 root      rt   0       0      0      0 S   0.0  0.0   0:00.00 migration/1
   11 root      20   0       0      0      0 S   0.0  0.0   0:00.05 ksoftirqd/1
   13 root       0 -20       0      0      0 S   0.0  0.0   0:00.00 kworker/1:0H
   14 root      rt   0       0      0      0 S   0.0  0.0   0:00.00 migration/2
[0] 0:sox- 1:top*                                  "raspberrypi" 19:21 27-Mar-16
```

A tmux session with two windows

Let's get back to the reason why we installed `tmux` in the first place-the ability to disconnect from the Pi while our recording command continues to run. Press *Ctrl + B* followed by *D* to detach from the `tmux` session. Getting accidentally disconnected from the SSH session would have the same effect.

Then type in the following command to attach to the `tmux` session again:

```
pi@raspberrypi ~ $ tmux attach
```

Use the following command to get a list of all the windows running inside `tmux`:

```
pi@raspberrypi ~ $ tmux lsw
```

When you want to stop the recording, you will need to connect to the relevant `tmux` session and press the *Ctrl + C* keys.

We've only covered the bare essentials of the `tmux` application here, so if you'd like to explore further, press *Ctrl + B* followed by *?* for a complete list of keyboard shortcuts.

# Making a covert wearable recorder with Pi Zero

Having a powerful device as small as the Pi Zero opens up all sorts of opportunities for covert operations. So why don't we build a voice recorder that we can take out with us and hide on our person—but which will also do everything else we'd expect from the Pi Zero? The low power requirement means that we can get hours of portable power from a small lithium-ion power bank.

Now, while the Pi Zero is very small, unfortunately the standard connector kit for power and USB makes it bulkier once we start plugging things into it:

Pi Zero connector kit

The bit that was bothering me was the bulky and long USB adapter to convert the Pi's micro-USB connector to a normal USB connector so I could plug in the audio adapter, but having a poke around on Amazon yielded the availability of very small form-factor converters:

eBoot low-profile OTG micro-USB converters

So this is what my Pi Zero looks like with my USB audio device connected to it using the small converter:

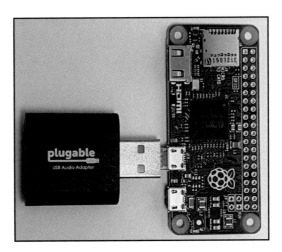

The drawback here, however, is I then didn't have enough room to put the power connector in that came with my power bank – unless I trimmed down the strain relief on the power cable, taking care not to damage the actual wires. This is what we now have:

Power cable strain relief has been trimmed to make it fit

To power the Pi Zero, I used a small USB power bank, such as the one available from RS Components (order number 775-7504) pictured here:

2200mAh lithium-ion USB power bank from RS Components

This particular one has enough juice to power our Pi Zero for about 5 hours when fully charged.

So let's take a look at our Pi Zero with all the bits connected:

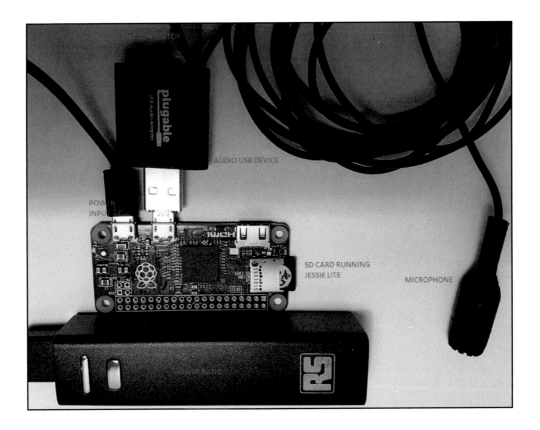

Our collection of components for our Pi Zero Wearable Edition

In order to protect the Pi Zero board, it's secured in an anti-static bag which can then be mounted to the power bank to make a compact, pocket-sized device that can be worn inside a jacket, or if you want, in secret agent style, taped to your body:

Our wearable Pi Zero protected in a little bag

# Listening in on conversations from a distance

What if we want to listen in on some event live as it goes down, but from a safe distance away from where the Pi's recording-exactly like a baby monitor?

We would need a way of broadcasting whatever is recorded across a network to another computer that we can listen to. Actually, we already have everything required to do this, SSH and SoX; one just has to know how to compose the command lines to wield these powerful tools.

## Listening in Windows

You should have the full PuTTY suite installed from the *Connecting to the Pi from Windows* section in `Chapter 1`, *Getting Up to No Good*, as we will be using the `plink` and `pscp` commands for this example.

If you didn't download the full PuTTY suite, then you can download the suite or the individual Plink and Pscp packages from here, `http://www.chiark.greenend.org.uk/~sgtatham/putty/download.html`.

To download SoX for Windows, visit `http://sourceforge.net/projects/sox/files/sox/` and click on the download link for the latest version (`sox-14.4.2-win32.exe` at the time of writing).

Run the installer to install SoX on your Windows PC.

To be able to play MP3 files with SoX, you can optionally download the decoder library file at `http://www.intestinate.com/libmad.dll` and put it in the `C:\Program Files (x86)\sox-14-4-2` folder.

Start a command prompt from the Start menu by clicking on the shortcut, or by typing `cmd` in the **Run/Search** field.

The following examples will be executed in the command prompt environment.

Note that the `C:\Program Files (x86)` directory in later versions of Windows might be called `C:\Program Files` on your computer. Just erase the `(x86)` part from the paths if the commands fail.

To start a recording on the Pi and send the output to our Windows machine, use the following command, but replace `[IP address]` with the IP address of your Pi and `[password]` with your login password:

```
C:\> "C:\Program Files (x86)\PuTTY\plink" pi@[IP address] -pw [password]
sox -t alsa plughw:1 -t sox - | "C:\Program Files (x86)\sox-14-4-1\sox" -q
-t sox - -d
```

SoX will behave just as if it was running locally on the Pi, with the volume meters moving on sound input.

Let's break down the command:

- `"C:\Program Files (x86)\PuTTY\plink"`: This is the full path to the `plink` application. The quotes are necessary because of the space in the `Program Files (x86)` directory name. `plink` is like a command-line version of PuTTY, but more suitable for interfacing with other applications, such as SoX in our example.
- `*` We specify that we want to log in as the user `pi@[IP address]` and to use the password `-pw [password]` because the command won't work if it has to pause and prompt us for that information.
- `*` `sox -t alsa plughw:1 -t sox -`: This starts `sox` on the Pi itself but sends the output to our Windows machine through the SSH link.
- `| "C:\Program Files (x86)\sox-14-4-1\sox" -q -t sox - -d` then pipes that output to our local `sox` application, to which we've given a `-q` or quiet mode argument for cosmetic reasons. Otherwise, SoX would show two competing progress displays.
- The two `-t sox` arguments instruct SoX to use its own native, uncompressed file format, which is especially useful for transporting audio between SoX pipes such as this one.

Let's look at a few additional tricks with PuTTY and SoX.

It's useful to be able to store the recording on your Windows machine instead of the SD card on the Pi. The following command will record from the Pi to `myrec.wav` on your local desktop:

```
C:\> "C:\Program Files (x86)\PuTTY\plink" pi@[IP address] -pw [password]
sox -t alsa plughw:1 -t wav - > %UserProfile%\Desktop\myrec.wav
```

 Note the > character instead of the pipe, which is used to redirect the output to a file.

You can simply copy files from your Pi using the `pscp` command. The following command copies `myrec.wav` from the `pi` user's home directory to your local desktop:

```
C:\> "C:\Program Files (x86)\PuTTY\pscp" pi@[IP address]:myrec.wav
%UserProfile%\Desktop\myrec.wav
```

Just reverse the argument order of the previous command to copy `myrec.wav` from your local desktop to the `pi` user's home directory:

```
C:\> "C:\Program Files (x86)\PuTTY\pscp"
%UserProfile%\Desktop\myrec.wav pi@[IP address]:myrec.wav
```

Finally, let's make sure you never have to type one of those long commands again by creating a simple shortcut on the desktop. Type in the following command from the command prompt:

```
C:\> notepad %UserProfile%\Desktop\PiRec.cmd
```

Click on **Yes** when a dialog box appears to create a new file, paste one of the long commands, then save and exit. You should now be able to double-click on the shortcut on your desktop to start a new listening or recording session.

# Listening in Mac OS X or Linux

Since Mac OS X and most Linux distributions include an SSH client, all we need is SoX. To install SoX on Linux, use the package manager of your distribution to add the `sox` package. For Mac, follow these steps:

1. Visit `http://sourceforge.net/projects/sox/files/sox/` and click on the download link for the latest version (`sox-14.4.2-macosx.zip` at the time of writing) and save it to your desktop.
2. Double-click on the SoX ZIP file to extract it.

1. Open up a Terminal (located in `/Applications/Utilities` on the Mac).
2. Type `cd ~/Desktop/sox-14.4.2` to change to the extracted SoX directory. Then type `sudo cp sox /usr/bin` to copy the `sox` binary to a location in our default path.

To be able to optionally encode and play MP3 files with SoX, the recommended method is to install SoX through **Homebrew**. Visit http://brew.sh and follow the installation instructions. Then type `brew install sox` to build and install an MP3-capable SoX.

To start a recording on the Pi and send the output to your computer, use the following command, but replace `[IP address]` with the IP address of your Pi:

```
$ ssh pi@[IP address] sox -t alsa plughw:1 -t sox - | sox -q -t sox - -d
```

SoX will behave just as if it was running locally on the Pi, with the volume meters moving on sound input.

Let's break down the command:

- \* `ssh pi@[IP address] sox -t alsa plughw:1 -t sox -` starts a `sox` command on the Pi itself but sends the output to our machine through the SSH link.
- `| sox -q -t sox - -d` then pipes that output to our local `sox` application, which we've given a `-q` or *quite mode* argument for cosmetic reasons. Otherwise, SoX would show two competing progress displays.
- The two `-t sox` arguments instruct SoX to use its own native, uncompressed file format, which is especially useful for transporting audio between SoX pipes like this one.

Let's look at a few additional tricks with SSH and SoX.

It's useful to be able to store the recording on your machine instead of the SD card on the Pi. The following command will record from the Pi to `myrec.wav` on your local desktop:

```
$ ssh pi@[IP address] sox -t alsa plughw:1 -t wav - > ~/Desktop/myrec.wav
```

Note the > character instead of the pipe, which is used to redirect the output to a file.

Simply copy files from your Pi using the `scp` command. The following command copies `myrec.wav` from the `pi` user's home directory to your local desktop:

```
$ scp pi@[IP address]:myrec.wav ~/Desktop/myrec.wav
```

Just reverse the argument order of the previous command to copy `myrec.wav` from your local desktop to the `pi` user's home directory:

```
$ scp ~/Desktop/myrec.wav pi@[IP address]:myrec.wav
```

To avoid having to remember those long commands, you could easily create aliases for them using the same techniques we covered previously in this chapter, only on Mac OS X, you need to put your lines in `~/.bash_profile` instead of `~/.bash_aliases`:

```
$ echo "alias pilisten='ssh pi@[IP address] sox -t alsa plughw:1 -t sox - |
sox -q -t sox - -d'" >> ~/.bash_profile
```

# Listening in over Bluetooth

Whilst it's good to be able to listen in on the action using our computer, we're dependent on having a network connection with the listening Pi, either through Ethernet or over Wi-Fi. This means it's not very portable or discreet, so wouldn't it be great if we could eavesdrop wirelessly from the next room or outside with just a **Bluetooth** headset or small speaker? Just like a bugging device.

## Introducing Bluetooth audio

Bluetooth is a short-range radio technology that allows wireless communication between devices such as mobile phones, computers and headset or speakers. As such, the Bluetooth system features an audio protocol as standard, which we make use of (called **Advanced Audio Distribution Profile** or **A2DP** for short). Standard Bluetooth gives us a range of up to about 10-20 meters between devices – enough to listen in from the next room or outside.

As an added bonus to make our system even simpler, the new Raspberry Pi version 3 boards include a Bluetooth radio on board, which means our listening box can be more compact and discreet than before. Of course, you can achieve the same results with other Pi boards by adding a compatible USB Bluetooth dongle, and the steps in this topic should work for that configuration also.

## Setting up Bluetooth on the Pi

We're now going to set up our Raspberry Pi as a listening device and relay the audio from the microphone to a Bluetooth headset or speaker.

If you don't have a Pi 3, then shut down your Pi and plug in a Bluetooth dongle. Power your Pi back up and when it's booted up and you're logged back in, we check that it can be seen by typing this:

```
pi@raspberrypi ~ $ lsusb
```

You should then see your device listed similar to this:

Bluetooth device shown in USB device list

Now that we have our Bluetooth radio connected, we need to install the Raspberry Pi Bluetooth support package (including Bluez 5). On the Pi 3 running Raspbian Jessie, you should already have it installed; otherwise type the following command:

```
pi@raspberrypi ~ $ sudo apt-get install pi-bluetooth
```

Raspbian Jessie is using Bluez 5, which has dropped support for ALSA (previously provided by the `bluez-alsa` package) so the alternative is to use PulseAudio, which we'll deal with a bit later.

With Bluez installed, let's check whether our Bluetooth hardware is working by typing:

```
pi@raspberrypi ~ $ hciconfig -a
```

You should now see the connected Bluetooth device(s) listed as follows:

```
pi@raspberrypi: ~                                          —    □    ×

pi@raspberrypi:~ $ hciconfig -a
hci0:   Type: BR/EDR  Bus: UART
        BD Address: B8:27:EB:0B:D4:35  ACL MTU: 1021:8  SCO MTU: 64:1
        UP RUNNING
        RX bytes:997 acl:0 sco:0 events:45 errors:0
        TX bytes:1544 acl:0 sco:0 commands:45 errors:0
        Features: 0xbf 0xfe 0xcf 0xfe 0xdb 0xff 0x7b 0x87
        Packet type: DM1 DM3 DM5 DH1 DH3 DH5 HV1 HV2 HV3
        Link policy: RSWITCH SNIFF
        Link mode: SLAVE ACCEPT
        Name: 'raspberrypi'
        Class: 0x000000
        Service Classes: Unspecified
        Device Class: Miscellaneous,
        HCI Version: 4.1 (0x7)  Revision: 0xb6
        LMP Version: 4.1 (0x7)  Subversion: 0x2209
        Manufacturer: Broadcom Corporation (15)

pi@raspberrypi:~ $
```

On the Raspberry Pi 3, the `Bus` setting will show as `UART` rather than `USB`, which it does when using a dongle.

Next we need to allow our `pi` account to access and make changes to Bluetooth configuration stuff:

```
pi@raspberrypi ~ $ sudo usermod -a -G lp pi
```

# Installing PulseAudio

PulseAudio is a sound proxy that takes audio from different inputs (*sources*) and routes them through to a single output (or *sink*). Think of it as a bit like the Volume Mixer on Windows, which sits between your applications and your sound hardware. We will use it to take our mic input from our sound card and route the audio to the Bluetooth adapter on our Raspberry Pi, which will send the audio to our headset or speaker using Bluetooth A2DP.

So let's install PulseAudio:

```
pi@raspberrypi ~ $ sudo apt-get install pulseaudio pulseaudio-module-
bluetooth
```

Now would be a good time to reboot our Pi:

```
pi@raspberrypi ~ $ sudo reboot
```

# Connect to your Bluetooth headset or speaker

In order to make a Bluetooth connection between your Pi and headset, you'll need to know its unique identifier or MAC address. To do this, put your headset or speaker into discoverable mode and then run the following command on your Pi:

```
pi@raspberrypi ~ $ hcitool scan
```

After a few seconds, you should see all discoverable devices, and in particular your audio device. In the following screenshot, you can see that my Pi has found my Plantronics 590 Bluetooth headset and provided me with its MAC address:

Take a note of the MAC address so that we can pair it with your Pi using the following steps:

1. Enter the Bluetooth Control console using this:

   ```
   pi@raspberrypi ~ $ bluetoothctl
   ```

2. Power up the Bluetooth radio by typing power on:

   ```
   [bluetooth]# power on
   ```

3. Ensure the agent is switched on by typing agent on:

   ```
   [bluetooth]# agent on
   ```

4. Ensure your headset is switched on and in discoverable mode.
5. Scan for the device using scan on:

   ```
   [Bluetooth]# scan on
   ```

6. Pair the Bluetooth headset using its MAC address, using pair followed by your device's address:

   ```
   [Bluetooth]# pair XX:XX:XX:XX:XX:XX
   ```

7. Add the Bluetooth headset to the list of trusted devices using trust followed by your device's address:

   ```
   [Bluetooth]# trust XX:XX:XX:XX:XX:XX
   ```

8. Now we can connect to the Bluetooth audio device using connect followed by your device's address:

   ```
   [Bluetooth]# connect XX:XX:XX:XX:XX:XX
   ```

Here's what the console should look like after entering these commands:

```
pi@raspberrypi: ~                                                    —

[bluetooth]# power on
[CHG] Controller B8:27:EB:0B:D4:35 Class: 0x0c0000
Changing power on succeeded
[CHG] Controller B8:27:EB:0B:D4:35 Powered: yes
[bluetooth]# agent on
Agent registered
[bluetooth]# scan on
Discovery started
[CHG] Controller B8:27:EB:0B:D4:35 Discovering: yes
[NEW] Device 60:03:08:AF:6D:03 60-03-08-AF-6D-03
[NEW] Device 00:03:89:93:8D:B4 590Plantronics
[bluetooth]# pair 00:03:89:93:8D:B4
Attempting to pair with 00:03:89:93:8D:B4
[CHG] Device 00:03:89:93:8D:B4 Connected: yes
[CHG] Device 00:03:89:93:8D:B4 UUIDs:
        00001108-0000-1000-8000-00805f9b34fb
        0000110b-0000-1000-8000-00805f9b34fb
        0000110e-0000-1000-8000-00805f9b34fb
        0000111e-0000-1000-8000-00805f9b34fb
[CHG] Device 00:03:89:93:8D:B4 Paired: yes
Pairing successful
[CHG] Device 00:03:89:93:8D:B4 Connected: no
[bluetooth]# trust 00:03:89:93:8D:B4
[CHG] Device 00:03:89:93:8D:B4 Trusted: yes
Changing 00:03:89:93:8D:B4 trust succeeded
[bluetooth]# connect 00:03:89:93:8D:B4
Attempting to connect to 00:03:89:93:8D:B4
[CHG] Device 00:03:89:93:8D:B4 Connected: yes
Connection successful
[CHG] Device 00:03:89:93:8D:B4 UUIDs:
        00001108-0000-1000-8000-00805f9b34fb
        0000110b-0000-1000-8000-00805f9b34fb
```

Now, that process can get a bit tedious if you want to do it often, so let's write a script that automates those steps for us (you can use Nano and save it in your home directory).

The script works by piping individual commands into the Bluetooth Control Console, assuming that we know the MAC address of the Bluetooth device and that it's on and ready to be connected to:

```sh
#!/bin/sh
DEV_MAC="00:03:89:93:8D:B4" #mac addr of headset
echo "power on" | bluetoothctl -a
echo "agent on" | bluetoothctl -a
echo "connect $DEV_MAC" | bluetoothctl -a
echo "exit" | bluetoothctl -a
bt-audio.sh
```

Before running the script, we need to make it executable using the following command:

```
pi@raspberrypi ~ $ chmod +x ./bt-audio.sh
```

Now run the script by typing this:

```
pi@raspberrypi ~ $ sudo ./bt-audio.sh
```

Once it's been run, you can check whether you are connected to your Bluetooth device with the following command:

```
pi@raspberrypi ~ $ hcitool con
```

Your device should be listed under **Connections**:

**Connections:**

**< ACL 00:03:89:93:8D:B4 handle 12 state 1 lm SLAVE AUTH ENCRYPT**

# Bluetooth by default

As it stands, our Raspberry Pi core is the default output device (*sink*), so we need to tell PulseAudio to direct audio to our Bluetooth headset or speaker. In order to do this, we need to find the device name according to PulseAudio.

First, we need to start the PulseAudio daemon so we can use it:

```
pi@raspberrypi ~ $ pulseaudio --start
```

Enter the following PulseAudio command:

You will then be presented with a long list of data about the devices PulseAudio knows about. In fact, since we only want to know the name at this time, we can limit what it returns by piping into grep, which will make our output a tad more palatable:

```
pi@raspberrypi ~ $ pacmd list-sinks short | grep -e 'name:'
```

You'll be looking for something like the name I've highlighted in the previous screenshot, in my case bluez_sink.00_03_89_93_8D_84.

So to set the default PulseAudio output device, we use the following command (you could include this in your previous automation script):

```
pi@raspberrypi ~ $ pactl set-default-sink bluez_sink.00_03_89_93_8D_B4
```

If you now play the recorded file we made earlier, you should hear it through the Bluetooth headset or speaker:

```
pi@raspberrypi ~ $ sox myrec.wav -d
```

To restore the default back to the Raspberry Pi jack output, use this command:

```
$ pactl set-default-sink alsa_output.0.analog-stereo
```

And now, to get your listening device working with your microphone, we can just start up the sox monitoring loop we used earlier:

```
pi@raspberrypi ~ $ sox -t alsa plughw:1 -d
```

If you get into a bit of mess with all these audio configurations, you can reset the ALSA configurations using this command:

```
sudo /etc/init.d/alsa-utils reset
```

Happy listening!

# Talking to people from a distance

Instead of listening in on the action, maybe you'd like to be the one creating all the noise by making the Pi an extension of your own voice. You'll be on a computer with a microphone, and the Pi can be somewhere else broadcasting your message to the world through a pair of speakers (or a megaphone). In other words, the roles of the Pi and your computer from the previous topic will be reversed.

## Talking in Windows

First, make sure SoX is added to Windows as per the instructions in the *Listening in Windows* section:

1. Connect your microphone and check the input volume of your device. You'll find the settings in **Control Panel | Hardware and Sound | Manage audio devices** under the **Recording** tab. Make your microphone the default device by selecting it and clicking on **Set Default**.
2. Start a command prompt from the Start menu by clicking on the shortcut or by typing cmd in the **Run/Search** field.
3. We can start a monitoring loop first to ensure our microphone works as intended:

```
C:\> "C:\Program Files (x86)\sox-14-4-2\sox" -d -d
```

4. Now, to send the audio from our microphone to the speakers on the Pi,
5. use the following command:

```
C:\> "C:\Program Files (x86)\sox-14-4-2\sox" -d -t wav - | "C:\Program
Files (x86)\PuTTY\plink" pi@[IP address] -pw [password] sox -q -t wav - -d
```

6. Maybe you'd like to broadcast some nice music or a prerecorded message instead of your own live voice? Use the following command to send `My Song.mp3` from your desktop to be played out of the speakers connected to the Pi:

```
C:\> type "%UserProfile%\Desktop\My Song.mp3" | "C:\Program Files
(x86)\PuTTY\plink" pi@[IP Address] -pw [password] sox -t mp3 - -d
```

7. Or why not broadcast an entire album with sweet tunes located in the `My Album` folder on the desktop:

```
C:\> type "%UserProfile%\Desktop\My Album\*.mp3" | "C:\Program Files
(x86)\PuTTY\plink" pi@[IP Address] -pw [password] sox -t mp3 - -d
```

# Talking in Mac OS X or Linux

First make sure SoX is added to your operating system as per the instructions in the *Listening in Mac OS X or Linux* section:

1. Connect your microphone and check the input volume of your device. On Mac, you'll find the settings in **System Preferences** | **Sound** under the **Input** tab. Make your microphone the default device by selecting it from the list. On Linux, use the default mixer application of your distribution or `alsamixer`.

2. Open up a Terminal (located in `/Applications/Utilities` on the Mac).

3. We can start a monitoring loop first to ensure our microphone works as intended, with the following command:

```
$ sox -d -d
```

4. Now, to send the audio from our microphone to the speakers on the Pi, use the following command:

```
$ sox -d -t sox - | ssh pi@[IP address] sox -q -t sox - -d
```

# Attention Mac users

You'll likely be flooded with warnings from the CoreAudio driver while SSH is waiting for you to input your password for the `pi` user. Just ignore the messages, type in your password anyway, and press the *Enter* key-the recording will proceed as normal:

1. Maybe you'd like to broadcast some nice music or a prerecorded message instead of your own live voice. Use the following command to send `My Song.mp3` from your desktop to be played out of the speakers connected to the Pi:

```
$ cat ~/"Desktop/My Song.mp3" | ssh pi@[IP address] sox -t mp3 - -d
```

2. Or why not broadcast an entire album with sweet tunes located in the `My Album` folder on the desktop:

```
$ cat ~/"Desktop/My Album/"*.mp3 | ssh pi@[IP address] sox -t mp3 - -d
```

# Talking in Bluetooth

Using Bluetooth makes it easy to be mischievous by using the techniques explored in the *Listening over Bluetooth* section. For example, you could set your Pi to remotely connect to the Bluetooth sound-bar connected to your TV in the living room, with you sitting in another room projecting your voice by speaking into the microphone attached to your Pi's soundcard.

Or, if your Pi is an integral part of the furniture in a particular room, you could use a Bluetooth headset with a microphone to send audio to a speaker connected to the Pi's jack output.

To do this, we need to tell PulseAudio what our default sound source and output is, and simply run the SoX monitoring loop again.

If PulseAudio isn't already running, then start it with:

```
pi@raspberrypi ~ $ pulseaudio --start
```

The following command will set your Pi's default audio output to the jack plug:

```
pi@raspberrypi ~ $ pactl set-default-sink alsa_output.0.analog-stereo
```

With my headset connected to the Pi (which has a built-in mic), I can find the source device name, according to PulseAudio, using:

```
pi@raspberrypi ~ $ pacmd list-sources short | grep -e 'name:'
```

In my case, this is:

```
bluez_sink.00_03_89_93_8D_B4.monitor
```

To set this as the default audio input device, use this command:

```
pi@raspberrypi ~ $ pactl set-default-source
bluez_sink.00_03_89_93_8D_B4.monitor
```

Set up the monitor loop to use the default devices and start talking:

```
pi@raspberrypi ~ $ sox -d -d
```

# Distorting your voice in weird and wonderful ways

Tired of your own voice by now? Let's make it more interesting by applying some cool SoX effects!

SoX comes with a number of sound effects that can be applied to your audio and optionally saved. Some effects are suitable to use on your live voice while others only make sense when applied to already recorded files.

To see a list of all the possible effects and their parameters, use the following command:

```
pi@raspberrypi ~ $ sox --help-effect=all | less
```

To apply an effect, specify the effect followed by any parameters after the output file or device.

In this example, we'll start a monitoring loop on the Pi and apply a reverb effect to our voice live as it plays back through the speakers:

```
pi@raspberrypi ~ $ sox -t alsa plughw:1 -d reverb
```

If you receive "under-run" warnings from ALSA whenever you run `sox`, these can be safely ignored.

How about that? Sounds like we're stuck in a cave. Let's see what parameters the reverb effect takes:

```
pi@raspberrypi ~ $ sox -t alsa plughw:1 -d reverb ?
usage: [-w|--wet-only] [reverberance (50%) [HF-damping (50%) [room-scale
(100%) [stereo-depth (100%) [pre-delay (0ms) [wet-gain (0dB)]]]]]]
```

The parameters inside the brackets are all optional, and the values inside the parentheses are the default values. By changing the `reverberance` parameter, we can turn the cave into a huge mountain hall:

```
pi@raspberrypi ~ $ sox -t alsa plughw:1 -d reverb 99
```

Or we could be stuck crawling in an air duct:

```
pi@raspberrypi ~ $ sox -t alsa plughw:1 -d reverb 99 50 0
```

Our next example is a cult classic-the freaky David Lynch phonetic reversal speech:

1. Write down a sentence that makes your skin crawl. (*The owls are not what they seem, and the cake is a lie too* will do.)
2. Read your sentence backwards, from right to left, and record it to a file named `myvoice.wav`:

```
pi@raspberrypi ~ $ sox -t alsa plughw:1 myvoice.wav
```

3. Now play back your recording using the reverse effect:

```
pi@raspberrypi ~ $ sox myvoice.wav -d reverse
```

4. Should you want to sneak this sample into your friend's playlist later, use the following command to save it with the effect applied:

```
pi@raspberrypi ~ $ sox myvoice.wav freaky.wav reverse
```

Here are some other effects you might enjoy experimenting with:

| Command | Description |
|---|---|
| `echo 0.8 0.9 1000 0.3` | Echoes of the Alps |
| `flanger 30 10 0 100 10 tri 25 lin` | Classic sci-fi robot voice |
| `pitch -500` | Creepy villain voice |
| `pitch 500` | Creepy smurf voice |

# Make your computer do the talking

Why should we humans have to exhaust ourselves yapping into microphones all day when we can make our computers do all the work for us? Let's install **eSpeak**, the speech synthesizer:

```
pi@raspberrypi ~ $ sudo apt-get install espeak
```

Now let's make the Pi say something:

```
pi@raspberrypi ~ $ espeak "I'm sorry, Dave. I'm afraid I can't do that."
```

If you receive warnings from ALSA whenever you run `espeak`, these can be safely ignored.

We could also make it read beautiful poetry in a French accent from a file:

```
pi@raspberrypi ~ $ espeak -f /etc/motd -v french
```

Or combine `espeak` with other applications for endless possibilities, as shown here:

```
pi@raspberrypi ~ $ ls | espeak --stdout | sox -t wav - -d reverb 99 50 0
```

To write the resulting speech to a WAV file, use the `-w` argument:

```
pi@raspberrypi ~ $ echo "It's a UNIX system. I know this." | espeak -w
iknow.wav
```

Finally, to get a list of the different voices available, use the `--voices` and `--voices=en` arguments.

# Scheduling your audio actions

In this section, we'll be looking at different techniques for triggering a recording or a playback, and optionally how to make it stop after a certain period of time.

# Start on power up

The first method we'll cover is also the bluntest: how to start a recording or playback directly when powering up the Raspberry Pi. There isn't really a standardized way of auto-starting regular user applications on boot, so we'll have to improvise a bit to come up with our own way of doing what we want.

The Raspbian boot process is basically a collection of shell scripts being run one after the other, with each script performing some important task. One of the last scripts to run is /etc/rc.local, which is a good starting point for our custom auto-run solution. Right now, the script doesn't do much, it just prints out the IP address of the Pi.

You can try running the script any time using the following command:

```
pi@raspberrypi ~ $ /etc/rc.local
```

We could just jam our list of commands right in there, but let's try to make our solution a little more elegant. We want the system to check whether there's an autorun script in our home directory, and if it exists, run it as the pi user. This will make sure our script doesn't accidentally wipe our entire SD card or write huge WAV files in random locations:

1. Let's start with the minor addition to rc.local:

   ```
   pi@raspberrypi ~ $ sudo nano /etc/rc.local
   ```

2. We're going to add the following block of code just above the final **exit 0** line:

```
if [ -x /home/pi/autorun.sh ]; then
  sudo -u pi /home/pi/autorun.sh
fi
```

> The preceding shell script means if there is an executable file named autorun.sh in the pi user's home directory, then run that script as the pi user (not as root, which would be the normal behavior for boot scripts).

> If we run `/etc/rc.local` right now, nothing new would happen-not
> until we create the `autorun.sh` script in our home directory and make
> it executable.

3. So let's create our autorun script:

```
pi@raspberrypi ~ $ nano ~/autorun.sh
```

4. After the first `#!/bin/sh` line, you're free to put anything in this script. Just keep
   in mind that you won't be able to use aliases here-you'll have to enter full
   commands. Here's an example record and playback script:

```
#!/bin/sh
#
# Auto-run script for Raspberry Pi.
# Use chmod +x ~/autorun.sh to enable.

PLAYORREC=P # Set to P for Playback or R for Record

INPUTFILE="playme.wav"
OUTPUTFILE="myrec.wav"
MICROPHONE="-t alsa plughw:1"
SPEAKERS="-t alsa plughw:0"

case "$PLAYORREC" in
  P|p) sox ~/"$INPUTFILE" $SPEAKERS ;;
  R|r) sox $MICROPHONE ~/"$OUTPUTFILE" ;;
  *) echo "Set the PLAYORREC variable to P for Playback or R for Record" ;;
esac
```

- The first `#!/bin/sh` line is called a **shebang** and is used to tell the system that
  any text that follows is to be passed on to the default shell (which is `dash` during
  boot and `bash` for logins on Raspbian) as a script.
- The other lines starting with # characters are comments, used only to convey
  information to anyone reading the script.
- The `PLAYORREC` variable is used to switch between the two operating modes of
  the script.
- `INPUTFILE` is what will be played if we are in the playback mode, and
  `OUTPUTFILE` is where we will record to if we are in the record
  mode. `MICROPHONE` and `SPEAKERS` lets us update the script easily for different
  audio gadgets.

- The case block compares the character stored in the PLAYORREC variable (which is P at the moment) against three possible cases:
  - If PLAYORREC contains a capital P or a lowercase p), then run this sox playback command a hint to the user about it.
  - If PLAYORREC contains a capital R or a lowercase r, then run this sox record command.
  - If PLAYORREC contains anything else or is left blank, then display a hint to user about it.
- The sox command is launched with the values of the variables inserted as arguments, and we assume that the file specified is located in the pi user's home directory.

5. Once we've saved the autorun.sh script and exited the editor, there's one last thing we need to do before we can actually run it. We need to give the script executable permission with the chmod command:

   **pi@raspberrypi ~ $ chmod +x ~/autorun.sh**

6. Now we can give the script a test run:

   **pi@raspberrypi ~ $ ~/autorun.sh**

If everything works fine now, it should also run fine when you reboot.

One major improvement we could do to the script is to have tmux start the playback or recording process in the background. That way we'll be able to log in remotely to check on sox as it runs. Simply change the two sox command lines as follows:

```
P|p) tmux new-session -s autostart -n $PLAYORREC -d "sox ~/"$INPUTFILE"
$SPEAKERS" ;;

R|r) tmux new-session -s autostart -n $PLAYORREC -d "sox $MICROPHONE
~/"$OUTPUTFILE"" ;;
```

Here we tell tmux to create a new session named autostart, create a new window named P or R depending on the mode, and start in a detached state. Then we specify the command we'd like to run inside the tmux session surrounded by double quotes. Because $INPUTFILE and $OUTPUTFILE are also surrounded by double quotes, we have to escape those characters by prefixing them with the \ character.

The easiest way to temporarily disable the script when you don't need to play or record anything on boot is to remove the executable permission from the script:

```
pi@raspberrypi ~ $ chmod -x ~/autorun.sh
```

# Scheduled start

When we simply want to postpone the start of something for a few minutes, hours, or days, the at command is a good fit.

Add it to the system using the following command:

```
pi@raspberrypi ~ $ sudo apt-get install at --no-install-recommends
```

The at command can optionally send e-mails with status reports, but since that would require a small local mail server to be installed and running, we've told apt-get not to install the additional recommended packages here.

Let's start with a demonstration of the basic at facilities. First, we specify the time we want something to occur:

```
pi@raspberrypi ~ $ at now + 5 minutes
```

Next, at will enter command input mode where we enter the commands we would like to execute, one per line:

```
at> sox ~/playme.wav -d
at> echo "Finished playing at $(date)" >> ~/at.log
```

We then press *Ctrl + D* to signal that we are done with our command list, and we'll get an output with our job's ID number and the exact time it has been scheduled to start.

After five minutes have passed, your job will start running in the background. Note that there won't be any visible output from the application on your console. If you need to be sure that your command ran, you could write a line to a log file, as was done in the previous example.

Alternatively, you may schedule commands for an exact date and time:

```
pi@raspberrypi ~ $ at 9am 1 April 2016
```

Jobs in the queue waiting to be executed can be viewed using the following command:

```
pi@raspberrypi ~ $ atq
```

Once you know the job ID, you can remove it from the queue by replacing # with your job ID:

```
pi@raspberrypi ~ $ atrm #
```

Another nifty trick is to specify a shell script to be executed instead of entering the commands manually:

```
pi@raspberrypi ~ $ at now + 30 minutes -f ~/autorun.sh
```

The Raspberry Pi board lacks a **real-time clock** (**RTC**), which computers use to keep track of the current time. Instead, the Pi has to ask other computers over the network what time it is when it boots up. Alternatively, it can obtain the correct time from a GPS module, as described in the *Using GPS as a time source* section of `Chapter 5`, *Taking Your Pi Off-Road*. The Pi is equally unable to keep track of the time that passes while it's powered off.

If we need to time something but know we won't have network access, we can combine the technique discussed in the *Start on power up* section with the `at` command. This allows us to implement the idea *Start the playback 1 hour after I plug in the Pi.*

All we have to do is modify one line in our `/etc/rc.local` script to add an `at` timer:

```
if [ -x /home/pi/autorun.sh ]; then
   sudo -u pi at now + 1 hour -f /home/pi/autorun.sh
fi
```

# Controlling recording length

An automated SoX recording will continue to run until the Pi runs out of SD card space. We can use the `trim` effect to stop the recording (or playback) after a certain amount of time has elapsed:

```
pi@raspberrypi ~ $ sox -t alsa plughw:1 myrec.wav trim 0 00:30:00
```

The previous command will record thirty minutes of audio to `myrec.wav` and then stop. The first zero tells the trim effect to start measuring from the beginning of the file. The position where you want to cut the recording is then specified as `hours:minutes:seconds`.

Another function useful for long recordings is to be able to split it into multiple files, each file with a certain duration. The following command will produce multiple WAV files, each file being one hour in length:

```
pi@raspberrypi ~ $ sox -t alsa plughw:1 myrec.wav trim 0 01:00:00 : newfile
: restart
```

# Start recording with noise detection

Wouldn't it be cool if the Pi could listen for activity in the room and only start recording when something or someone makes a sound? Once again SoX comes to the rescue.

Our noise detection method works in two simple steps:

1. Start listening for one second and measure the noise level during that second.
2. If the measured noise was above a certain threshold, start recording for 5 minutes; if not, start over and listen for another second.

First, let's calibrate the microphone and figure out a good amplitude threshold value:

```
pi@raspberrypi ~ $ sox -t alsa plughw:1 -n stat trim 0 00:00:01 : restart
```

This command starts monitoring your microphone, but the -n argument tells SoX to discard the output since we are only interested in the statistics produced by the stat effect. The trim effect then cuts of the monitoring after one second, the important statistics are printed, and a new monitoring second starts thanks to the restart argument.

Now, keep your eyes on the **Maximum amplitude** value in the statistics output. As long as you stay quiet, the value shouldn't fluctuate too much from one readout to the other.

Next, make a loud noise and watch the **Maximum amplitude** value jump. Now try moving further away from the microphone and say something in your normal tone of voice. If there was a significant change in amplitude value, write that value down as a rough starting point for your threshold value. If not, try raising the capture volume of your microphone in alsamixer until you see a significant increase in the amplitude value.

Alright, now all we need to do is translate the theory into program logic with the following script:

```
#!/bin/bash
#
# Noise activated recorder script for Raspberry Pi.
# Use chmod +x ~/noisedetect.sh to enable.
```

```
THRESHOLD=0.010000

noise_compare() {
  awk -v NOISE=$1 -v THRESHOLD=$2 'BEGIN {if (NOISE > THRESHOLD) exit 0;
exit 1}'
}

while true ; do
  NOISE=$(sox -t alsa plughw:1 -n stat trim 0 00:00:01 2>&1 > /dev/null |
grep 'Maximum amplitude' | cut -d ':' -f 2 | tr -d ' ')
  if noise_compare $NOISE $THRESHOLD; then
    echo "Noise detected ($NOISE) - Recording..."
    sox -t alsa plughw:1 $(date +%Y%m%d-%H%M%S).wav trim 0 00:05:00
  fi
done
noise-detect.sh
```

Be careful not to introduce line breaks within each of your lines of script, or the script will not work – breaks are only shown here for display reasons.

The THRESHOLD variable holds, of course, the threshold amplitude value that you found out by calibrating your microphone. Next comes the noise_compare function. A function is a piece of code that can be called from other places in a script. In this case, we use it to compare two floating point numbers by passing them to the awk command, since bash doesn't have this ability built in.

Then we enter an infinite loop, which means our script will continue to run until we press Ctrl + C to break out of the loop. Next, we chain together a series of commands to extract the **Maximum amplitude** value from sox and store it in the NOISE variable, which is then compared with our THRESHOLD variable with the help of the noise_compare function.

If the NOISE value is larger than the THRESHOLD value, we start a 5-minute recording with the current date and time as the filename.

Now that you know how to do sound detection, you can easily swap out the sox recording command to play an alarm bell or send an e-mail warning about a possible noisy intruder, as described in the *Sending e-mail updates* section of Chapter 5, *Taking Your Pi Off-Road*.

# Calling your fellow agents

When you're out in the field and need to call in a favor from a fellow agent or report back to HQ, you don't want to depend on the public phone network if you can avoid it. Landlines and cell phones alike can be tapped by all sorts of shady characters and to add insult to injury, you have to pay good money for this service. We can do better.

Welcome to the wonderful world of **Voice-over IP** (**VoIP**). VoIP is a blanket term for any technology capable of delivering speech between two end users over IP networks. There are plenty of services and protocols out there that try to meet this demand, most of which force you to connect through a central server that you don't own or control.

We're going to turn the Pi into the central server of our very own phone network.

To aid us with this task, we'll deploy **GNU SIP Witch**-a peer-to-peer VoIP server that uses **Session Initiation Protocol** (**SIP**) to route calls between phones.

While there are many excellent VoIP servers available (Asterisk, FreeSwitch, Yate, and so on), SIP Witch has the advantage of being very lightweight on the Pi because its only concern is connecting phones and not much else.

# Setting up SIP Witch

Once we have the SIP server up and running, we'll be adding one or more software phones or **softphones**. It's assumed that server and phones will all be on the same network, so if you're away from home with your Pi, you might want to have a look at the *Turning the Pi into a Wi-Fi hotspot* section in `Chapter 5`, *Taking Your Pi Off-Road* first. Let's get started!

1. Install SIP Witch using the following command:

   `pi@raspberrypi ~ $ sudo apt-get install sipwitch`

2. Once installed, we have to define `PLUGINS` in `/etc/default/sipwitch` before running SIP Witch. Let's open it up for editing:

   `pi@raspberrypi ~ $ sudo nano /etc/default/sipwitch`

   Find the line that reads `#PLUGINS="zeroconf scripting subscriber forward"` and remove the # character to uncomment the line. This directive tells SIP Witch that we want the standard plugins to be loaded.

3. Next we'll have a look at the main SIP Witch configuration file:

```
pi@raspberrypi ~ $ sudo nano /etc/sipwitch.conf
```

Note how some blocks of text are between `<!--` and `-->` tags. These are comments in XML documents and are ignored by SIP Witch. Whatever changes you want to make, ensure they go outside of those tags.

4. Now we're going to add a few softphone user accounts. It's up to you how many phones you'd like on your system, but each account needs a username, an extension (short phone number) and a password. Find the `<provision>` tag, make a new line and add your users:

```xml
<user id="phone1">
  <extension>201</extension>
  <secret>SecretSauce201</secret>
  <display>Agent 201</display>
</user>
<user id="phone2">
  <extension>202</extension>
  <secret>SecretSauce202</secret>
  <display>Agent 202</display>
</user>
```

The user ID will be used as a user/login name later from the softphones. In this default configuration, the extensions can be any number between 201 and 299. The secret is the password that will go together with the username on the softphones. We will look into a better way of storing passwords later in this chapter. Finally, the display string defines an identity to present to other phones when calling.

5. One more thing that we need to configure is how SIP Witch should treat local names. This makes it possible to call a phone by user ID, in addition to the extension. Find the `<stack>` tag, make a new line and add the following directive, but replace `[IP address]` with the IP address of your Pi:

```
<localnames>[IP address]</localnames>
```

Those are all the changes we need to make to the configuration at the moment.

```
pi@raspberrypi: ~                                           —   □   ×
GNU nano 2.2.6           File: /etc/sipwitch.conf              Modified
<?xml version="1.0"?>
<sipwitch>
  <provision>
    <user id="phone1">
      <extension>201</extension>
      <secret>SecretSauce201</secret>
      <display>Agent 201</display>
    </user>
    <user id="phone2">
      <extension>202</extension>
      <secret>SecretSauce202</secret>
      <display>Agent 202</display>
    </user>
  </provision>

  <stack>
    <localnames>192.168.0.106</localnames>
    <mapped>200</mapped>
    <threading>2</threading>
    <interface>*</interface>
    <dumping>false</dumping>
    <system>system</system>
    <anon>anonymous</anon>
  </stack>

  <timers>
    <!-- ring every 4 seconds -->
    <ring>4</ring>
    <!-- call forward no answer after x rings -->
    <cfna>4</cfna>
    <!-- call reset to clear cid in stack, 6 seconds -->
    <reset>6</reset>
  </timers>

  <registry>
    <prefix>200</prefix>
    <range>100</range>
    <keysize>77</keysize>
    <mapped>200</mapped>
  </registry>
</sipwitch>

^G Get Help  ^O WriteOut  ^R Read File ^Y Prev Page ^K Cut Text  ^C Cur Pos
^X Exit      ^J Justify   ^W Where Is  ^V Next Page ^U UnCut Tex ^T To Spell
```

Basic SIP Witch configuration for two phones

6. With our configuration in place, let's start up the SIP Witch service:

**pi@raspberrypi ~ $ sudo service sipwitch start**

On Raspbian Jessie, I found that **sipwitch** wouldn't start properly unless I rebooted the Pi after it was installed. Also it seemed that it started up automatically on boot-up. If you want to stop it from automatically starting up, use the command:
```
$ sudo systemctl disable sipwitch
```
You can then manually start it when you need to with:
```
$ sudo systemctl start sipwitch
```

The SIP Witch server runs in the background and only outputs to a log file viewable with this command:

**pi@raspberrypi ~ $ sudo cat /var/log/sipwitch.log**

7. Now we can use the `sipwitch` command to interact with the running service. Type `sipwitch` for a list of all possible commands. Here's a short list of particularly handy ones:

| Command | Description |
|---|---|
| sudo sipwitch dump | Shows how the SIP Witch server is currently configured. |
| sudo sipwitch registry | Lists all currently registered softphones. |
| sudo sipwitch calls | Lists active calls. |
| sudo sipwitch message [extension] "[text]" | Sends a text message from the server to an extension. Perfect for sending status updates from the Pi through scripting. |

# Connecting the softphones

Running your own telecommunications service is kind of boring without actual phones to make use of it. Fortunately, there are softphone applications available for most common electronic devices out there.

The configuration of these phones will be pretty much identical no matter which platform they're running on. This is the basic information that will always need to be specified when configuring your softphone application:

- **User/Login name**: `phone1` or `phone2` in our example configuration
- **Password/Authentication**: The user's secret in our configuration
- **Server/Host name/Domain**: The IP address of your Pi

Once a softphone is successfully registered with the SIP Witch server, you should be able to see that phone listed using the `sudo sipwitch registry` command.

What follows is a list of verified decent softphones that will get the job done.

# Windows (MicroSIP)

MicroSIP is an open source softphone that also supports video calls. Visit `http://www.mic rosip.org/downloads` to obtain and install the latest version (`MicroSIP-3.12.1.exe` at the time of writing, which supports Windows 10):

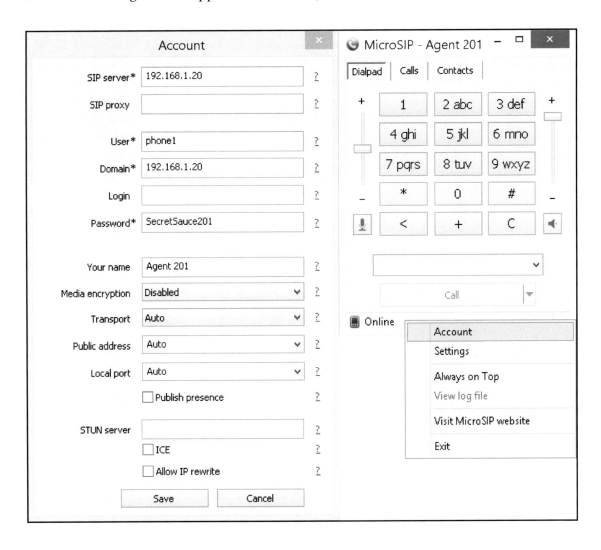

# Configuring the MicroSIP softphone for Windows

Right-click on either the status bar in the main application window or the system tray icon to bring up the menu that lets you access the **Account** settings.

# Mac OS X (Telephone)

Telephone is a basic open source softphone that is easily installed through the Mac App store:

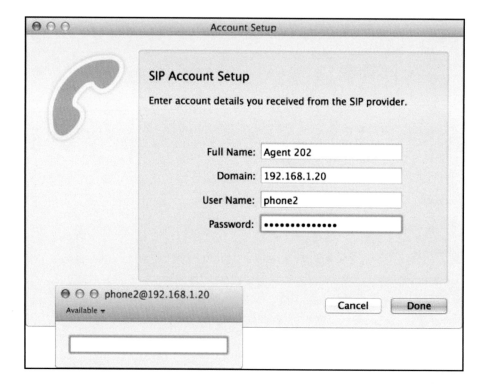

Configuring the Telephone softphone for Mac OS X

# Linux (Ring)

Ring (formally SFLphone) is an open source softphone with packages available for all major distributions and client interfaces for both GNOME and KDE. Instructions on how to download and install it for your particular distribution can be found at `https://ring.cx/en/download/gnu-linux`.

# Android (CSipSimple)

CSipSimple is an excellent open source softphone available from the Google Play store. When adding your account, use the basic generic wizard:

Configuring the CSipSimple softphone on Android

# iPhone/iPad (Linphone)

Linphone is an open source softphone that is easily installed through the iPhone App Store. Select **I have already a SIP-account** to go to the setup assistant:

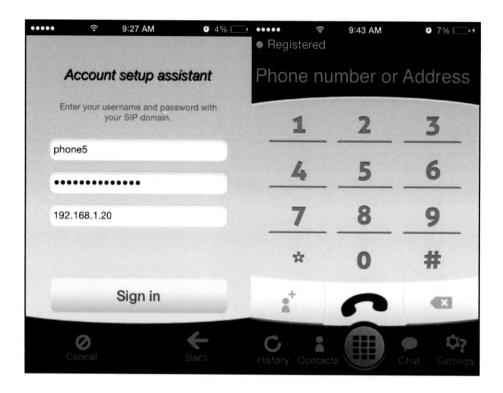

Configuring Linphone on the iPhone

# Running a softphone on the Pi

It's always good to be able to reach your agents directly from HQ, that is, the Pi itself. Proving once again that anything can be done from the command line, we're going to install a softphone called Linphone that will make good use of your USB microphone.

This new softphone obviously needs a user ID and password just like the others. We will take this opportunity to look at a better way of storing passwords in SIP Witch.

# Encrypting SIP Witch passwords

Type `sudo sipwitch dump` to see how SIP Witch is currently configured. Find the **Accounts** section and note how there's already a user ID named `pi` with extension `200`.

This is the result of a SIP Witch feature that automatically assigns an extension number to certain Raspbian user accounts. You may also have noticed that the **display** string for the `pi` user looks empty. We can easily fix that by filling in the full name field for the Raspbian `pi` user account with the following command:

```
pi@raspberrypi ~ $ sudo chfn -f "Agent HQ" pi
```

Now restart the SIP Witch server with `sudo service sipwitch restart` and verify with `sudo sipwitch dump` that the **display** string has changed.

So how do we set the password for this automatically added `pi` user? For the other accounts, we specified the password in clear text inside `<secret>` tags in `/etc/sipwitch.conf`. This is not the best solution from a security perspective if your Pi happens to fall into the wrong hands. Therefore, SIP Witch supports specifying passwords in encrypted digest form. Use the following command to create an encrypted password for the `pi` user:

```
pi@raspberrypi ~ $ sudo sippasswd pi
```

We can then view the database of SIP passwords that SIP Witch knows about:

```
pi@raspberrypi ~ $ sudo cat /var/lib/sipwitch/digests.db
```

Now you can add digest passwords for your other SIP users as well, and then delete all `<secret>` lines from `/etc/sipwitch.conf` to be completely free of clear text.

# Setting up Linphone

With our `pi` user account up and ready to go, let's proceed to set up Linphone:

1. Linphone does actually have a graphical user interface, but we'll specify that we want the command-line only client:

```
pi@raspberrypi ~ $ sudo apt-get install linphone-nogtk
```

2. Now we fire up the Linphone command-line client:

```
pi@raspberrypi ~ $ linphonec
```

3. You will immediately receive a warning that reads:

```
 Warning: Could not start udp transport on port 5060, maybe this port is
already used.
```

That is, in fact, exactly what is happening. The standard communication channel for the SIP protocol is UDP port 5060, and it's already in use by our SIP Witch server. Let's tell Linphone to use port 5062 with this command:

```
linphonec> ports sip 5062
```

4. Next we'll want to set up our microphone. Use these three commands to list, show, and select what audio device to use for phone calls:

```
linphonec> soundcard list
linphonec> soundcard show
linphonec> soundcard use [number]
```

5. For the softphone to perform reasonably well on the Pi, we'll want to make adjustments to the list of codecs that Linphone will try to use. The job of a codec is to compress audio as much as possible while retaining high quality. This is a very CPU-intensive process, which is why we want to use the codec with the least amount of CPU load on the Pi, namely **PCMU** or **PCMA**. Use the following command to list all currently supported codecs:

```
linphonec> codec list
```

Now use this command to disable all codecs that are not PCMU or PCMA:

```
linphonec> codec disable [number]
```

6. It's time to register our softphone to the SIP Witch server. Use the following command but replace [IP address] with the IP address of your Pi, and [password] with the SIP password you set earlier for the pi user:

```
linphonec> register sip:pi@[IP address] sip:[IP address] [password]
```

7. That's all you need to start calling your fellow agents from the Pi itself.
8. Type `help` to get a list of all commands that Linphone accepts.

> The basic commands are `call [user id]` to call someone, `answer` to pick up incoming calls, and `quit` to exit Linphone. All the settings that you've made will be saved to `~/.linphonerc` and loaded the next time you start `linphonec`.

## Playing files with Linphone

Now that you know the Linphone basics, let's explore some interesting features not offered by most other softphones.

At any time (except during a call), you can switch **Linphone** into file mode, which lets us experiment with alternative audio sources. Use this command to enable file mode:

```
linphonec> soundcard use files
```

Do you remember eSpeak from earlier in this chapter? While you rest your throat, eSpeak can provide its soothing voice to carry out entire conversations with your agents. If you haven't already got it, install eSpeak first:

```
pi@raspberrypi ~ $ sudo apt-get install espeak
```

Now we tell Linphone what to say next:

```
linphonec> speak english Greetings! I'm a Linphone, obviously.
```

This sentence will be spoken as soon as there's an established call. So you can either make an outgoing call or answer an incoming call to start the conversation, after which you're free to continue the conversation in Italian:

```
linphonec> speak italian Buongiorno! Mi chiamo Enzo Gorlami.
```

Should you want a message to play automatically when someone calls, just toggle **auto answer**:

```
linphonec> autoanswer enable
```

How about playing a pre-recorded message or some nice grooves? If you have a WAV or MP3 file that you'd like to play over the phone, it has to be converted to a suitable format first. A simple SoX command will do the trick:

```
pi@raspberrypi ~ $ sox "original file.mp3" -c 1 -r 48000 playme.wav
```

Now we can tell Linphone to play the file:

```
linphonec> play playme.wav
```

Finally, you can also record a call to file. Note that only the remote part of the conversation can be recorded, which makes this feature more suitable for leaving messages and such. Use the following command to record:

```
linphonec> record message.wav
```

# Using your voice to control things

Starting and stopping our listening device to record what's going on might be a bit tricky when our device is hidden, so wouldn't it be great if we could use a voice command to start recording when something interesting is happening?

Well, using a tool called Voice Command installed on our Pi allows us to do this. It was created for the Raspberry Pi by a guy called Steven Hickson and it's based on the Google Voice API, and as such is pretty reliable and accurate.

Because it uses the Google Voice API, Voice Command requires Internet access to be able to process your voice. If you want to use *offline* voice recognition, then look at something like Jasper (http://jasperproject.github.io), although it needs plenty of storage space and is not as accurate as online systems.

# Give your Pi some ears

There's no install package for Voice Command so we need download the code and build it on our Pi. To do this, we need to ensure that we have `git-core` installed so that we can download it from the Git repository, although on the latest version of Raspbian Jessie you should already have it. Check and install with the following command:

```
pi@raspberrypi ~ $ sudo apt-get install git-core
```

It also needs this library, as it doesn't automatically include it in its dependency script:

```
pi@raspberrypi ~ $ sudo apt-get install libboost-regex1.49.0
```

Now we can download the Voice Command files:

```
pi@raspberrypi ~ $ git clone
git://github.com/StevenHickson/PiAUISuite.git
```

Once downloaded we can install it:

```
pi@raspberrypi ~ $ cd PiAUISuite/Install/
pi@raspberrypi ~ $ ./InstallAUISuite.sh
```

As part of the installation, it will ask if you want to install dependencies too. Press Y when you're asked this. It will then download a bunch of libraries it requires to run.

The installer will also ask lots of questions about installing other stuff as well. Say N to not to install them and just say *Y* to the `voicecommand` option at the end.

When Voice Command has finished installing (it may take a while), it will ask you if you want it to help you set it up. Say Y to this. You can also do this at any time by using the `voicecommand -s` command if you want to change the options.

The configuration process will ask you the following questions. Respond to them as shown:

```
pi@raspberrypi:~ $ voicecommand -s
Opening config file...
Do you want to permanently set the continuous flag so that it always
runs continuously? (y/n)
n
Do you want to permanently set the verify flag so that it always
verifies the keyword? (y/n)
y
Do you want to permanently set the ignore flag so that it never looks
for answers outside the config file? (y/n)
y
Do you want to permanently set the quiet flag so that it never uses
```

```
audio out to speak? (y/n)
    n
    Do you want to permanently change the default duration of the speech
recognition (3 seconds)? (y/n)
    n
    Do you want to permanently change the default command duration of the
speech recognition (2 seconds)? (y/n)
    n
    Do you want to set up and check the text to speech options? (y/n)
    n
    Do you want to set up and check the speech recognition options? (y/n)
    y
    First I'm going to make sure you have the correct hardware device
    Everything seems right with the hardware config
    Would you like me to try to get the proper audio threshold? (y/n)
    y
    I'm going to record you once while you are silent and then once while
you say the command in order to determine the threshold
    Getting ready for silent recording, just don't say anything while this
is happening, press any key when ready
    Recording WAVE '/dev/shm/noise.wav' : Signed 16 bit Little Endian, Rate
16000 Hz, Stereo
    Getting ready for command recording, try saying the command while this
is happening, press any key when ready
    Recording WAVE '/dev/shm/noise.wav' : Signed 16 bit Little Endian, Rate
16000 Hz, Stereo
    I detected that your default thresh: 12.180400 is different than the
thresh I detected that you should use: 1.492800
    Should I set that in the config file? (y/n)
    y
    The default keyword of the system is "pi"
    Do you want to change the keyword? (y/n)
    n
    Done setting everything up!
    pi@raspberrypi:~ $
```

We can now configure Voice Command to respond to our, umm, voice commands:

To edit the configuration file, type:

```
pi@raspberrypi ~ $ voicecommand -e
```

After displaying some blurb, it will take you into Nano so that you can change its settings. You might want to read the documentation for Voice Command by running the following command, which loads the manual pages:

```
pi@raspberrypi ~ $ voicecommand -h
```

However, here's a basic configuration file I have set up which will get you started. It's a little bit more straightforward and simpler than the default one that's set up during installation. You can replace that one with this:

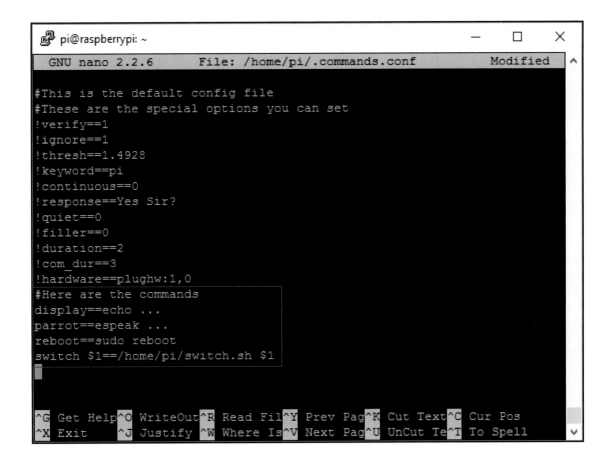

Voice Command configuration file

If you take a look at the highlighted part of the screenshot, you'll see that I've added four voice commands. Add these commands to your file so that you can try them for yourself. The format of the configuration is `voice_command==action`, so in the first example, by saying `display` it will echo to the console whatever is said after `display` - that's what the ellipses (…) means. So if I said `display hello world`, I would expect the words **hello world** to be output onto the terminal console.

The second command will have `espeak` say back whatever I say after the command `parrot`.

The third command will simply reboot the Pi after saying `reboot`.

And the last one is just an example of how to run a given script, passing in the parameter that I give after saying the word `switch`. So if I say `switch on` it will run the equivalent of running this:

**/home/pi/switch.sh on**

Let's take a look at a basic `switch.sh` script that responds to our voice commands. When we pass in the parameter `on`, it will begin to record in the background using the `sox` command we explored earlier. When we use the parameter `off`, it will kill the `sox` process if it's running:

```
#!/bin/bash
# switch.sh $1

#get the parameter that was passed in
case "$1" in
  "on" )
    #record using SoX
    sox -t alsa plughw:1 -t wav - | lame - myrec.mp3 &
  ;;

  "off" )
    pkill sox
  ;;

  * )
    echo "Option not recognised"
esac
Voice controlled switch.sh script
```

The keyword to activate the voice commander is `pi` by default, so in our switch example we operate it like this:

1. Start off by running Voice Command in continuous mode:

```
pi@raspberrypi ~ $ voicecommand -c
```

1. Say `pi` clearly into your microphone
2. Wait for the Pi to response with `Yes Sir?`
3. Say `switch on`. Your switch script should now run, switching **on** whatever it's supposed to do – in this case the recording command from earlier.
4. Say `switch off`. Your switch script should now run switching **off** the recording process by killing the process.

As you can see, this has massive scope for us secret agents to be mischievous in a very covert manner.


# Bonus one-line sampler

Let's wrap up the chapter with a trivial project that's got big pranking potential.

First, make nine short samples, each sample being one second in length, using the following command:

```
pi@raspberrypi ~ $ sox -t alsa plughw:1 sample.wav trim 0 00:00:01 :
newfile : restart
```

Now, enter this one-line sampler command and use your number keys 1 to 9 to trigger the samples and *Ctrl + C* to quit:

```
pi@raspberrypi ~ $ while true; do read -n 1 -s REPLY;
sox~/sample00$REPLY.wav -d; done
```

This is a small piece of Bash script, where the commands have been separated with the `;` character instead of spreading over multiple lines. It starts off with a `while true` **infinite loop**, which makes the commands that follow repeat over and over again forever.

The next command is `read -n 1 -s REPLY`, which reads one character from the keyboard and stores it in the `REPLY` variable. We then trigger the `sox` command to play the sample associated with the number by inserting the `$REPLY` value as part of the filename.

When you get tired of your own voice, replace your samples with small clips of movie dialog!

# Summary

In this chapter, you learned a great deal about audio under Linux in general and about the ALSA sound system in particular. You know how to configure and test the audio output of the Raspberry Pi board itself and how to set up your USB audio gadgets for recording.

You learned how to use SoX to record sound and store it in multiple formats, how you can avoid typing the same thing over and over with aliases, and how to keep a recording session running with `tmux` even when network connectivity is spotty.

Armed with only SoX and SSH software, we turned our Pi into a very capable radio; we can put it in a room and listen in, like a baby monitor, or we can let it broadcast our voice and music to the world. In addition, we can use Bluetooth to connect to wireless headsets and speakers for ultimate covert listening using the built-in Bluetooth found on the latest Raspberry Pi 3.

You also learned how to apply SoX effects to spice up your voice, or let the Pi make the noise using eSpeak. Then we looked at a few different techniques to control the timing of our sound-related mischief including noise detection.

We then set up our very own phone network using SIP Witch and connected softphones running on a wide variety of platforms, including the Pi itself.

Finally, we gave our Pi some ears so that it could listen to us and do what we tell it with the help of Voice Command.

In the upcoming chapter, we'll explore the world of video streaming and motion detection, so get your webcam out and ready to roll.

# 3

# Webcam and Video Wizardry

Aha, good! Still with us, our sly grasshopper is! For our second day of spy class, we'll switch our gear of perception from sound to sight.

You're going to learn how to get the most out of your USB webcam or official Raspberry Pi camera module, secure your perimeter, and then end it on a high note with some mindless mischief. Specifically, we will:

- Take a look at the official Raspberry Pi Camera Module and how to connect it
- Use the camera module to take video and still images
- Connect webcams to the USB port, and capture video and still images
- Build a video surveillance and capture system with built-in motion detection
- Expand the video surveillance to support multiple cameras and remotely monitor it over the Internet
- Build a wearable covert video recording device using the Pi Zero
- Switch your TV on and off with scripts using the HDMI connection

## Meet the USB Video Class drivers and Video4Linux

Just as the ALSA system provides kernel drivers and a programming framework for your audio gadgets, there are two important components involved in getting your cameras to work under Linux:

- The Linux **USB Video Class (UVC)** drivers provide the low-level functions for your USB webcam, which are in accordance with a specification followed by most webcams produced today.

- **Video4Linux (V4L)** is a video capture framework used by applications that record video from cameras, TV tuners, and other video producing devices. There's an updated version of V4L called V4L2, which we'll want to use whenever possible.

# Raspberry Pi Camera Module

The Raspberry Pi Camera Module is an official Raspberry Pi accessory that works with all models of the Pi, and can be used to take high-definition still and video images. It connects directly to the Pi board's **CSI (Camera Serial Interface)** port, dedicated for these modules to enable high-speed operation.

The first release of the Raspberry Pi Zero didn't have a dedicated CSI port for the camera, but the latest v1.3 of the Pi Zero board now features this connector, opening all sorts of possibilities by connecting the official camera module. Note that the connector is actually smaller than the one on the standard-sized Pi boards, so you will need a different flat cable to connect to your camera. You can get these from your usual Pi-friendly online stores, such as pimoroni.com.

The latest version 2 of the camera itself is an 8-megapixel fixed-focus sensor supporting 1080p, 720p, and VGA video modes and still captures. The original version was 5 mega-pixels and even that gave great results:

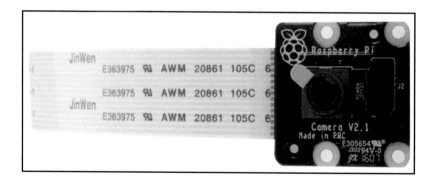

Official Raspberry Pi Camera Module – Version 2

You can also obtain housings for the camera modules, which, unless you're going to build your own enclosure for the camera system, I recommend you use:

Raspberry Pi camera housings come in various colors and styles

# Connecting the camera module

The camera module connects directly to the Raspberry Pi board via its dedicated camera interface, as shown in the following image. When connecting the camera, the contact side of the ribbon cable is towards the HDMI connector and the blue side of the cable is toward the network connector:

Connect the camera module to the dedicated interface

Here's a step-by-step guide for connecting it:

1. Before handling the camera module, ground yourself to get rid of any static electricity you might have picked up, by touching a radiator or a PC chassis.
2. The flexible flat cable connects to the CSI connector located between the Ethernet and HDMI ports on the Pi board.
3. Open up the connector by pulling the plastic tab upward.
4. With the blue side facing the Ethernet port, push the flex cable into the connector.
5. While holding the flex cable in place, push down on the plastic tab to secure the cable. Make sure the cable is evenly pushed into the connector. There might be a small piece of translucent blue plastic film covering the camera lens to protect it during transportation. This should be peeled off and discarded.
6. The camera module is now connected to Raspberry Pi:

Camera module housed within an enclosure

# Setting up the camera module

Before we can use the camera module, we need to enable camera support on the Raspberry Pi. To do this, we use the *raspi-config* tool:

1. Connect to your Raspberry Pi in the normal lazy way from your sofa using SSH or directly, using a keyboard and monitor.

2. Once you've logged in, launch the config tool with:

   ```
   $ sudo raspi-config
   ```

3. Select option **6 Enable Camera**...:

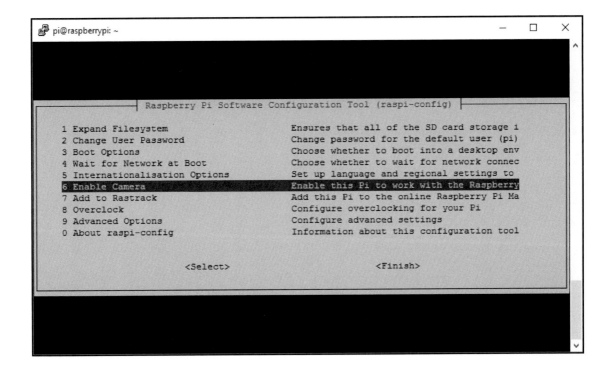

4. Select **Enable.**

5. Then select **Finish** and reboot your Pi to enable the camera settings (use the *Tab* key to navigate between the menu options):

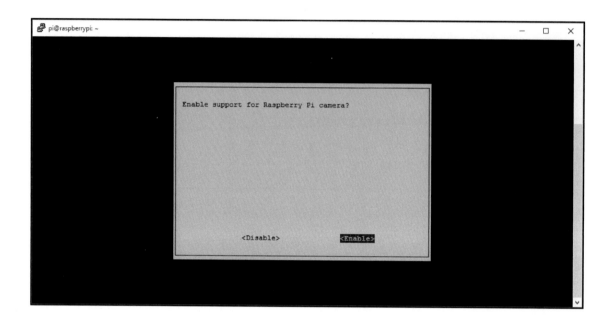

6. Test the camera module.

Once your Raspberry Pi has rebooted, your camera should be enabled. To check this, we can test this by taking a still image using the raspistill utility:

```
$ raspistill -v -o test.jpg
```

This will delay for 5 seconds then take a picture, while displaying various pieces of information, such as that shown in the following screenshot:

 The camera module needs at least 128 MB of GPU memory to operate properly. If you experience any issues, first ensure that the **gpu_mem** setting in the /boot/config.txt configuration file is set to at least **128**.

```
pi@raspberrypi: ~                                                    —    □    ×

pi@raspberrypi ~ : raspistill -v -o test.jpg

raspistill Camera App v1.3.8

Width 2592, Height 1944, quality 85, filename test.jpg
Time delay 5000, Raw no
Thumbnail enabled Yes, width 64, height 48, quality 35
Link to latest frame enabled  no
Full resolution preview No
Capture method : Single capture

Preview Yes, Full screen Yes
Preview window 0,0,1024,768
Opacity 255
Sharpness 0, Contrast 0, Brightness 50
Saturation 0, ISO 0, Video Stabilisation No, Exposure compensation 0
Exposure Mode 'auto', AWB Mode 'auto', Image Effect 'none'
Metering Mode 'average', Colour Effect Enabled No with U = 128, V = 128
Rotation 0, hflip No, vflip No
ROI x 0.000000, y 0.000000, w 1.000000 h 1.000000
Camera component done
Encoder component done
Starting component connection stage
Connecting camera preview port to video render.
Connecting camera stills port to encoder input port
Opening output file test.jpg
Enabling encoder output port
Starting capture 0
Finished capture 0
Closing down
Close down completed, all components disconnected, disabled and destroyed

pi@raspberrypi ~ :  ▉
```

All being well, you should find that the file **test.jpg** is in your home folder. As you're connected via the shell, you wouldn't have seen the five-second preview image displayed when the command was running.

If you download the image file to your PC, you should see a nice quality snap taken by the camera module.

If you find that **raspistill** outputs errors when you run it, ensure that the camera is connected properly at both ends of the ribbon cable. One other *gotcha* is that sometimes the ribbon connecting the actual camera lens component to the tiny connector on the camera board can come loose. Just ensure that this is securely connected too. I've had this issue a couple times  of after the camera modules have been taken out of my box of random test bits to be used.

**raspistill** has loads of options for manipulating the images it captures; to see the available options, run **raspistill** without any options and they will be listed:

```
$ raspistill
```

We can also test its video capability by recording a 10 second test video using `raspivid`, as follows:

```
pi@raspberrypi ~ $ raspivid -o camtest.h264 -t 10000
```

Then play it back through the HDMI port to an attached monitor:

```
pi@raspberrypi ~ $ omxplayer camtest.h264
```

You can send any recorded audio through the HDMI port by using this version of the command:

```
pi@raspberrypi ~ $ omxplayer -o hdmi camtest.h264
```

Finally, we need to make our Camera Module accessible to other applications, via a standardized V4L interface. We need to make sure that a certain kernel module gets loaded at boot time.

To do this, open up /etc/modules for editing using `nano`:

```
pi@raspberrypi ~ $ sudo nano /etc/modules
```

Add this line:

```
bcm2835-v4l2
```

Now press *Ctrl + X* to exit and select *Y* when prompted to save the modified buffer, then press the *Enter* key to confirm the filename to write to.

Reboot your Pi and use the following commands to confirm that your camera module is now accessible through a V4L interface:

```
pi@raspberrypi ~ $ v4l2-ctl --list-devices
```

The output should show a mmal service accessible through /dev/video0:

```
pi@raspberrypi:~ $ v4l2-ctl --list-devices
mmal service 16.1 (platform:bcm2835-v4l2):
/dev/video0
```

Type this command to enable a preview video overlay on your monitor connected to your HDMI connector (when in the GUI desktop):

```
pi@raspberrypi ~ $ v4l2-ctl --overlay=1
```

If your camera is upside down, just flip it with the following command:

```
pi@raspberrypi ~ $ v4l2-ctl -c vertical_flip=1
```

Explore the cool camera effects by supplying a number from 1 to 15:

```
pi@raspberrypi ~ $ v4l2-ctl -c color_effects=5
```

Type the following command to disable the overlay window:

```
pi@raspberrypi ~ $ v4l2-ctl --overlay=0
```

For optimal use, in stealthy situations, you may also want to consider disabling the red LED to avoid leading any intruders straight to the camera. Open up /boot/config.txt for editing:

```
pi@raspberrypi ~ $ sudo nano /boot/config.txt
```

Make a new line and add the following configuration directive, then reboot:

```
disable_camera_led=1
```

# Using USB cameras

Instead of using the Raspberry Pi Camera Module, it's also possible to use a standard USB **webcam** to take still images. You should be aware, though, that the dedicated camera module is far superior to most USB webcams in terms of image quality, although you may already have a webcam knocking about in your box of bits, so plug it in and boot up your Pi.

# Connecting the webcam

After you've plugged your webcam into a USB port on your Pi, you can check it's been recognized using the lsusb command:

```
pi@raspberrypi ~ $ lsusb
```

I'm using a reasonably small and discreet Logitech C270 webcam, which gets reported on my Raspberry Pi 3 as follows with `lsusb` (`Device 004`):

```
pi@raspberrypi:~ $ lsusb
Bus 001 Device 004: ID 046d:0825 Logitech, Inc. Webcam C270
Bus 001 Device 003: ID 0424:ec00 Standard Microsystems Corp. SMSC9512/9514
Fast Ethernet Adapter
Bus 001 Device 002: ID 0424:9514 Standard Microsystems Corp.
Bus 001 Device 001: ID 1d6b:0002 Linux Foundation 2.0 root hub
```

Not all webcams will work with the Raspberry Pi. Even though it may be recognized as a USB device, it might not actually work properly with the operating system and create a video device (for example, `/dev/video0`). For example, an old cheap Trust webcam I had appeared as a USB device, but wouldn't capture any images.

 You can check whether your webcam is likely to work with the Pi by checking the make and model here: `http://elinux.org/RPi_USB_Webcams`.

So now that the Pi knows that we have a webcam device attached, we can use the `fswebcam` utility to capture image frames. You can find out more about **fswebcam** from the developer's site at `http://www.sanslogic.co.uk/fswebcam/`.

Install **fswebcam** with:

```
pi@raspberrypi ~ $ sudo apt-get install fswebcam
```

Take a snap. You can now test the webcam by capturing a still image, done by running the following command:

```
pi@raspberrypi ~ $ fswebcam test.jpg
```

You should expect to see output similar to the following:

```
pi@raspberrypi: ~                                        —    □    ×
pi@raspberrypi:~ $ lsusb
Bus 001 Device 004: ID 046d:0825 Logitech, Inc. Webcam C270
Bus 001 Device 003: ID 0424:ec00 Standard Microsystems Corp. SMSC9512/9514 Fa
st Ethernet Adapter
Bus 001 Device 002: ID 0424:9514 Standard Microsystems Corp.
Bus 001 Device 001: ID 1d6b:0002 Linux Foundation 2.0 root hub
pi@raspberrypi:~ $ fswebcam test.jpg
--- Opening /dev/video0...
Trying source module v4l2...
/dev/video0 opened.
No input was specified, using the first.
Adjusting resolution from 384x288 to 352x288.
--- Capturing frame...
Captured frame in 0.00 seconds.
--- Processing captured image...
Writing JPEG image to 'test.jpg'.
pi@raspberrypi:~ $ ▊
```

If you have both the Pi camera module and a USB camera attached, you need to check which device is assigned to which by using this command again:

```
pi@raspberrypi ~ $ v4l2-ctl --list-devices
```

If it's /dev/video1, for example, then use the device parameter with fswebcam to specify this:

```
pi@raspberrypi ~ $ fswebcam test.jpg -d /dev/video1
```

> **fswebcam** has lots of options for things like the resolution and quality of the image. It can also do things like overlay text and timestamps on image captures. Use the command fswebcam -? to get a list of all options.

If you experimented with the dwc_otg.speed parameter to improve the audio quality during the previous chapter, you should change it back now by changing its value from 1 to 0, as chances are that your webcam will perform worse or will not perform at all, because of the reduced speed of the USB ports.

# Finding out your webcam's capabilities

Before we start grabbing videos with our webcam, it's very important that we find out exactly what it is capable of in terms of video formats and resolutions. To help us with this, we'll add the uvcdynctrl utility to our arsenal, using the following command:

```
pi@raspberrypi ~ $ sudo apt-get install uvcdynctrl
```

Let's start with the most important part—the list of supported frame formats.

To see this list, type in the following command:

```
pi@raspberrypi ~ $ uvcdynctrl -f
```

Or, if specifying a particular device:

```
pi@raspberrypi ~ $ uvcdynctrl -f -d /dev/video1
pi@raspberrypi:~ $ uvcdynctrl -f
Listing available frame formats for device video0:
Pixel format: YUYV (YUYV 4:2:2; MIME type: video/x-raw-yuv)
Frame size: 640x480
Frame rates: 30, 25, 20, 15, 10, 5
Frame size: 160x120
Frame rates: 30, 25, 20, 15, 10, 5
Frame size: 176x144
Frame rates: 30, 25, 20, 15, 10, 5
Frame size: 320x176
Frame rates: 30, 25, 20, 15, 10, 5
Frame size: 320x240
Frame rates: 30, 25, 20, 15, 10, 5
... blah blah blah ...
Frame size: 1280x960
Frame rates: 30, 25, 20, 15, 10, 5
Pixel format: MJPG (Motion-JPEG; MIME type: image/jpeg)
Frame size: 640x480
Frame rates: 30, 25, 20, 15, 10, 5
Frame size: 160x120
Frame rates: 30, 25, 20, 15, 10, 5
... blah blah....
Frame size: 1280x960
Frame intervals: 2/15, 1/5
```

According to the output of this particular webcam, there are two main pixel formats that are supported. The first format, called YUYV, or YUV 4:2:2, is a raw, uncompressed video format; the second format, called MJPG, or MJPEG, provides a video stream of compressed JPEG images.

Below each pixel format, we find the supported frame sizes and frame rates for each size. The frame size, or image resolution, will determine the amount of detail visible in the video. Three common resolutions for webcams are 320 x 240, 640 x 480 (also called **VGA)**, and 1024 x 768 (also called **XGA**).

The frame rate is measured in **Frames Per Second (fps)**, and will determine how fluid the video will appear. Various frame rates, from 5 fps to 30 fps, are available for each frame size on this particular webcam.

If you happen to be the unlucky owner of a camera that doesn't support the MJPEG pixel format, you can still go along, but don't expect more than a slideshow of images at 320 x 240 from your webcam. Video processing is one of the most CPU-intensive activities you can do with the Pi, so you need your webcam to help with this by compressing the frames first.

# Capturing your target on film

Right, let's see what our sneaky glass eye can do!

For our camera surveillance and capturing needs, we're going to use some excellent software called **Motion** and **MotionEye**. Motion, written by Kenneth Lavrsen, is a rather clever application that takes a feed from one or more cameras and can monitor the feed to see if areas of the image have changed. The official Motion site is here: http://www.lavrsen.dk/foswiki/bin/view/Motion/WebHome.

Motion is a command-line based service, which can be quite tricky to work with, so we're going to use MotionEye, which is a rather good, web-based frontend, which sits on top of the Motion daemon. MotionEye was developed by a guy called Calin Crisan, and the official Wiki site can be found here: https://github.com/ccrisan/motioneye/wiki.

So let's get our surveillance system set up. First install the Motion package with:

```
pi@raspberrypi ~ $ sudo apt-get install motion
```

On the current version of Raspbian Jessie, dependent packages such as `v4l-utils` should already be pre-installed.

MotionEye is written using Python, so we now need to install some Python packages and other libraries that it needs:

```
pi@raspberrypi ~ $ sudo apt-get install python-dev
```

And then:

```
pi@raspberrypi ~ $ sudo apt-get install libssl-dev libjpeg-dev
```

We then install the actual `motioneye` package using the Python Package Manager:

```
pi@raspberrypi ~ $ sudo pip install motioneye
```

Once it's installed, we start the `motioneye` service with:

```
pi@raspberrypi ~ $ sudo systemctl start motioneye
```

MotionEye should install nicely, using the preceding steps, however, it does require a few dependencies, and there could be some conflicts with some of the packages. If you have any issues, then take a step back and follow these Raspbian-specific instructions on the MotionEye Wiki at: https://github.com/ccrisan/motioneye/wiki/Install-On-Raspbian.

Now the MotionEye server is running, we can access our surveillance console through our web browser. The web server, by default, runs on port 8765, so accessing it is as simple as typing the IP address of your Pi plus the port number, into the URL bar of your browser: http://<my-ip>:8765.

I'm currently eyeing up the comings and goings of vehicles in the car park on the estate grounds:

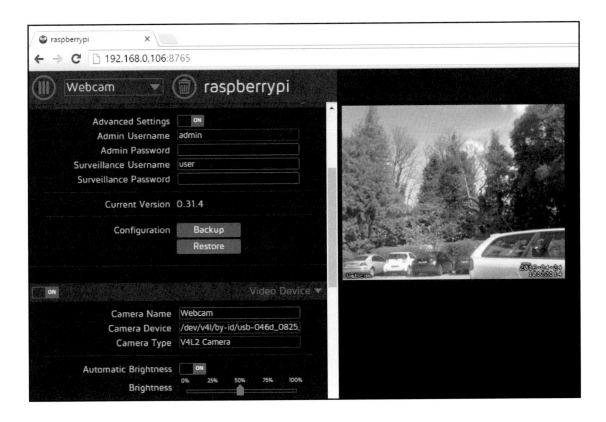

MotionEye web console with a live feed keeping a beady eye on the car park

The default login for the MotionEye is the username *admin* and a blank password.

The MotionEye interface allows us to configure how we want to capture the video stream—either by continuously recording or by taking snapshot images. Switch the **Advanced Settings** to **On** to see all of the settings available to you in the interface—you'll soon see how easy it is to set up your covert camera surveillance options with MotionEye:

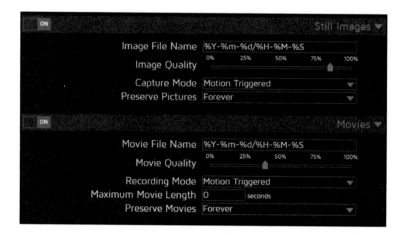

MotionEye still and video capture options

If you want to access the live stream from an external application, such as VLC player or within your own web pages, you can do so with the alternative direct video stream feed offered by the Motion daemon. The access URLs can be seen in the Video Streaming section of the **MotionEye** settings. More about this in the next section:

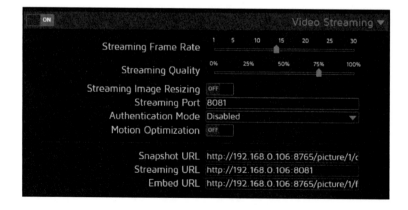

The MotionEye video streaming port by default is 8081

# Viewing your camera in VLC media player

You might be perfectly content with your current camera setup and viewing the stream in your browser, but for those of you who prefer to watch all videos inside your favorite media player, this section is for you. Also note that we'll be using VLC for other purposes further in this chapter, so we'll go through the installation here.

## Viewing in Windows

Let's install VLC and open up the camera stream by following these steps:

1. Visit `http://www.videolan.org` and download the latest version of the VLC installer package (`vlc-2.2.2-win32.exe`, at the time of writing).
2. Install VLC media player using the installer.
3. Launch VLC using the shortcut on the desktop or from the **Start** menu.
4. From the **Media** drop-down menu, select **Open Network Stream...**
5. Enter the direct stream URL shown in the MotionEye settings above (`http://<my-ip>:8081`), and click on the **Play** button:

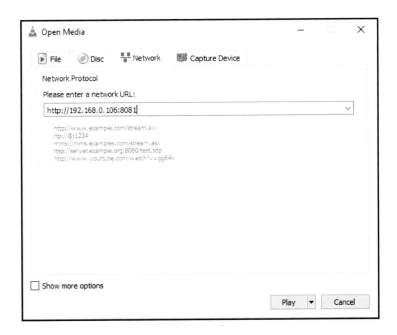

Open Media dialogue in VLC Player allows access to your streams

Viewing our feed in the VLC player

# Viewing in Mac OS X

Let's install VLC and open up the camera stream:

1. Visit `http://www.videolan.org/` and download the latest version of the VLC installer package (`vlc-2.2.2.dmg`, at the time of writing).
2. Double-click on the VLC disk image and drag the VLC icon to the **Applications** folder.
3. Launch VLC from the **Applications** folder.
4. From the **File** drop-down menu, select **Open Network**…
5. Enter the direct stream URL shown in the MotionEye settings above (`http://<my-ip>:8081`), and click on the **Play** button.

6. (Optional) You can add live audio monitoring from the webcam by opening up a terminal window (located in **Applications | Utilities**), and typing in the command line you learned from the *Listening in on conversations from a distance* section in `Chapter 2`, *Audio Antics*:

```
$ ssh pi@[IP address] sox -t alsa plughw:1 -t sox - | sox -q -t sox - -d
```

# Viewing in Linux

Let's install VLC or MPlayer and open up the camera stream:

1. Use your distribution's package manager to add the VLC or MPlayer package.
2. For VLC, either use the GUI to open a network stream, or launch it from the command line with this command:

```
$ vlc http://[IP address]:8081
```

3. For MPlayer, you need to tag on an MJPG file extension to the stream using the following command:

```
$ mplayer -demuxer lavf "http://[IP address]:8081"
```

4. (Optional) You can add live audio monitoring from the webcam by opening up a Terminal and typing in the command line you learned in the *Listening in on conversations from a distance* section of `Chapter 2`, *Audio Antics*:

```
$ ssh pi@[IP address] sox -t alsa plughw:1 -t sox - | sox -q -t sox - -
d
```

# Recording the video stream

The best way to save a video clip from the stream is to record it with VLC, and save it into an AVI file container. With this method, we get to keep the MJPEG compression while retaining the frame rate information.

Unfortunately, you won't be able to record the webcam video with sound. There's no way to automatically synchronize audio with the MJPEG stream. The only way to produce a video file with sound would be to grab video and audio streams separately and edit them together manually in a video editing application such as **VirtualDub.**

# Recording in Windows

We're going to launch VLC from the command line to record our video:

1.  Open up a **command prompt** window from the **Start** menu by clicking on the shortcut or by typing in **cmd** in the **Run/Search** field. Then type in the following command to start recording the video stream to a file called `myvideo.avi`, located on the desktop:

```
C:\> "C:\Program Files (x86)\VideoLAN\VLC\vlc.exe" http://[IP
address]:8081 --
sout="#standard{mux=avi,dst=%UserProfile%\Desktop\myvideo.avi,access=file}"
```

> If your particular Windows version doesn't have a `C:\Program Files` `(x86)` folder, just erase the (x86) part from the path on the command line.

2.  It may seem like nothing much is happening, but there should now be a growing `myvideo.avi` recording on your desktop. To confirm that VLC is indeed recording, we can select **Media Information** from the **Tools** drop-down menu and then select the **Statistics** tab.

3.  To stop the recording, simply close VLC.

# Recording in Mac OS X

We're going to launch VLC from the command line to record our video:

1.  Open up a **Terminal** window (located in **Applications | Utilities**) and type in the following command to start recording the video stream to a file called `myvideo.avi`, located on the desktop:

```
$ /Applications/VLC.app/Contents/MacOS/VLC http://[IP address]:8081 --
sout='#standard{mux=avi,dst=/Users/[username]/Desktop/myvideo.avi,access=fi
le}'
```

> Replace [username] with the name of the account you use to log in to your Mac, or remove the directory path to write the video to the current directory.

2.  It may seem like nothing much is happening, but there should now be a growing `myvideo.avi` recording on your desktop. To confirm that VLC is indeed recording, we can select **Media Information** from the **Window** drop-down menu and then select the **Statistics** tab.

3.  To stop the recording, simply close VLC.

# Recording in Linux

We're going to launch VLC from the command line to record our video:

1. Open up a **Terminal** and type in the following command to start recording the video stream to a file called `myvideo.avi`, located on the desktop:

```
$ vlc http://[IP address]:8081 --
sout='#standard{mux=avi,dst=/home/[username]/Desktop/myvideo.avi,access=fil
e}'
```

> Replace `[username]` with your login name, or remove the directory path to write the video to the current directory.

2. It may seem like nothing much is happening, but there should now be a growing `myvideo.avi` recording on your desktop. To confirm that VLC is indeed recording, we can select `Media Information` from the `Tools` drop-down menu and then select the **Statistics** tab.
3. To stop the recording, simply close VLC.

# Detecting an intruder and setting off an alarm

Let's dive right into the wonderful world of motion detection!

The basic idea of motion detection is pretty simple from a computer's point of view—the motion detection software processes a continuous stream of images and analyzes the positions of the pixels that make up the image. If a group of contiguous pixels above a certain threshold starts to change from one frame to the next, that must mean that something is moving. The tricky part of motion detection is weeding out false positives triggered by naturally occurring changes in light and weather conditions.

We've already installed the Motion software above, which will do the motion detection work for us, and the MotionEye web frontend will help us to easily set this up.

# Creating a motion detection configuration

The Video Device section of the MotionEye settings allows us to configure the camera that will be used for our motion detection scheme:

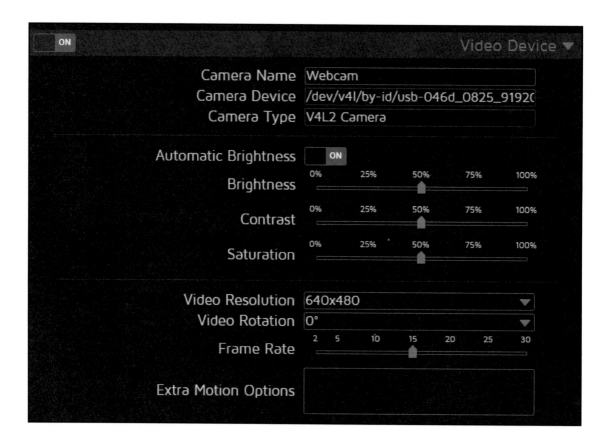

Video settings for our motion detection device

In the preceding settings, I'm using my USB webcam and have set a VGA video resolution with a frame rate of 15fps.

 You can get a summary of each setting by hovering over the associated question mark on the right-hand side of the panel.

The `Motion` package itself has an overwhelming number of options, but we can use the MotionEye front-end to setup the key ones for us:

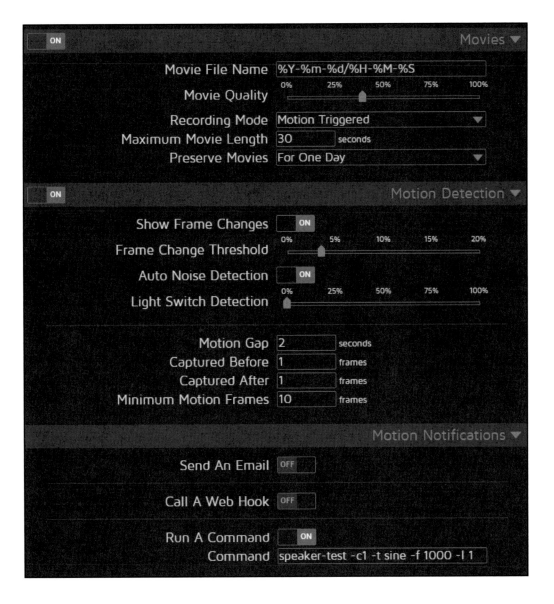

Motion detection settings in MotionEye

In the preceding configuration, we're telling Motion to start recording a video when motion is detected. It will also run the following command (in **Motion** Notifications), which is our temporary alarm sound until we find something better in a minute:

```
pi@raspberrypi ~ $ speaker-test -c1 -t sine -f 1000 -l 1
```

Once you've entered your settings, click the **Apply** button at the top of the page and they will take effect.

# Trying out Motion

Alright, let's take our motion detection system out for a spin by following this procedure:

1. Point your webcam away from yourself and any movement in view of the camera.
2. Now try waving your hand in front of the webcam. If your Pi sent out a high-pitched note through the speakers, and you see messages from the speaker test application on the console, we have managed basic motion detection! Even if you didn't trigger anything, keep reading to find out what's going on with the detection system.
3. In your web browser, view the live video feed from your camera in MotionEye. You should see the clock in the lower-right corner and the number of changed pixels in the upper-right corner. (If you're looking, instead, at a gray image with the text *unable to open video device*, there's most likely a problem with stream.)

Studying the number of changed pixels is one of the best ways to understand the motion detection system. The number will spike whenever you move the camera, but should come to rest at zero as Motion learns about light sources and applies an automatic noise filter to minimize the risk of false positives.

Now if you wave your hand in front of the camera, the pixel counter should climb and a rectangle will be drawn onto those areas in the image where Motion detected the largest changes in pixels.

If the number of pixels climbs over the set frame threshold value (roughly 9,200 when set at 3%), an event will fire, which is currently set to play the high-pitched tone.

When no motion has been detected for the number of seconds specified by the gap value (currently two), the event ends and a new event can begin.

The MotionEye maintains a library of clips it has collected when it detects movement in the camera. To access the library, click on the actual camera feed to view some options and click the triangular **Play** button at the top:

MotionEye video feed options overlay the video

You'll then be presented with your library of movies recorded by the webcam.

In the preceding image, you'll notice that a new car appeared in the scene. I can access and download the movie in which it was first detected, with the red square highlighting the moving vehicle, as you can see in the following video screenshot. Pretty cool eh?

Motion has detected the vehicle moving into the view of the camera

# Collecting the evidence

Now that we've established an initial working Motion setup, we have to decide what actions we want the system to take upon detection. Sounding an alarm, saving images and videos of the detected activity, logging the activity to a database, or alerting someone via e-mail are all valid responses to detection.

Let's create a directory to hold our evidence:

```
pi@raspberrypi ~ $ mkdir ~/evidence
```

We're going to revisit the MotionEye settings web panel, but this time, we're setting up the system for use in the real world. Once again, we'll go through the configuration file and pause to explain or change options.

Under the **Video Device** section, change the following settings to keep our CPU usage low:

- **Video Resolution**: 640x480
- **Frame Rate**: 5

We'll change the **Root Directory** setting under the **File Storage** section to: /home/pi/evidence

Ensure the **Still Images** section is enabled, so that a snapshot is taken when motion is detected:

- **Image Quality**: 50%
- **Capture Mode**: Motion Triggered

Ensure the **Movies** section is enabled so that video is recorded:

- **Movie Quality**: 30%
- **Recording Mode**: Motion Triggered

Under the **Motion Detection** section:

- Switch **Show Frame Changes** to Off to prevent the rectangle from being drawn onto our evidence.
- **Motion Gap**: 30 seconds

Under **Motion Notifications**:

- Run a command. It's up to you whether you want to keep the alarm tone, but you could generate a better one yourself with `espeak`—perhaps a robot voice saying *intruder alert!*—and then play it back with a simple `sox` command.

Now if you click **Apply** to save your settings and trigger a detection, a video file will start recording the event to your `~/evidence` directory, and after the 30 second gap, a JPG snapshot with the largest change in motion will be written to the same location.

# Viewing and e-mailing the evidence

Whenever a new file is recorded, the filename will be shown in the image and movies library, accessible by clicking the camera feed as shown previously.

To view the videos on the Pi itself, use VLC or an other compatible player and specify a filename, for example:

```
pi@raspberrypi ~ $ vlc ~/evidence/2016-04-24/15-26-49.avi
```

Having the images stored on your Raspberry Pi is not really much if you're not glued to the monitoring web page. Ideally, you would want the motion-triggered images sent to you straightaway, as soon as they are captured, so that you can view them on your smartphone. This would be pretty handy if you wanted to know if you had any visitors while you were out.

Fortunately, this is nice and simple in MotionEye—just enable the **Email** settings in the **Motion Notification** section of the settings panel:

MotionEye e-mail notification settings allow us to be sent evidence as it happens

# Hooking up more cameras

If you've got an extra webcam at home, perhaps built into a laptop, it would be a shame not to let it help out with the motion detection mission, right?

We're going to look at how to connect more camera streams to MotionEye. These streams might come from conventional IP security cameras, but the same method works equally well for webcams on Windows and Mac computers, with some tinkering.

## Preparing a webcam stream in Windows

We'll use **webcamXP** to add additional cams in Windows. The following are the necessary steps:

1. Visit `http://www.webcamxp.com/download.aspx` to download the latest webcamXP free application installer (`wxpfree590.exe` at the time of writing). Free for private use, webcamXP also allows two camera streams.
2. Install webcamXP using the installer.
3. Launch webcamXP using the shortcut (webcamXP 5) from the **Start** menu.
4. Right-click on the large image frame and select your webcam from the list; it will most likely be located under PCI / USB (WDM Driver).

You should be able to confirm that the stream is working by opening up a new tab in your browser and entering the following address in the address bar, but change [WinIP] to the IP address of your Windows computer: `http://[WinIP]:9090/cam_1.cgi`.

If the stream is working all right, proceed to add it to the Motion setup.

You may quit webcamXP to stop the stream at any time.

## Preparing a webcam stream in Mac OS X

We'll be using VLC to add additional cams in Mac OS X:

1. You should have VLC installed already as per the instructions in the *Viewing your webcam in VLC media player* section in this chapter.
2. Launch VLC from the **Applications** folder.
3. From the **File** drop-down menu, select **Open Capture Device**....

4. Check the **Video** checkbox and select your webcam from the list.

5. Show **Media Resource Locator** (MRL) and copy the string that starts with `qtcapture://`, followed by the ID number of your particular webcam. You will need this ID string next.

6. Now quit VLC and open up a **Terminal** window (located in **Applications | Utilities**) and type in the following command, replacing [ID] with the ID of your webcam and adjusting the width and height to suit your camera:

```
/Applications/VLC.app/Contents/MacOS/VLC qtcapture://[ID] --qtcapture-width
640 --qtcapture-height 480 --
sout='#transcode{vcodec=mjpg}:duplicate{dst=std{access=http{mime=multipart/
x-mixed-replace;boundary=-
-7b3cc56e5f51db803f790dad720ed50a},mux=mpjpeg,dst=:8080/stream.mjpg}}'
```

7. VLC will start serving a raw M-JPEG stream over HTTP on port 8080, suitable to feed into Motion.

You should be able to confirm that the stream is working by opening up a new tab in your browser and entering the following address in the address bar, but change [MacIP] to the IP address of your Mac: `http://[MacIP]:8080/stream.mjpg`.

If the stream is working all right, proceed to add it to the Motion setup.

You may quit VLC to stop the stream at any time.

## Configuring MotionEye for multiple input streams

MotionEye does all of the hard work of configuring the underlying Motion daemon to support multiple streams. To add a new camera feed into MotionEye, select **Add Camera...** from the camera list drop-down at the top of the page. You'll then get a dialog box in which to enter your remote camera details:

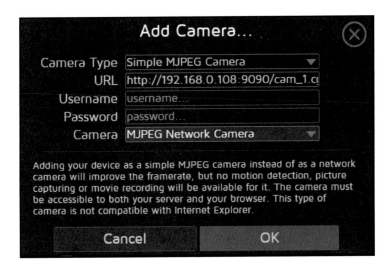

For the **Camera Type**, select `Simple MJPEG Camera` for it to work with our feed.

In the URL field, enter either `http://[WinIP]:9090/cam_1.cgi` or `http://[MacIP]:8080/stream.mjpg`.

You should now see the new camera feed added to the monitoring panel in the MotionEye web page.

To stop the MotionEye service, use the command:

```
pi@raspberrypi ~ $ sudo systemctl stop motioneye
```

As you can see, MotionEye gives us a proper villain's security monitoring wall, with all of our camera feeds being shown at once. But MotionEye also rather helpfully adds a unique embed URL too in the Video Streaming section, so that we can access each camera image individually. Handy if we want to build our own video surveillance wall.

# Watching your camera over the Internet

What if you'd like to monitor your headquarters from afar, or invite a fellow agent to keep an eye out for trouble while you're away on a mission? Well it just so happens that our MotionEye installation can help us with this

You could try to make the Pi accessible directly over the Internet, but it's much more convenient to let a stream broadcasting service pick up the Pi camera feed and make it available to any number of viewers.

There are a few different stream-broadcasting services to choose from, and we'll be looking at one called Ustream, but the method described here should be applicable to other companies as well.

Follow this procedure to get started with Ustream:

1. Visit `http://www.ustream.tv/` and sign up for a new account.
2. After verifying your e-mail address and signing in, click on **Go live!** You're signing up for the free Basic broadcasting service, which is fine for our purposes.
3. Pick a name for your channel—make it something easy to remember. Your unique channel URL will be shown underneath the **Channel Name** in the **Channel Info** section.
4. With your channel created, click your user icon at the top of the page and select **Dashboard** from the menu.
5. Under the **Channel** options, click on **Broadcast settings** and then the **View** link in the **Encode** settings section.
6. The RTMP URL and Stream Key fields shown will be copied to the command line to deliver the camera stream to the broadcasting service.

# The link between the Pi and the broadcasting service

To transmit the camera feed over **Real-Time Messaging Protocol (RTMP)**, we'll need to use an application called `avconv` that's part of the `ffmpeg` package. If you installed Motion earlier in this chapter, you already have this package; otherwise, install it now with the following command:

```
pi@raspberrypi ~ $ sudo apt-get install ffmpeg
```

Now let's try broadcasting. You'll get the best performance if you let the avconv utility grab the video straight from the camera, without Motion running in the background. Enter the following command, but replace [RTMP URL] and [Stream Key] with the values copied previously:

```
pi@raspberrypi ~ $ avconv -f video4linux2 -s 480x270 -r 15 -i
/dev/video0 -f flv [RTMP URL]/[Stream Key]
```

These are the lowest recommended broadcast settings for resolution and frame rate. You might have to adjust them slightly to fit your camera's capabilities.

You should now be able to tune in to your camera feed from any web browser by visiting your channel URL, which can be found in the *Info* section of your Channel Manager.

If you want to run MotionEye at the same time, start it up again with the following command:

**pi@raspberrypi ~ $ sudo systemctl start motioneye**
If you want the MotionEye service to start up automatically on boot, then use the following command:

```
$ sudo systemctl enable motioneye
To disable the service:
$ sudo systemctl disable motioneye
```

We can now make the avconv utility read the camera stream as input from MotionEye instead:

```
pi@raspberrypi ~ $ avconv -f mjpeg -r 1 -i "http://localhost:8081" -f flv
[RTMP URL]/[Stream Key]
```

All being well, you should now see the video stream in the MotionEye browser window being replicated on the Ustream broadcast, complete with text overlays.

The following screen shows a video stream of my rather inanimate giraffe in front of my webcam—but it shows the possibilities!

Your giraffe can be a TV star too, with a Pi webcam broadcast viewed in a browser

 If you don't want to broadcast out, but still want to be able to access your video streams and the MotionEye security wall remotely, then you can set up port forwarding on your Internet router in order to access the Raspberry Pi directly from outside on port 8765.

You'll learn about port forwarding and dynamic DNS setups in the next chapter.

# Night vision

The standard Raspberry Pi camera and webcams are great for taking daytime snaps of cars driving past, but when it comes to nighttime surveillance, these are not really suitable. One way to counter this and give your camera night-vision is to use the Raspberry Pi **NoIR camera module** along with an infrared LED array to let the camera *see* in the dark.

If you don't want to illuminate an area with bright lights before capturing an image, you can use **infrared lighting** in conjunction with a compatible camera. The standard Raspberry Pi camera module, and many webcams, won't work with infrared lighting, however, because they contain infrared filters; but we can use the NoIR version of the camera module instead.

The Raspberry Pi NoIR camera module is exactly the same as the standard one, except that it doesn't have an infrared filter built in, which means it will see in the dark with the aid of infrared lighting:

The Kingbright BL0307-50-63 infrared LED cluster runs from a 6V supply, which means you can connect two in series—one either side of the camera from a separate 12V supply

If you're interested in controlling the infrared LEDs from the Pi using a motion detector, then my previous book, *Building a Home Security System with Raspberry Pi* published by *Packt Publishing* will show you how: `https://www.packtpub.com/hardware-and-creative/building-home-security-system-raspberry-pi`.

# Make a covert wearable recorder with Pi Zero

In the same way that we used the Pi Zero in `Chapter 2`, *Audio Antics*, to create a covert audio record with a small battery pack and some low-profile USB adapters, we can do exactly the same with a small USB camera. In the following image, you can see that I have replaced the audio adapter and microphone with my USB webcam, again protected in a little bag:

Our wearable Pi Zero with camera connected

The Pi Zero with the battery pack shown should have enough current to power a small webcam as well as the Pi board. However, if you ever need to have the maximum power available from the USB port, you can add the following entry to the /boot/config.txt file: max_usb_current=1.

Again, our little low-profile micro-USB adapter helps us to keep our bag of tricks nice and compact.

# Turning your TV on or off using the Pi

For this example, we are relying on a technology called **Consumer Electronics Control (CEC),** which is a feature of the HDMI standard to send control messages to your home electronics equipment.

To help us send these messages, we'll need a software package called libCEC. While previously we had to build the libCEC package ourselves, we can now download a version for Raspbian Jessie using the installer:

```
pi@raspberrypi ~ $ sudo apt-get install libcec3 cec-utils
```

We will be using a utility called cec-client to send CEC messages to the TV. Issue the following command to switch off your TV:

```
pi@raspberrypi ~ $ echo "standby 0" | cec-client -d 1 -s
```

Use the following command to turn your TV on again:

```
pi@raspberrypi ~ $ echo "on 0" | cec-client -d 1 -s
```

Note that your TV must be able to support these commands. Not all TVs support the standby command through the HDMI port. You can play around with the cec-client console to discover the devices and their features connected to the HDMI bus on your setup.

# Scheduling a playback scare

At this stage, you already know all the individual techniques used for this example. It's simply a matter of combining what you've learned so far to achieve the effect you want.

We'll try to illustrate a bit of everything with one sweet prank: you will prepare your Pi at home, take it over to your friend's house, and sneakily hook it up to the living room TV. In the middle of the night, the TV will turn itself on and a creepy video of your choice will start to play. This freaky incident might repeat itself a couple of times during the night, or we could take the prank to phase two: whenever someone walks into the room, their presence is detected and the video is played.

Let's start prepping the Pi! We will assume that no network connection is available at your friend's house, so we'll have to create a new ~/autorun.sh script to perform our prank, together with a timer in /etc/rc.local that starts counting down when the Pi is plugged in at your friend's house.

Here's the new ~/autorun.sh script:

```
#!/bin/sh
#
# Raspberry Pi Video Prank Script
# Use chmod +x ~/autorun.sh to enable.

CREEPY_MOVIE="AJn5Y65GAkA.mp4" # Creepy movie to play, located in the Pi
home directory

MOVIE_LOOPS="1" # Number of times to play creepy movie (1 by default)

MOVIE_SLEEP="3600" # Number of seconds to sleep between movie plays (1 hour
by default)

WEBCAM_PRANK="y" # Set to y to enable the motion detection prank

tv_off() {
  if [ "$(echo "pow 0" | cec-client -d 1 -s | grep 'power status:
    on')" ]; then # If TV is currently on
  echo "standby 0" | cec-client -d 1 -s # Send the standby command
  fi
}

prepare_tv() {
  tv_off # We switch the TV off and on again to force the
    active channel to the Pi
  sleep 10 # Give it a few seconds to shut down
  echo "on 0" | cec-client -d 1 -s # Now send the on command
```

```
    sleep 10 # And give the TV another few seconds to wake up
    echo "as" | cec-client -d 1 -s # Now set the Pi to be the
      active source
}

play_movie() {
    if [ -f ~/"$CREEPY_MOVIE" ]; then # Check that the creepy movie
      file exists
    omxplayer -o hdmi ~/"$CREEPY_MOVIE" # Then play it with sound
      going out through HDMI
    fi
}


case "$1" in
    prankon) # Signal from Motion that event has started
      prepare_tv
      play_movie
      tv_off
      ;;

    prankoff) # Signal from Motion that event has ended
      ;;

    *) # Normal start up of autorun.sh script
for i in $(seq $MOVIE_LOOPS) # Play creepy movie in a loop the number of
times specified
do
      prepare_tv
      play_movie
      tv_off
      sleep "$MOVIE_SLEEP" # Sleep the number of seconds specified
done

      start_webcam_prank # Begin prank phase 2
      ;;
esac
```

Don't forget to give the script executable permission using the following:

```
pi@raspberrypi ~ $ chmod +x ~/autorun.sh.
```

Now all we need to do is adjust/etc/rc.local to set a timer for our autorun.sh script using the at command. Type in `sudo nano /etc/rc.local` to open it up for editing, and adjust the following block:

```
if [ -x /home/pi/autorun.sh ]; then
    sudo -u pi at now + 9 hours -f /home/pi/autorun.sh
fi
```

So if you plug in the Pi at your friend's house at 6pm, strange things should start happening right around 3am in the morning.

As for what creepy movie to play, we leave that entirely up to you. There's a tool called `youtube-dl` that you might find useful. Install it and update it with the following sequence of commands:

```
pi@raspberrypi ~ $ sudo apt-get install youtube-dl
pi@raspberrypi ~ $ sudo wget https://yt-dl.org/latest/youtube-dl
-O /usr/bin/youtube-dl
```

 Be careful not to introduce line breaks within each of the command lines; otherwise, they will not run—breaks are only present in these ones for display reasons.

Now you could use it to fetch videos like this:

```
pi@raspberrypi ~ $ youtube-dl
http://www.youtube.com/watch?v=[creepyvideoid]
```

# Summary

In this chapter, we got acquainted with the two components involved in camera handling under Linux: the USB Video Class drivers and the Video4Linux framework. You learned how to obtain important information about your camera's capabilities; you also learned a bit about pixel formats, image resolution, and frame rates.

We proceeded to set up a video feed, accessible directly via a web browser or through VLC media player, which we could also use to record the stream for permanent storage.

Then we jumped head first into surveillance and motion detection systems with the help of the Motion and MotionEye applications. You learned how to create an initial configuration suitable to verify and tweak the motion detection mechanism, and how to set off alarms upon detection. We also explored how to view that evidence and have it delivered to our smartphone by e-mail.

Not content with letting any unused webcams in the home go to waste, we explored how to hook up additional camera streams to the MotionEye system to take advantage of its security monitoring wall.

We then made our camera feed easily viewable over the Internet, with the help of a broadcasting service that picked up our camera feed through an RTMP stream.

We also looked at how to make use of CEC technology to remotely control the TV connected to the Pi, a neat trick that came in handy for our last and boldest prank: the creepy playback scare.

In the upcoming chapter, we'll dive deep into the world of computer networks and you'll learn how to be in complete control over your Wi-Fi access point.

# 4
# Wi-Fi Pranks – Exploring Your Network

In this age of digital information, a secret agent must be able to handle computer networks with ease. The intricate details of protocols and network packets are still shrouded in mystery to most people. With this chapter, you'll gain the advantage by simply picking up, and looking closely at, the network signals that surround all of us every day.

We'll start off by analyzing the Wi-Fi traffic around the house, and then we'll map out your local network in more detail so that you can pick out an interesting target for your network pranks. You'll not only learn how to capture, manipulate, and spy on your target's network traffic, but also how to protect yourself and your network from mischief.

In this chapter, we will:

- Get an overview of all computers on your network
- Find out what the other computers are up to
- Protect your network against Ettercap
- Analyze packet dumps with Wireshark
- Explore dynamic DNS, port forwarding, and tunneling
- Keep Facebook conversations secret with encryption

# Getting an overview of all the computers on your network

When analyzing Wi-Fi networks in particular, we have to take the borderless nature of radio signals into account. For example, someone could be parked in a car outside your house, running a rogue access point, and tricking the computers inside your home to send all their traffic through this nefarious surveillance equipment. To be able to detect such attacks, you need a way of monitoring the airspace around your house.

## Monitoring Wi-Fi airspace with Kismet

Kismet is a Wi-Fi spectrum and traffic analyzer that relies on your Wi-Fi adapter's ability to enter something called **monitor mode**. You should be aware that not all adapters and drivers support this mode of operation, but those based on the Atheros or Ralink chipset are a good bet.

You can test whether your Wi-Fi adapter supports monitor mode; attempt to put it into this mode with the following commands:

```
pi@raspberrypi ~ $ sudo ifconfig wlan0 down
pi@raspberrypi ~ $ sudo iwconfig wlan0 mode monitor
```

If your device doesn't support this mode, you'll get a response something like:

```
Error for wireless request "Set Mode" (8B06) :
 SET failed on device wlan0 ; Operation not supported.
```

If you don't get this message then it's probably supported and set. You can check this with the following command:

```
pi@raspberrypi ~ $ sudo iwconfig
```

Look for your device in the output, which should confirm that it's switched into monitor mode with:

```
wlan0 IEEE 802.11bgn Mode:Monitor Tx-Power=20 dBm
 Retry short limit:7 RTS thr:off Fragment thr:off
 Power Management:off
```

Note that the Wi-Fi chip built into the new Raspberry Pi 3 **does not** support monitor mode, therefore you'll have to plug in an external USB Wi-Fi dongle, which does support monitor mode, such as the **Farnell element14 Wi-Pi** device shown in the following image. This will be seen by the Pi 3 as device `wlan1` rather than `wlan0` as on the previous versions.

Farnell element14's nice little Wi-Pi device is based on the Ralink chipset and supports monitor mode

Since your Wi-Fi adapter will be busy monitoring the airwaves, you'll want to work directly on the Pi itself with a keyboard and monitor, or log in to the Pi over a wired connection. See the *Setting up point-to-point networking* section of `Chapter 5`, *Taking Your Pi Off-road*, if you would like to set up a direct wired connection without a router.

We'll have to build Kismet ourselves from source code, as the package in the Raspbian repository is an ancient version from 2013, whereas the latest version was released in February 2016. The following are the steps to build Kismet:

1. First, add some developer headers and code libraries that Kismet relies on:

```
pi@raspberrypi ~ $ sudo apt-get install libncurses5-dev           libpcap-dev
libpcre3-dev libnl-3-dev libnl-genl-3-dev libcap-dev libwireshark-data
```

2. Next, download the Kismet source code from the project's web page:

```
pi@raspberrypi ~ $ wget
http://www.kismetwireless.net/code/kismet-2016-01-R1.tar.xz
```

Now extract the source tree and build the software using the following sequence of commands:

```
pi@raspberrypi ~ $ tar -xvf kismet-2016-01-R1.tar.xz
pi@raspberrypi ~ $ cd kismet-2016-01-R1
pi@raspberrypi ~/kismet-2016-01-R1 $ ./configure --prefix=/usr --
sysconfdir=/etc --with-suidgroup=pi
pi@raspberrypi ~/kismet-2016-01-R1 $ make
```

At this point you'll notice that a large amount of text output is generated by the `make` process—this is normal!

```
pi@raspberrypi ~/kismet-2016-01-R1 $ sudo make suidinstall
```

3. The Kismet build process is quite lengthy and will eat up about half an hour of a Pi 3's time, and longer on earlier models. Once it's finished, you may exit the source directory and delete it:

```
pi@raspberrypi ~/kismet-2016-01-R1 $ cd .. && rm -rf kismet-20136-01-R1
```

# Preparing Kismet for launch

When a Wi-Fi adapter enters monitor mode, it means that it's not associated with any particular access point and is just listening for any Wi-Fi traffic that happens to whizz by in the air. On Raspbian, however, there are utility applications running in the background that try to automatically associate your adapter with Wi-Fi networks. We'll have to temporarily disable two of these helper applications to stop them from interfering with the adapter while Kismet is running.

1. Open up `/etc/network/interfaces` for editing:

```
pi@raspberrypi ~ $ sudo nano /etc/network/interfaces
```

2. Find the block that starts with `allow-hotplug wlan0` and put a # character in front of each line, like we've done here:

```
#allow-hotplug wlan0
#iface wlan0 inet manual
#    wpa-conf /etc/wpa_supplicant/wpa_supplicant.conf
```

On the Pi 3 with the dongle showing as `wlan1`, comment out those lines instead.

Press *Ctrl + X* to exit and select **y** when prompted to save the modified buffer, then press the *Enter* key to confirm the filename to write to. This will prevent the `wpa_supplicant` utility from interfering with Kismet.

2. Now, reboot your Pi. Once logged back in, you can verify that your adapter has not associated with any access points by using the following command:

```
pi@raspberrypi ~ $ iwconfig
```

```
pi@raspberrypi:~ $ iwconfig
wlan0     IEEE 802.11bgn  ESSID:off/any
          Mode:Managed  Access Point: Not-Associated   Tx-Power=31 dBm
          Retry short limit:7   RTS thr:off   Fragment thr:off
          Power Management:on
```

Wi-Fi adapter showing no associated access point

Kismet has the option to geographically map access points using a connected GPS. If you have a GPS that you'd like to use with Kismet, read the *Tracking the Pi's whereabouts using GPS* section of `Chapter 5`, *Taking Your Pi Off-road*, to learn how to set up your GPS adapter, then continue reading from here.

Kismet is also capable of alerting you to new network discoveries using sound effects and synthesized speech. The SoX and eSpeak software from `Chapter 2`, *Audio Antics*, works well for these purposes. In case you haven't got them installed, use the following command to add them to your system now:

```
pi@rasypberrypi ~ $ sudo apt-get install sox
libsox-fmt-mp3 espeak
```

Another very important function of Kismet is to generate detailed log files. Let's create a directory to hold these files using the following command:

```
pi@raspberrypi ~ $ mkdir ~/kismetlogs
```

Before we start Kismet, we need to open up the configuration file to adjust a few settings to our liking, using the following command:

```
pi@raspberrypi ~ $ sudo nano /etc/kismet.conf
```

We will go through the configuration and make stops to explain or change options from top to bottom:

- `logprefix`: Uncomment and change the `logprefix` line so that the log files generated by Kismet will be stored in a predictable location:

    **logprefix=/home/pi/kismetlogs**

- `ncsource`: Uncomment and change the `ncsource` line so that Kismet knows what Wi-Fi interface to use for monitoring. There are many options for this directive and Kismet should pick sensible defaults for the most part, but we've specified two options here that have proved necessary in some cases on the Pi:

    **ncsource=wlan0:forcevap=false,validatefcs=true**

Or:

**ncsource=wlan1:forcevap=false,validatefcs=true**

For the Pi 3:

- `gps`: Change this line to read `gps=false` if you don't have a GPS attached; otherwise, leave it as it is and check that your `gpsd` is up and running.
- Save the file and exit `nano`.

# First Kismet session

The Kismet application is actually made up of a separate server component and client interface, which means that you could let the Pi run only the Kismet server and then attach a client interface to it from another computer.

In this case, we'll run both server and client on the Pi, using the following command:

**pi@raspberrypi ~ $ kismet**

You'll be greeted by a colorful console interface and a series of pop-up dialog boxes asking you questions about your setup. Use your *Tab* key to switch between answers and press the *Enter* key to select. The first question about color just tweaks the color scheme used by the Kismet interface, depending on your answer. Select **Yes** to the second question about starting the Kismet server, then accept the default options for the Kismet server and select **Start**.

This is the crucial point where you'll find out if your particular Wi-Fi adapter will successfully enter monitoring mode so that Kismet can work its magic. If your adapter doesn't support monitor mode, it will tell you so on the Kismet Server Console:

```
INFO: Kismet starting to gather packets
INFO: Deferring opening of packet source 'wlan0' to IPC child
INFO: kismet_capture pid 2917 synced with Kismet server, starting service
      loop
INFO: Enabling FCS frame validation on packet source 'wlan0'
INFO: Enabling FCS frame validation on packet source 'wlan0'
INFO: Source 'wlan0' forced into non-vap mode, this will modify the
      provided interface.
INFO: Started source 'wlan0'
INFO: Kismet server accepted connection from 127.0.0.1
INFO: Detected new managed network "MiFi", BSSID 9C:D6:43:CF:23:DD,
      encryption yes, channel 2, 54.00 mbit
      [ Kill Server ]                              [ Close Console Window ]
```

First detected network reported on the Kismet Server Console

When you see messages about new detected networks starting to pop up in the log, you know that everything is working fine and you may close the server console by pressing the *Tab* key to select **Close Console Window,** and then pressing the *Enter* key.

You're now looking at the main Kismet screen, which is composed of different **View** areas with **Network List** being the most prominent. You'll see any number of access points in the near vicinity and should be able to spot your own access point in the list:

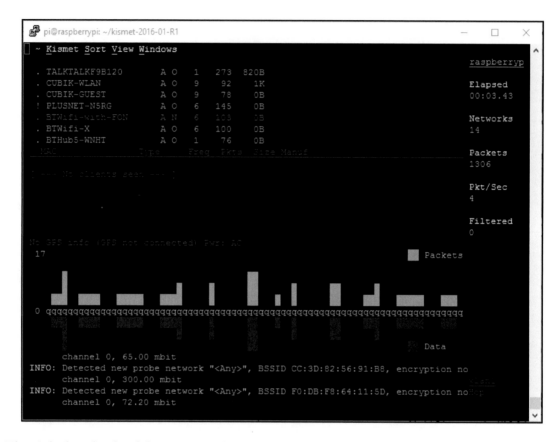

The right-hand side of the screen is the **General Info** area, which provides a grand overview of the Kismet session, and **Packet Graph** across the middle provides a real-time activity monitor of the packet capture process.

The **Status** area at the bottom contains the latest messages from the **Kismet Server** console and makes it easy to spot when new access points are discovered and added to the list.

To toggle the drop-down menu at the top of the screen, press the ~ key (usually located under the *Esc* key), and then use your arrow keys to navigate through the menus and press the *Enter* key to select. Press the same ~ key to close the menu. There are also underlined letters and shortcut letters that you can use to navigate faster through the menus.

Let's look at the **Sort** menu. When you start out, **Network List** is set to the **Auto-fit** sorting. To be able to select individual access points in the list for further operations, you need to choose one of the available sorting methods. A good choice is **Packets (descending)** since it makes the most active access points visible at the top of the list:

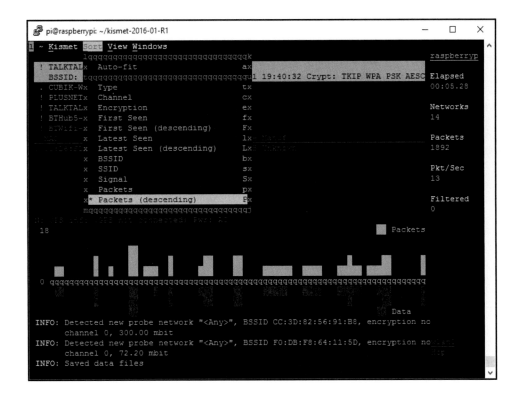

Kismet showing the sort menu

Now you'll be able to use your arrow keys in the **Network** list to select your access point and get a closer look at the connected computers by viewing the **Client** list from the **View** or **Windows** drop-down menu. Each Wi-Fi adapter associated with the access point has a unique hardware identifier called a MAC address. While these addresses can be faked (spoofed), it does give you an idea of how many computers are actively sending and receiving network packets on your network, as indicated by the ! character in front of active MACs. Just keep in mind that the access point itself appears in the list as a **Wired/AP** type.

# Adding sound and speech

Most aspects of the Kismet user interface can be changed from the **Preferences** panel under the **Kismet** drop-down menu. To add sound effects or synthesized speech, select the **Audio...** option.

Use your *Tab* and *Enter* keys to enable **Sound** and/or **Speech**. To make the speech work, select **Configure Speech** and change the **Speech Player** command to `espeak`. Now close the dialogs and your changes should take effect immediately.

# Enabling rogue access point detection

Kismet not only monitors the Wi-Fi airspace, it also includes some **Intrusion Detection System** (**IDS**) functionality. When Kismet detects something fishy going on, it will let you know with special alert messages (and an optional siren sound effect). To help Kismet detect the rogue access point attack we mentioned in the introduction to this section, we need to specify the correct MAC address of our access point in the Kismet configuration file.

You can obtain the MAC of your access point through Kismet. Verify that it stops sending packets when you turn it off to be sure it's really your access point.

Come out of Kismet *(Ctrl + ~)* and open up the Kismet configuration file for editing:

```
pi@raspberrypi ~ $ sudo nano /etc/kismet.conf
```

Locate the two example lines starting with `apspoof=` and comment them out. Then add your own line below according to the following format:

```
apspoof=RogueAPAlert:ssid="[AP Name]",validmacs="[MAC address]"
```

Replace `[AP Name]` with the name (SSID) of your access point and `[MAC address]` with the MAC of your access point, then save and exit `nano`.

Whenever Kismet detects any inconsistencies involving your access point, you'll receive alerts in the **Kismet Server Console** and under the special **Alerts** window:

```
GNU nano 2.2.6              File: /etc/kismet.conf              Modified
# Controls behavior of the APSPOOF alert.  SSID may be a literal match (ssid=) or
# a regex (ssidregex=) if PCRE was available when kismet was built.  The allowed
# MAC list must be comma-separated and enclosed in quotes if there are multiple
# MAC addresses allowed.  MAC address masks are allowed.
# apspoof=Foo1:ssidregex="(?i:foobar)",validmacs=00:11:22:33:44:55
# apspoof=Foo2:ssid="Foobar",validmacs="00:11:22:33:44:55,aa:bb:cc:dd:ee:ff"
apspoof=RougeAPAlert:ssid="MiFi",validmacs="C0:3F:0E:DC:83:11"


ALERT: APSPOOF Unauthorized device (C0:3F:0E:DC:83:1F) advertising for
       SSID 'MiFi', matching APSPOOF rule RougeAPAlert with SSID which
       may indicate spoofing or impersonation.
```

Kismet showing a rogue AP alert

This concludes our Kismet crash course. We'll cover how to analyze the captured network traffic that we logged to `~/kismetlogs` later, in the *Analyzing packet dumps with Wireshark* section.

# Mapping out your network with Nmap

While Kismet gave us a broad overview of the Wi-Fi airspace around your home, it's time to get an insider's perspective of what your network looks like.

For the rest of this chapter, you can stay associated with your access point or connected to your router via Ethernet as usual. You'll need to revert any changes you made to the `/etc/network/interfaces` file earlier during the Kismet section. Then, reboot your Pi and check that you are indeed associated with your access point using the `iwconfig` command:

```
pi@raspberrypi ~ $ iwconfig
wlan0     IEEE 802.11bgn  ESSID:"MiFi"
          Mode:Managed  Frequency:2.457 GHz  Access Point: C0:3F:0E:DC:83:11
          Bit Rate=13.5 Mb/s   Tx-Power=20 dBm
          Retry  long limit:7   RTS thr:off    Fragment thr:off
          Power Management:off
          Link Quality=69/70  Signal level=-41 dBm
          Rx invalid nwid:0  Rx invalid crypt:0  Rx invalid frag:0
          Tx excessive retries:0  Invalid misc:3   Missed beacon:0
```

Wi-Fi adapter associated with the MiFi access point

We'll be using the highly versatile **Nmap** application to gather information about everything that lives on your network. Let's install Nmap together with two other packages that will come in handy:

```
pi@raspberrypi ~ $ sudo apt-get install nmap
xsltproc elinks
```

Nmap, as well as the other applications we'll be using in this chapter, will want to know what IP address or range of addresses to focus this attention on. Nmap will gladly start scanning the entire Internet if you tell it to, but that's neither practical nor helpful to you or the Internet. What you want to do is pick a range from the private IPv4 address space that is in use on your home network.

These are the three IP address blocks reserved for use on private networks:

- 10.0.0.0 to 10.255.255.255 (Class A network)
- 172.16.0.0 to 172.31.255.255 (Class B network)
- 192.168.0.0 to 192.168.255.255 (Class C network)

The Class C network is the most common range for home routers, with 192.168.1.1 being a typical IP address for the router itself. If you're unsure of the range in use on your network, you can look at the IP address and route information that was handed to the Wi-Fi interface by the DHCP service of your router:

```
pi@raspberrypi ~ $ ip addr show wlan0
pi@raspberrypi ~ $ ip route show
```

```
pi@raspberrypi ~ $ ip addr show wlan0
3: wlan0: <BROADCAST,MULTICAST,UP,LOWER_UP> mtu 1500 qdisc mq state UP qlen 1000
    link/ether 64:70:02:25:16:15 brd ff:ff:ff:ff:ff:ff
    inet 192.168.1.20/24 brd 192.168.1.255 scope global wlan0
       valid_lft forever preferred_lft forever
pi@raspberrypi ~ $ ip route show
default via 192.168.1.1 dev wlan0
192.168.1.0/24 dev wlan0  proto kernel  scope link  src 192.168.1.20
```

Wi-Fi interface in the 192.168.1.0/24 address range

The Wi-Fi interface, as shown in the previous screenshot, has been handed an IP address in the 192.168.1.0/24 range, which is a shorter way (called **CIDR** notation) of saying between 192.168.1.0 and 192.168.1.255.

We can also see that the default gateway for the Wi-Fi interface is 192.168.1.1. The default gateway is where the Wi-Fi interface sends all its traffic to talk to the Internet, which is very likely to be the IP address of your router.

So, if you find that your interface has been given, for example, 10.1.1.20, the IP addresses of the other computers on your network are most likely somewhere in the 10.1.1.1 to 10.1.1.254 range. Now that we know what range to scan, let's see what Nmap can find out about it.

The simplest, yet surprisingly useful, scan technique offered by Nmap is called the List Scan. It's one way of finding computers on the network by doing a host name lookup for each IP address in the range that we specify, without sending any actual network packets to the computers themselves. Try it out using the following command, but replace [target] with a single IP address or range:

```
pi@raspberrypi ~ $ sudo nmap -v -sL [target]
```

```
pi@raspberrypi ~ $ sudo nmap -v -sL 192.168.1.0/24

Starting Nmap 6.00 ( http://nmap.org ) at 2014-10-18 15:37 EDT
Initiating Parallel DNS resolution of 256 hosts. at 15:37
Completed Parallel DNS resolution of 256 hosts. at 15:37, 8.73s elapsed
Nmap scan report for 192.168.1.0
Nmap scan report for dlinkrouter (192.168.1.1)
Nmap scan report for MacBook (192.168.1.2)
Nmap scan report for EeePC (192.168.1.3)
Nmap scan report for BobXP (192.168.1.4)
Nmap scan report for PS3 (192.168.1.5)
...
Nmap scan report for 192.168.1.253
Nmap scan report for 192.168.1.254
Nmap scan report for 192.168.1.255
Nmap done: 256 IP addresses (0 hosts up) scanned in 9.08 seconds
```

Nmap performing the List Scan

We always want to run Nmap with sudo, since Nmap requires root privileges to perform most of the scans. We also specify -v for some extra verbosity and -sL to use the List Scan technique. At the end comes the target specification, which can be a single IP address or a range of addresses. We can specify ranges using the short CIDR notation such as in the preceding screenshot, or with a dash in each group (called an octet) of the address. For example, to scan the first 20 addresses, we could specify 192.168.1.1-20.

The List Scan tells us which IP address is associated with what host name, but it doesn't really tell us if the computer is up and running at this very moment, which is why is reports **0 hosts up** at the end. To check if a host is alive, we'll move on to the next technique: the ping scan. In this mode, Nmap will send out packets to each IP in the range to try to determine whether the host is alive or not. Try it out using the following command:

```
pi@raspberrypi ~ $ sudo nmap -sn [target]
```

You'll get a list of all the computers that are currently running, along with their MAC address and the hardware manufacturer of their network adapter. On the last line, you'll find a summary of the total number of IP addresses scanned and how many of them are alive.

The other functions offered by Nmap can be viewed by starting nmap without arguments. To give you a taste of the powerful techniques available, try the following series of commands:

```
pi@raspberrypi ~ $ sudo nmap -sS -sV -sC -O -oX report.xml [target]
pi@raspberrypi ~ $ xsltproc report.xml -o report.html
pi@raspberrypi ~ $ elinks report.html
```

This nmap command might take a while to finish, depending on the number of computers on your network; On a Pi 3 across a /24 subnet it can take more than half an hour, as it launches four different scanning techniques:

- -sS: for port scanning
- -sV: for service version detection
- -sC: for script scan
- -O: for OS detection

We've also specified -oX to get a detailed report in XML format, which we then transform to an HTML document, viewable on the console with the Elinks web browser. Press Q to quit Elinks when you're done viewing the report.

# Finding out what the other computers are up to

Now that we have a better idea of the computer behind each IP address, we can begin to target the network traffic itself as it flows through our network.

For these experiments, we'll be using an application called **Ettercap**. The act of listening in on network traffic is commonly known as **sniffing,** and there are several great sniffer applications to choose from. What sets Ettercap apart is its ability to combine man-in-the-middle attacks with network sniffing and a bunch of other useful features, making it an excellent tool for network mischief.

You see, one obstacle that sniffers have to overcome is how to obtain network packets that aren't meant for your network interface. This is where Ettercap's man-in-the-middle attack comes into play. We will launch an **ARP poisoning** attack that will trick any computer on the network into sending all its network packets through the Pi. Our Pi will essentially become the man in the middle, secretly spying on and manipulating the packets as they pass through.

Let's install the command-line version of Ettercap using the following command:

```
pi@raspberrypi ~ $ sudo apt-get install
ettercap-text-only
```

Before we begin, make a few small adjustments to the Ettercap configuration file:

```
pi@raspberrypi ~ $ sudo nano /etc/ettercap/etter.conf
```

Find the two lines that read **ec_uid = 65534** and **ec_gid = 65534**. Now change the two lines to read `ec_uid = 0` and `ec_gid = 0`. This changes the user/group ID used by Ettercap to the `root` user. Next, find the line that starts with **remote_browser** and replace the whole line with:

remote_browser = "elinks -remote 'openURL(http://%host%url)'"

Then save the configuration and exit `nano`.

For our first Ettercap experiment, we'll try to capture every single host name lookup made by any computer on the local network. For example, your browser makes a host name lookup behind the scenes when you visit a website for the first time. Use the following command to start sniffing:

```
pi@raspberrypi ~ $ sudo ettercap -T -i wlan0
-M arp:remote -V ascii -d ///53
```

You can also use the Ethernet connection if you want by changing the interface parameter, such as:

```
pi@raspberrypi ~ $ sudo ettercap -T -i eth0
-M arp:remote -V ascii -d ///53
```

```
pi@raspberrypi:~ $ sudo ettercap -T -i eth0 -M arp:remote -V ascii -d ///53

ettercap 0.8.1 copyright 2001-2014 Ettercap Development Team

Listening on:
  eth0 -> B8:27:EB:A1:7E:9F
          192.168.0.106/255.255.255.0
          fe80::baf5:7fe8:d8e1:e1c8/64

SSL dissection needs a valid 'redir_command_on' script in the etter.conf file
Privileges dropped to UID 0 GID 0...

  33 plugins
  42 protocol dissectors
  57 ports monitored
19839 mac vendor fingerprint
1766 tcp OS fingerprint
2182 known services
Lua: no scripts were specified, not starting up!

Randomizing 255 hosts for scanning...
Scanning the whole netmask for 255 hosts...
\ |===============>                          |  29.41 %

Mon May  2 16:23:57 2016 [136940]
UDP  192.168.0.254:3995 --> 208.67.222.222:53 |
```

Ettercap sniffing for DNS requests

Depending on the level of activity on your network, the messages could be flooding your screen or trickle in once in a while. You can verify that it is indeed working by opening up a command prompt on any computer on the network and trying to ping a made-up address, for example:

```
C:\> ping connectingobjects.com
```

The address should show up as part of a DNS request (UDP packet to port 53) in your Ettercap session:

```
Mon May  2 16:23:57 2016 [827765]
UDP  192.168.0.108:55494 --> 192.168.0.1:53 |

...........connectingobjects.com.....
\ |============================>                     |  56.08 %

Mon May  2 16:23:57 2016 [848552]
UDP  192.168.0.1:53 --> 192.168.0.108:55494 |

...........connectingobjects.com................b|.,
| |============================>                     |  56.47 %

Mon May  2 16:23:57 2016 [855058]
UDP  192.168.0.108:55495 --> 192.168.0.1:53 |

...........connectingobjects.com.....
- |============================>                     |  57.25 %

Mon May  2 16:23:57 2016 [877327]
UDP  192.168.0.1:53 --> 192.168.0.108:55495 |

...........connectingobjects.com..............D.dns1.name-services.com..info.name-services.c
om.V;...............
* |===============================================>|  100.00 %
```

Ettercap finding DNS requests

Note that Ettercap is in interactive mode here. You can press the H key to get a menu with several interesting key commands to help you control the session. It's very important that you quit Ettercap by pressing the Q key. This ensures that Ettercap will clean up your network after the ARP poisoning attack.

 If your PC has a decent security product installed, you might notice it alerting you about ARP poison attacks on your network—it may also prevent Ettercap from seeing anything sent from your computer—so for the benefit of the experiments in this section involving Ettercap, you might need to temporarily switch of the Network Protection module of your security product.

Let's go over the arguments:

We pass -T on the command line for interactive text mode, and -i wlan0 means we want to use the Wi-Fi interface for sniffing—use eth0 to sniff on a wired connection.

The `-M arp:remote` specifies that we'd like to use an ARP poisoning man-in-the-middle attack, the `-V ascii` dictates how Ettercap will display the network packets to us, and `-d` specifies that we would prefer to read host names instead of IP addresses.

Last comes the target specification, which is of the `[MAC address or IP address]//[Port number]` form. So for example, `/192.168.0.1//80` will sniff traffic to and from `192.168.0.1` on port number `80` only. Leaving something out is the same as saying all of them. You may also specify ranges, for example, `/192.168.1.10-20//` will sniff the ten IPs from `192.168.1.10` to `192.168.1.20`. Often, you'll want to specify two targets, which is excellent to watch; for example, all the traffic between two hosts, the router and one computer.

# How encryption changes the game

Before we move on to the next example, we need to talk about encryption. As long as the network packets are sent in plaintext (unencrypted—in the clear), Ettercap is able to dissect and analyze most packets. It will even catch and report the usernames and passwords used to log in to common network services. For example, if a web browser is used to log in to your router's administration interface over regular unencrypted HTTP, Ettercap will spit out the login credentials that were used immediately.

This all changes with encrypted services such as SSH and the HTTPS protocol in your web browser. While Ettercap is able to log these encrypted packets, it can't get a good look at the contents inside. There are some experimental features in Ettercap that will try to trick web browsers with fake SSL certificates, but this will usually result in a big red warning from your browser saying that something is wrong. If you still want to experiment with these techniques, uncomment the `redir_command_on` and `redir_command_off` directives under these if you use an `iptables` header in the Ettercap configuration file.

After experimenting with Ettercap and understanding the implications of unencrypted communications, you might reach the conclusion that we need to encrypt everything, and you'd be absolutely right—welcome to the club and tell your friends! Fortunately, several large web service companies such as Google and Facebook have started to switch over to encrypted HTTPS traffic by default.

# Traffic logging

For our next example, we will capture and log all communications between the router and one specific computer on your network. Use the following command, but replace [Router IP] with the IP address of your router and [PC IP] with the IP address of one particular computer on your network. In this example we are capturing using the Ethernet device:

```
pi@raspberrypi ~ $ sudo ettercap -q -T -i eth0
-M arp:remote -d -L mycapture /[Router IP]// /[PC IP]//
```

Here, we're still in interactive mode and can use the key commands, but we've also specified the -q flag for quiet mode. This prevents packets from flooding our screen, but we will still receive notices about captured login credentials. The -L mycapture argument enables the logging mechanism and will produce two log files:

mycapture.eci, containing only information and captured log in credentials and

mycapture.ecp, containing all the raw network packets.

The log files can then be filtered and analyzed in different ways with the etterlog command. For example, to print out all HTTP communications with Google, use the following command:

```
pi@raspberrypi ~ $ sudo etterlog -e
"google.com" mycapture.ecp
```

Use etterlog --help to get a list of all the different options to manipulate the log files.

# Shoulder surfing in Elinks

Ettercap offers additional functionality in the form of plugins that can be loaded from the interactive mode with the *P* key or directly on the command line using the -P argument.

We'll be looking at the sneaky remote_browser plugin that allows us to create a shadow browser that mimics the surfing session of the browser on a remote computer. When the remote computer surfs to a site, the plugin will instruct your elinks to also go to that site.

To try this out, you need to start `elinks` first in one terminal session, as root:

```
pi@raspberrypi ~ $ sudo elinks
```

Then we start Ettercap with `-P remote_browser` in another terminal session:

```
pi@raspberrypi ~ $ sudo ettercap -q -T -i wlan0
-M arp:remote -P remote_browser /[Router IP]//
/[PC IP]//
```

As soon as Ettercap picks up a URL request from the sniffed PC, it will report this on the Ettercap console and your Elinks browser should follow along. Press the H key in `elinks` to access the history manager and Q to quit `elinks`.

If you have decent security software installed on the PC being monitored, then you may not get any success with some of these examples as the security software will protect the PC against these kinds of attacks. You may need to disable the software beforehand. Don't forget to re-enable it afterwards though!

# Pushing unexpected images to browser windows

Not only do man-in-the-middle attacks allow us to spy on the traffic as it passes by, we also have the option of modifying the packets before we pass them on to their rightful owner. To manipulate packet contents with Ettercap, we will first need to build some filter code in nano:

```
pi@raspberrypi ~ $ nano myfilter.ecf
```

The following is our filter code:

```
if (ip.proto == TCP && tcp.dst == 80) {
  if (search(DATA.data, "Accept-Encoding")) {
    replace("Accept-Encoding", "Accept-Mischief");
  }
}

if (ip.proto == TCP && tcp.src == 80) {
  if (search(DATA.data, "<img")) {
    replace("src=", "src=\"http://files.raspiplace.com/agentpi/tux.png"
alt=");
    msg("Mischief Managed!\n");
  }
}
```

The first block looks for any TCP packets with a destination of port 80, that is, packets that a web browser sends to a web server to request for pages. The filter then peeks inside these packages and modifies the `Accept-Encoding` string in order to stop the web server from compressing the returned pages. You see, if the pages are compressed, we wouldn't be able to manipulate the HTML text inside the packet in the next step.

The second block looks for TCP packets with a source port of 80. Those are pages returned to the web browser from the web server. We then search the package data for the opening of HTML `img` tags, and if we find such a packet, we replace the `src` attribute of the `img` tag with a URL to an image of your choice. Finally, we print out an informational message to the Ettercap console to signal that our image prank was performed successfully.

The next step is to compile our Ettercap filter code into a binary file that can be interpreted by Ettercap, using the following command:

```
pi@raspberrypi ~ $ etterfilter myfilter.ecf
-o myfilter.ef
```

Now all we have to do is fire up Ettercap and load the filter. Replace `[Router IP]` with the IP address of your router and `[PC IP]` with the IP address of the computer that will have the unexpected images pop up in its web browser:

```
pi@raspberrypi ~ $ sudo ettercap -q -T -i wlan0
-M arp:remote -F myfilter.ef:1 /[Router IP]//
/[PC IP]//
```

The `-F myfilter.ef:1` argument was used to enable our filter from the start. You can also press the F key to toggle filters on and off in Ettercap:

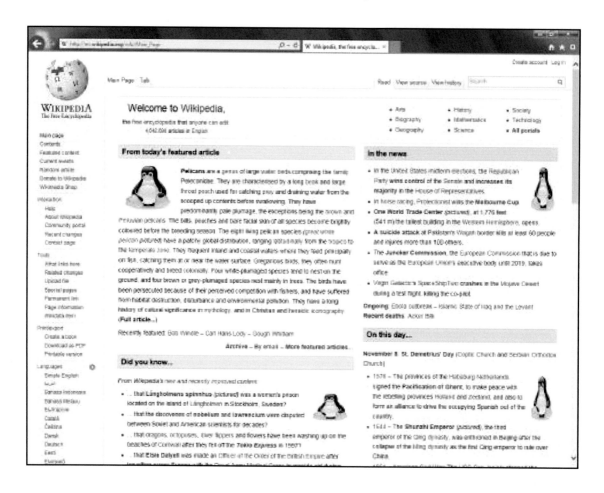

Wikipedia with four images replaced in transit

# Knocking all visitors off your network

There are times in every network owner's life when we just need that little extra bandwidth to watch the latest cat videos on YouTube in glorious HD resolution, right?

With the following Ettercap filter, our Pi will essentially become a very restrictive firewall and drop every single packet that comes our way, thus forcing the guests on our network to take a timeout:

```
pi@raspberrypi ~ $ nano dropfilter.ecf
```

Here is our minimalistic drop filter:

```
if (ip.proto == TCP || ip.proto == UDP) {
  drop();
  msg("Dropped a packet!\n");
}
```

The next step is to compile our Ettercap filter code into a binary file that can be interpreted by Ettercap, using the following command:

```
pi@raspberrypi ~ $ etterfilter dropfilter.ecf
-o dropfilter.ef
```

Now all we have to do is fire up Ettercap and load the filter. You can either target one particularly pesky network guest or a range of IP addresses:

```
pi@raspberrypi ~ $ sudo ettercap -q -T -i wlan0
-M arp:remote -F dropfilter.ef:1 -P repoison_arp
/[Router IP]// /[PC IP]//
```

# Protecting your network against Ettercap

By now you might be wondering if there's a way to protect your network against the ARP poisoning attacks we've seen in this chapter.

The most common and straightforward defense is to define static ARP entries for important addresses on the network. You could do this on the router, if it has support for static ARP entries, and/or directly, on each machine connected to the network:

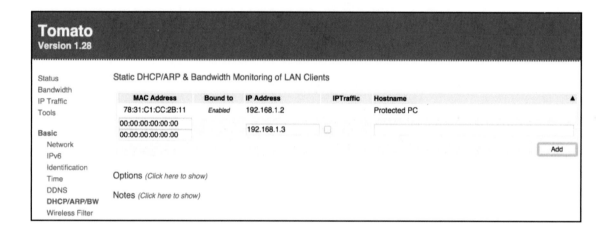

Defining static ARP entries on a router running Tomato firmware

Most operating systems will display the ARP table with the `arp -a` command.

To turn a dynamic ARP entry for your router into a static entry in Windows, open a Command Prompt as `Administrator` and type in the following command, but replace `[Router IP]` and `[Router MAC]` with the IP and MAC address of your router:

```
C:\> netsh -c "interface ipv4" add neighbors
"Wireless Network Connection" "[Router IP]"
"[Router MAC]"
```

The `Wireless Network Connection` argument might need to be adjusted to match the name of your interface. For wired connections, the common name is `Local Area Connection`.

The equivalent command for Mac OS X or Linux is:

```
$ sudo arp -s [Router IP] [Router MAC]
```

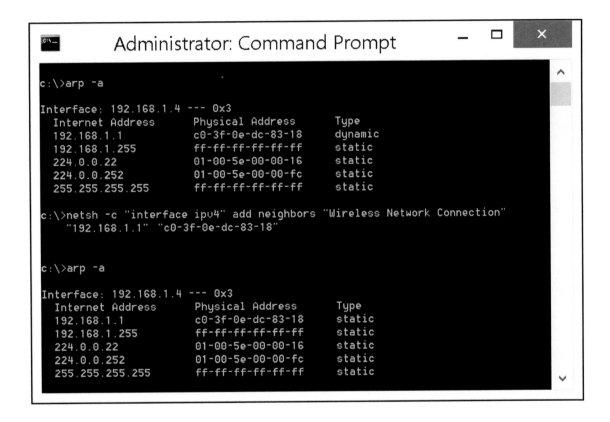

```
Administrator: Command Prompt                          — □  ×

c:\>arp -a

Interface: 192.168.1.4 --- 0x3
  Internet Address      Physical Address      Type
  192.168.1.1           c0-3f-0e-dc-83-18     dynamic
  192.168.1.255         ff-ff-ff-ff-ff-ff     static
  224.0.0.22            01-00-5e-00-00-16     static
  224.0.0.252           01-00-5e-00-00-fc     static
  255.255.255.255       ff-ff-ff-ff-ff-ff     static

c:\>netsh -c "interface ipv4" add neighbors "Wireless Network Connection"
   "192.168.1.1" "c0-3f-0e-dc-83-18"


c:\>arp -a

Interface: 192.168.1.4 --- 0x3
  Internet Address      Physical Address      Type
  192.168.1.1           c0-3f-0e-dc-83-18     static
  192.168.1.255         ff-ff-ff-ff-ff-ff     static
  224.0.0.22            01-00-5e-00-00-16     static
  224.0.0.252           01-00-5e-00-00-fc     static
  255.255.255.255       ff-ff-ff-ff-ff-ff     static
```

Setting a static ARP entry for the router in Windows

To verify that your static ARP entries mitigate the ARP poisoning attacks, start an Ettercap session and use the `chk_poison` plugin:

```
Plugin name (0 to quit): chk_poison
Activating chk_poison plugin...

chk_poison: Checking poisoning status...
chk_poison: No poisoning at all :(
```

Ettercap plugin checking ARP poisoning status

# Analyzing packet dumps with Wireshark

Most sniffers have the capability to produce some kind of log file or raw packet dump containing all the network traffic that it picks up. Unless you're *Neo* from *The Matrix*, you're not expected to stare at the monitor and decipher the network packets live as they scroll by. Instead, you'll want to open up your log file in a good traffic analyzer and start filtering the information so that you can follow the network conversation you're interested in.

Wireshark is an excellent packet analyzer that can open up and dissect packet logs in a standard format called **pcap**. Kismet already logs to the pcap format by default and Ettercap can be told to do so with the `-w` argument, as in the following command:

```
pi@raspberrypi ~ $ sudo ettercap -q -T -i wlan0 -M arp:remote -d -w
mycapture.pcap /[Router IP]// /[PC IP]//
```

The only difference running Ettercap with pcap logging is that it logs every single packet it can see, whether it matches the target specification or not, which is not necessarily a bad thing if you want to analyze traffic that Ettercap itself cannot dissect.

There is a command line version of Wireshark called `tshark` that can be installed with `apt-get`, but we want to explore the excellent user interface that Wireshark is famous for and we want to keep our Pi headless:

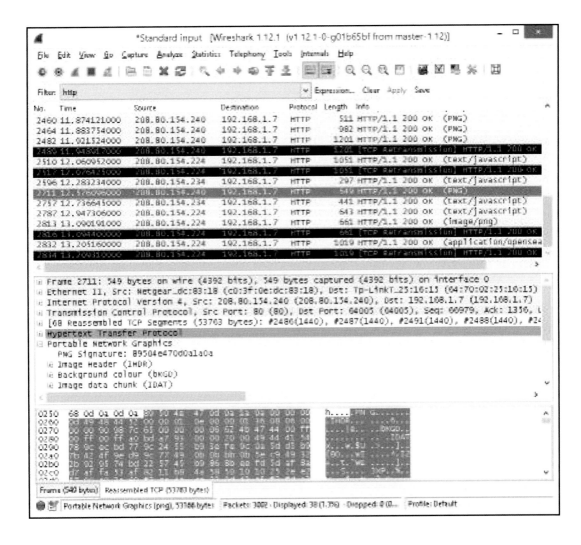

Dissecting a HTTP conversation in Wireshark

In the preceding screenshot, we have entered a simple filter to single out HTTP protocol conversations. Wireshark's filtering facilities are highly advanced and can be tweaked to locate the needle in any network haystack. We have selected a PNG image data packet that was sent from Wikipedia to `192.168.1.7` and we can right-click on the **Portable Network Graphics** layer and select **Export Selected Packet Bytes** to save that image to our desktop. Another nice feature is **Follow TCP Stream**, which allows us to follow along in the conversation between the web server and web browser.

# Running Wireshark in Windows

Let's get Wireshark up and running by following these steps:

1. Visit `http://www.wireshark.org/download.html` to download the latest stable Windows Installer for your version of Windows (`Wireshark-winXX-1.12.11` at the time of writing).

2. Run the installer to install Wireshark. Note that installing the WinPcap component is optional, and is only needed if you plan to sniff on the Windows machine itself.

3. Start a command prompt from the Start menu by clicking on the shortcut, or by typing `cmd` in the **Run/Search** field.

Now type in the following command to open up the `mycapture.pcap` packet log from the previous Ettercap example over the network via SSH:

```
C:\> "C:\Program Files (x86)\PuTTY\plink"
pi@[IP address] -pw [password] cat
~/mycapture.pcap | "C:\Program
Files\Wireshark\wireshark.exe" -k -i -
```

Note that it's generally a bad idea to try to read this file live while Ettercap is running.

The same method can be used to read packet dumps from Kismet:

```
C:\> "C:\Program Files (x86)\PuTTY\plink"
pi@[IP address] -pw [password] cat
~/kismetlogs/Kismet-XXXX.pcapdump | "C:\Program
Files\Wireshark\ wireshark.exe" -k -i -
```

# Running Wireshark in Mac OS X

Let's get Wireshark up and running with the help of these steps:

1. Wireshark on the Mac requires an X11 environment to be installed. If you're running Mountain Lion or later, go to `http://xquartz.macosforge.org` to download and install the latest version of **XQuartz**.

2. Visit `http://www.wireshark.org/download.html` to download the latest stable OS X DMG package for your Mac model (`Wireshark 1.12.11 Intel XX.dmg` at the time of writing).

3. Double-click on the Wireshark disk image and run the installer package inside.
4. Open up a `Terminal` located in `/Applications/Utilities`.
5. Now type in the following command to open up the `mycapture.pcap` packet log from the previous Ettercap example over the network via SSH:

```
$ ssh pi@[IP address] cat /home/pi/mycapture.pcap |
/Applications/Wireshark.app/Contents
/Resources/bin/wireshark -k -i -
```

- The same method can be used to read packet dumps from Kismet:

```
$ ssh pi@[IP address] cat /home/pi/kismetlogs/Kismet-
XXXX.pcapdump | /Applications/Wireshark.app/Contents
/Resources/bin/wireshark -k -i -
```

Note that Wireshark takes a few minutes to open up the first time you run it in Mac OS X.

## Running Wireshark in Linux

Use your distribution's package manager to add the `wireshark` package. Now type in the following command to open up the `mycapture.pcap` packet log from the previous Ettercap example over the network via SSH:

```
$ ssh pi@[IP address] cat /home/pi/mycapture.pcap
| wireshark -k -i -
```

The same method can be used to read packet dumps from Kismet:

```
$ ssh pi@[IP address] cat /home/pi/kismetlogs/Kismet-XXXX.pcapdump |
wireshark -k -i
```

Connecting an SSH session between machines assumes that you have already set up a SSH key between them, as you cannot specify your password in the command line. Alternatively, you can just SCP the file to your PC and run it locally.

## Exploring dynamic DNS, port forwarding, and tunneling

In this section, you'll learn the exact opposite of what we've done throughout this book when it comes to network security. We are going to make the Pi available to the big bad Internet, and not only on your local network.

There are plenty of reasons why one would like to do this. Perhaps you'd like to log in to your Pi from work, school, or from an Internet cafe around the globe. Maybe you'd like to run your own instant messaging service for only yourself and your group of friends.

There's absolutely nothing wrong with these goals, as long as you understand that there are certain risks associated with inviting outside traffic inside your home network. As we speak, there are thousands of automated attacks running wild on the Internet, scanning for badly configured services and vulnerable software to exploit for fun and profit.

If a malicious human or application manages to compromise your Pi, the best-case scenario is that you notice it and re-image your SD card. One of many possible worst-case scenarios is that your relatives' credit card numbers get stolen from another computer attached to your network and your Pi starts sending out millions of spam e-mails while you scratch your head wondering why your Internet connection feels so sluggish lately.

With that grim disclaimer out of the way, let's see what we can do to minimize the risks and keep uninvited guests at bay.

# Dynamic DNS

Let's say that you are over at your friend's house and you'd very much like to log in to your Pi through SSH to show your friend all the neat experiments you've been working on.

You know that your Pi is up and running at your house. You even remember the IP address is 192.168.1.20. So why can't you seem to connect with PuTTY from your friend's computer?

Well, there are multiple obstacles to overcome here. First of all, 192.168.1.20 is from a private address range and has no meaning outside of your home network. These are the three private address ranges:

- 10.0.0.0 to 10.255.255.255 (Class A network)
- 172.16.0.0 to 172.31.255.255 (Class B network)
- 192.168.0.0 to 192.168.255.255 (Class C network)

You need to find out what the external IP (also called WAN IP or Internet IP) of your home network is. You can usually find out by logging in to your home router, but it's easy to use one of the many free services available on the Internet. For example, visit http://ipogre.com, or use the following command on the Pi:

```
pi@raspberrypi ~ $ curl ipogre.com
```

So now you know your external IP. Here's the next obstacle: the external IP address usually changes once in a while. Unless you pay extra for a static IP address, your Internet Service Provider usually gives you a dynamic IP address that changes.

This is where a free dynamic DNS service comes in handy. It allows you to associate a domain name with your IP, which will be automatically updated every time your IP changes. So wherever you may be in the world, all you need to remember is a name like `gimmepi.mooo.com` and it will always point to your home network's current external IP address.

# Choosing your domain name

Start by signing up with a dynamic DNS service. There are quite a few to choose from, but we're going to look closer at **FreeDNS**. Follow these steps to get started with FreeDNS:

1. Head over to `http://freedns.afraid.org` and click on the **Sign Up!** link at the bottom of the page.
2. Select the Basic (Starter) package, fill out the form and keep an eye out for an e-mail from dnsadmin@afraid.org.
3. Click on the account activation link in that e-mail to activate your FreeDNS account.
4. Once you're logged in at FreeDNS, click on **Subdomains** in the menu to the left, and then click on **Add a subdomain** to add a new subdomain.
5. Leave the **Type** as **A**.
6. The **Subdomain** field is the part of the domain name where you get to put whatever you want—preferably something short, unique, and easy for you to remember.
7. From the **Domain** drop-down list you pick the second part that makes up your domain name. The most popular ones are in this list, while another thousand names or so can be picked from the **Registry** page in the menu to the left.
8. Your current external IP goes into the **Destination** field. This is the field that we'll be updating continuously as your IP changes.
9. That's all there is to it. Click on **Save!**

# Verifying your domain name

To verify that your domain name has been added correctly and to find out what IP address it's currently pointing to, we'll use the `nslookup` utility because it works equally well on the Pi, on Windows, and on Mac OS X. The following are the steps to verify the domain name:

1. Install the `nslookup` utility on the Pi with the following command:

   ```
   pi@raspberrypi ~ $ sudo apt-get install dnsutils
   ```

2. Start by querying the DNS server of the dynamic DNS service that you're using. For FreeDNS, that DNS server is called `ns1.afraid.org`. Type the following command, but replace `[gimmepi.mooo.com]` with your subdomain and domain you picked:

   ```
   pi@raspberrypi ~ $ nslookup [gimmepi.mooo.com]
   ns1.afraid.org
   ```

3. If the previous query returned your external IP as expected, you can continue to query Google's DNS server (`8.8.8.8`) to see if your domain name has successfully propagated across the Internet:

   ```
   pi@raspberrypi ~ $ nslookup [gimmepi.mooo.com] 8.8.8.8
   ```

   Just be patient with DNS, it can take a while for updates to reach your Internet Service Provider's name servers.

# Updating your domain name

So how do we make sure that your new domain name stays up to date when your external IP changes? A few home routers have started to include support to update DDNS services, but it's not hard to set up on the Pi. The following are the steps to update the domain name:

1. The `inadyn` client has good support for FreeDNS; install it with the following command:

   ```
   pi@raspberrypi ~ $ sudo apt-get install inadyn
   ```

2. Next we need to obtain the hash string for our domain name. On the FreeDNS site, click on the **Dynamic DNS** link in the menu on the left. Find your record on the page, right-click on the **Direct URL** link and copy the link address, then paste the link into a temporary text document. Your hash is the string of characters after `update.php?`

3. Now try running the `inadyn` client manually to ensure everything is working, but replace [mydomain] with your registered sub-domain:

```
pi@raspberrypi ~ $ sudo inadyn -u [username]
-p [password] -a [mydomain] --dyndns_system
default@freedns.afraid.org --verbose 5
```

To have `inadyn` run automatically and in the background after the next reboot, add the following command to /etc/rc.local:

```
sudo inadyn -u [username] -p [password] -a [mydomain] --background --
dyndns_system default@freedns.afraid.org --verbose 5
```

# Port forwarding

So, once again, you're over at your friend's house trying to connect to your Pi at your own house through SSH. This time, you come prepared with a snazzy domain name, that you know for a fact points to the external IP of your home network, thanks to the wonders of dynamic DNS... and yet PuTTY complains about not being able to connect. What gives?

Well, home routers usually put up one or two barriers preventing you from connecting from outside (through the Internet) to the inside of your home network. One such barrier is called **Network Address Translation (NAT)** and is a common solution for sharing one external IP address among several computers. The other barrier is the **firewall**, which is a more explicit way of allowing or denying traffic to pass based on certain criteria.

**Port forwarding** is a way of telling your router to forward certain packets coming in through the Internet to a specific computer on your home network. To set up a port forward rule, we need to know the following three things:

- The IP address of the computer that will receive the packets (your Pi in this case)
- Which IP protocol to expect:
    - **TCP**: This is the most common, used by services like SSH, HTTP, and XMPP
    - **UDP**: This is the other common protocol, used for DNS queries and audio/video transportation for VoIP applications and so on
    - **CMP**: This is used primarily by the ping utility and is usually blocked by the firewall and not forwarded

- Which destination port to expect

  To find out which network interface, port, and protocol a certain service is using on the Pi, issue the following command:

```
pi@raspberrypi ~ $ sudo netstat -tulpn
```

```
pi@raspberrypi ~ $ sudo netstat -tulpn
Active Internet connections (only servers)
Proto Recv-Q Send-Q Local Address          Foreign Address         State       PID/Program name
tcp        0      0 0.0.0.0:8080           0.0.0.0:*               LISTEN      3139/mjpg_streamer
tcp        0      0 0.0.0.0:8081           0.0.0.0:*               LISTEN      3176/motion
tcp        0      0 0.0.0.0:22             0.0.0.0:*               LISTEN      2392/sshd
tcp        0      0 0.0.0.0:7070           0.0.0.0:*               LISTEN      3176/motion
udp        0      0 0.0.0.0:26252          0.0.0.0:*                           2108/dhclient
udp        0      0 0.0.0.0:68             0.0.0.0:*                           2108/dhclient
udp        0      0 192.168.1.10:123       0.0.0.0:*                           2362/ntpd
udp        0      0 127.0.0.1:123          0.0.0.0:*                           2362/ntpd
udp        0      0 0.0.0.0:123            0.0.0.0:*                           2362/ntpd
```

List of network services running on the Pi

The **Local Address** column shows the network interface, a colon, and the port number of each service. The addresses in the previous screenshot have the following meanings:

- `0.0.0.0` means that the service is listening on *all* network interfaces.
- `127.0.0.1` means that the service is bound to `localhost`, and cannot be accessed from any other computer. If you're trying to port forward to a service that's only listening on `localhost`, you need to edit the configuration for that application and tell it to listen on all interfaces or the IP of your primary interface.
- `192.168.1.10` means that the service is listening on the interface with this specific IP. For example, you could configure the SSH service to listen only on your Ethernet connection but not on your Wi-Fi connection.

## Adding the forwarding rule

We now know the three things required to add a port forwarding rule for the SSH service running on the Pi:

- It's listening on the IP address of the Pi (`192.168.1.10` in this example)
- It's using the `tcp` protocol
- It's listening for connections on port `22`

You now have two options: either log in to your home router and add the port forwarding rule manually, or try to add it through UPnP, which is a protocol supported by many home routers.

The exact procedure for port forwarding differs slightly between router brands, but in general, the input fields are like in the following screenshot:

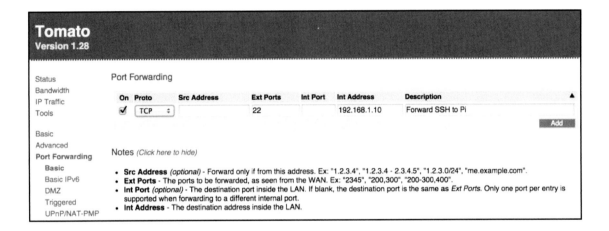

Adding port forwarding rules on a router running Tomato firmware

To add a port forwarding rule via UPnP, follow this procedure:

1.  First we need to install the `miniupnpc` package:

    ```
    pi@raspberrypi ~ $ sudo apt-get install miniupnpc
    ```

2.  Issue the following command to verify that your router supports UPnP:

    ```
    pi@raspberrypi ~ $ upnpc -s
    ```

    If the utility reports that no IGD UPnP device was found on the network, you may have to enable UPnP support on your router first.

3. Now we can try to add a port forwarding rule for the SSH service on the Pi:

```
pi@raspberrypi ~ $ upnpc -r 22 tcp
```

```
pi@raspberrypi ~ $ upnpc -r 22 tcp
upnpc : miniupnpc library test client. (c) 2006-2010 Thomas Bernard
Go to http://miniupnp.free.fr/ or http://miniupnp.tuxfamily.org/
for more information.
List of UPNP devices found on the network :
 desc: http://192.168.1.1:19650/rootDesc.xml
 st: urn:schemas-upnp-org:device:InternetGatewayDevice:1

Found valid IGD : http://192.168.1.1:19650/ctl/IPConn
Local LAN ip address : 192.168.1.10
ExternalIPAddress = 175.175.231.128
InternalIP:Port = 192.168.1.10:22
external 175.175.231.128:22 TCP is redirected to internal 192.168.1.10:22
```

Adding port forwarding rules via UPnP

Some routers won't allow you to add rules for ports below 1024 for security reasons; if that's the case for you, keep reading to find out how to move the SSH service to a non-standard port above 1024.

# Verifying your port forwarding

To confirm that your port forward is working correctly, and that nothing else (like a firewall or your Internet service provider) is blocking incoming connections, you need to try connecting through the Internet.

An easy way of doing that is the online port scanner at http://ipogre.com. You'll find it under the **IPV4 Tools** menu. Simply fill in your external IP or dynamic DNS name and the port number that you would like to test, then click on **Scan:**

**IPv4 Port Scanner**

Enter the Target Domain Name or IP Address, and Target Port:

**Target Domain Name or IP**   175.175.231.128

**Target Port**   22

☑   I agree to the Terms of Service

**Scan**

Scanned "175.175.231.128:22"
PORT OPEN

Verifying port forwarding online

# Port forwarding security

Many Internet service providers have started to block incoming traffic on standard ports, normally below 1024. They usually do this for security reasons (and not just to stop you from hosting your own servers). The vast majority of automated attacks running rampant on the Internet only scan for listening ports on these standard numbers.

Therefore, you can minimize the risk of having your Pi flooded with automated break-in attempts by either creating port forwarding rules that forward traffic from non-standard ports, or alternatively, you can configure the service itself to bind to a non-standard port.

If your router allows it, the first method is much easier. Simply add a port forwarding rule like in the earlier example, but specify a different external port, for example, `2222`.

To do the same thing through UPnP, you would use this command but replace `[IP address]` with the IP address of your Pi:

```
pi@raspberrypi ~ $ upnpc -a [IP address] 22 2222 tcp
```

To make the actual service listen on another port, we usually need to edit the configuration for the service and restart it. We'll take a look at SSH as an example:

1. Open up the SSH service configuration for editing:

```
pi@raspberrypi ~ $ sudo nano /etc/ssh/sshd_config
```

2. Find the line near the top that reads **Port 22**, and change the port number to something else, for example `2222`. Then save and exit `nano`.
3. Now reload the SSH service configuration with the following command:

```
pi@raspberrypi ~ $ sudo service ssh reload
```

# Connected at last

So, you're over at your friend's house, again, and you should finally be able to log in to your Pi through SSH. Just remember to specify the port if you changed it to something other than `22`. In PuTTY, simply change the **Port** field.

In Linux and Mac OS X, you would use the following command but replace `[port]` with your port number and `[gimmepi.mooo.com]` with your domain name:

```
$ ssh -p [port] pi@[gimmepi.mooo.com]
```

Now that you're running an Internet facing service, it's also a good idea to keep an eye on your log files for any login attempts that you don't recognize. Use the following command to view the log file where SSH records the login information:

```
pi@raspberrypi ~ $ cat /var/log/auth.log
```

# Tunneling

In computer networking lingo, tunneling means to embed one protocol inside another. In this section, we'll be embedding HTTP traffic inside the SSH protocol. Two good uses for SSH tunneling are:

- Encrypting traffic that would otherwise be sent in the clear to evade prying eyes that might be snooping on the network traffic. For example, this could be web content filtering software at your school/workplace or an oppressive regime spying on its citizens.
- Tunneling through firewalls to access the computers on the inside as if you were a computer on the local network. You could use this to safely access a web/file server on your local home network from a distance, or even print something on your printer in your home from somewhere else.

All you need to start tunneling is an SSH server reachable through the Internet and your regular SSH client.

## Port tunneling in Windows

In this example scenario, you're over at your friend's house, and you would like to access the web interface of your home router to make some adjustments to the configuration. The following are the steps to access the web interface:

1. Start PuTTY and select **Connection**, then **SSH**, then **Tunnels** from the **Category** tree on the left.
2. In the **Source port** field, enter any port number above `1024` that you think is available on the local Windows machine.
3. In the **Destination field**, enter the IP address of the computer and port of the service you would like to reach through the tunnel, then click on **Add**. In this example, the computer in question is the router and the web interface is on port `80`, so we would fill in `192.168.1.1:80`.
4. Now select **Session** from the **Category** tree on the left and log in to your Pi like you usually would. The tunnel is being set up in the background.
5. Finally, open up a web browser and enter the following URL, but replace `[localport]` with the port you chose in step 2: `http://localhost:[localport]`.

6. You should now be looking at the web interface of your home router just as if you were sitting at home:

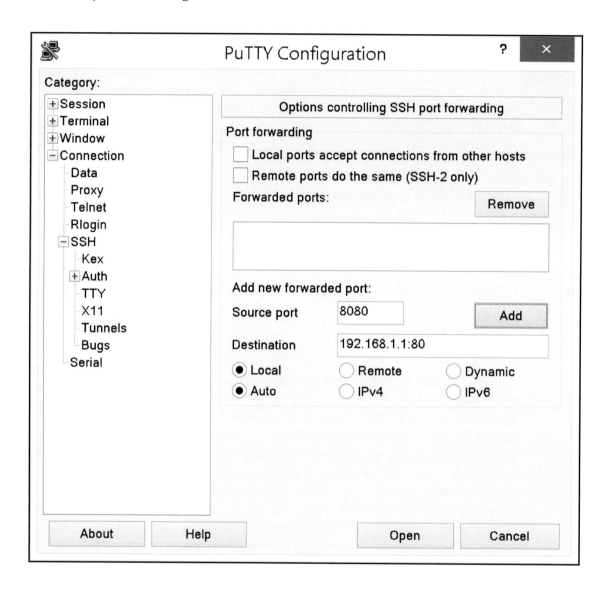

Adding a tunnel in PuTTY

The previous example can be applied to any situation where you need to reach something on a single TCP port on your home network.

However, there are situations in which you don't know in advance all the destination addresses that you'll want to reach. When evading content filtering or web censorship for example, you'll want to send all HTTP requests through the SSH tunnel. Fortunately, SSH can act as a **SOCKS proxy**, where it will tunnel traffic to and from any address that you specify in your web browser.

Follow this procedure to enable the SOCKS proxy support:

1. Start PuTTY and select **Connection**, then **SSH**, then **Tunnels** from the **Category** tree on the left.
2. In the **Source port** field, enter any port number above `1024` that you think is available on the local Windows machine.
3. Leave the **Destination field** blank and select the **Dynamic** radio button, then click on **Add**.
4. Now select **Session** from the **Category** tree on the left and log in to your Pi like you usually would. The tunnel is being set up in the background.
5. Finally, you need to configure your browser to use a SOCKS proxy. The procedure differs slightly between browsers. Both Chrome and Internet Explorer use the system-wide proxy settings, which can be found in **Internet Options** in **Control Panel**.
6. Under the **Connections** tab, click on **LAN settings**. Check **Use a proxy server for your LAN** and click on the **Advanced** button.
7. Make sure all the fields are cleared, then enter `localhost : [localport]` in the **Socks** field, but replace `[localport]` with the number you chose in step 2.

8. Now you can verify that you're connecting from your home IP address by visiting `http://ipogre.com`:

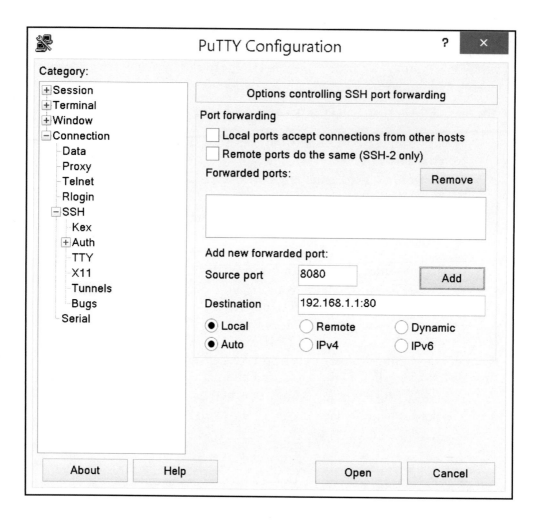

Adding an SSH SOCKS proxy in PuTTY

# Port tunneling in Linux or Mac OS X

In this example scenario, you're over at your friend's house, and you would like to access the web interface of your home router to make some adjustments to the configuration.

Enter the following command to enable the tunnel, but replace [gimmepi.mooo.com] with your domain name, and [192.168.1.1] with the IP address of your home router:

```
$ ssh pi@gimmepi.mooo.com -L 8080:192.168.1.1:80
```

So you're connecting to your Pi via SSH as usual, but the -L argument tells SSH to open a tunnel in the background. 8080 is a port on the local machine and can use any free port you like above 1024. Finally, 192.168.1.1:80 is the device and port on your home network that you would like to reach—in this case the router and its web interface.

Now, open up a web browser and enter the http://localhost:8080 URL. You should be looking at the web interface of your home router just as if you were sitting at home. The previous example can be applied to any situation where you need to reach something on a single TCP port on your home network.

However, there are situations in which you don't know in advance all the destination addresses that you'll want to reach. When evading content filtering or web censorship for example, you'll want to send all HTTP requests through the SSH tunnel. Fortunately, SSH can act as a SOCKS proxy, where it will tunnel traffic to and from any address that you specify in your web browser.

Enter this command to enable the SOCKS proxy support:

```
$ ssh pi@gimmepi.mooo.com -D 8080
```

Now you need to tell your web browser or underlying operating system to use localhost:8080 as a SOCKS proxy. Consult the documentation for your browser and platform. Finally, you can verify that you're connecting from your home IP address by visiting http://ipogre.com.

# Creating a diversion using a chat bot

Ever wish you could run a quick errand during a conversation without the other party noticing you've gone away? Ever wanted to create the illusion that you've been sitting in front of your computer all day long? Perhaps you'd just like to freak out your friends or co-workers? All noble causes for sure. Whatever your reasons may be, running a chat bot is always a good laugh and a great way to experiment with instant messaging protocols.

A chat bot or chatter robot is a computer program that tries to have an intelligent conversation with a human by analyzing the input text received from a human and replying with output text that hopefully makes sense to humans.

These applications are one of the classic topics of *artificial intelligence* and the famous *Turing Test*. To create a convincing chat bot from scratch is far outside the scope of this book. Instead, we will create an interface between three great existing chat bots and a few popular chat services.

## Introducing XMPP

The **Extensible Messaging and Presence Protocol (XMPP)**, or **Jabber**, as it was originally named, is an open communications protocol, and is compatible with the chat services at Google. There's also a large network of free to use XMPP servers, as anyone can run their own XMPP server and there is no central master server.

 The Facebook chat service used to support open XMPP, but has recently removed this support, so the client used in this section (and other XMPP clients) will no longer work with Facebook Chat.

## Useful Profanity

Profanity is a console-based XMPP client that will be the gateway between our chat bot and your buddies on the chat network. Don't worry about the name—no actual profanity will be spouted unless your friends manage to anger the chat bot with something awful.

As our chat bot interface will be in the form of a plugin for Profanity, written in the Python programming language, we need a special build of Profanity that is not yet available in the Raspbian repository.

Download and install the Profanity package with the following commands:

```
pi@raspberrypi ~ $ wget
http://files.raspiplace.com/agentpi/profanity_0.5.0_plugins-1_armhf.deb
pi@raspberrypi ~ $ sudo dpkg -i profanity_0.5.0_plugins-1_armhf.deb
```

We also need to download and install a required package that may not already be installed in your distribution of Raspbian Jessie. Use the following commands to do this:

```
pi@raspberrypi:~ $ wget
http://files.raspiplace.com/agentpi/libgcrypt11_1.5.3-5_armhf.deb
pi@raspberrypi:~ $ sudo dpkg -i libgcrypt11_1.5.3-5_armhf.deb
```

Now let's fire up Profanity and learn the basics:

```
pi@raspberrypi ~ $ profanity
```

Connecting to Google Chat with Profanity

The first thing to note is that all Profanity commands start with a slash, and you can always get more information on a particular command or topic by typing /help followed by the command. Profanity will also auto-complete commands when you press *Tab*.

# Connecting to Google chat

For a regular Gmail account, type the following command to connect, but replace `[username]` with your username:

> `/connect [username]@gmail.com`

You will then be prompted for your Gmail password. If the login fails, it's likely that you've received an e-mail in your Gmail inbox with the subject *Sign-in attempt blocked*. To allow Profanity to connect, you will need to enable less secure apps by visiting the link in that e-mail. Alternatively, you can find it under the security settings of your Gmail account:

Allowing Profanity to connect to Google chat

Once successfully connected, your online status indicator in the upper-right corner of the screen will change accordingly.

If you have a **Google Apps** account, the connection procedure is slightly different. Use the following command, but replace `[username@company.com]` with your address:

> `/connect [username@company.com] server talk.google.com`

# Connecting to XMPP servers

First, you'll need to register for a free XMPP account at one of the public XMPP servers listed on `https://xmpp.net/directory.php`.

Pick a server with A grade security from the list and follow the link to learn how to register. You should end up with an account username and a password.

Type the following command to connect, but replace `[username@someservice.com]` with your account username:

```
> /connect [username@someservice.com]
```

You will then be prompted for your password, and once successfully connected, your online status indicator in the upper-right corner of the screen will change accordingly.

# Getting around Profanity

Now that you're connected, we need to find your friends. When anyone in your contact list signs in or out of chat, you'll receive status notifications. To view your contact list, use the `/who` command, or type `/who online` to list friends who are currently signed in.

To send a friend a message and open up a conversation, use the following command:

```
> /msg "Your Friend" Greetings friend!
```

Note that your friend's name needs to be in quotes if there's a space. Profanity will wrap it in quotes for you if you type the first few letters and press Tab.

A new chat window will open up and come into focus, as indicated in the window activity bar in the lower-right corner of the screen. Any text you type in this window will be sent to your friend when pressing Enter. Window number **1** is used for system messages and output from commands, while the rest are designated chat windows.

Press Alt + 1 through 9 to change windows, or alternatively, use the `/win [number]` command. To get a list of all your windows, use the `/wins` command.

This marks the end of our Profanity crash course. Let's exit Profanity using the `/quit` command and see how to set up our chat bot.

# Project AgentBot

As mentioned earlier, we'll be passing chat messages between our friends and one of three existing chat bots. The default one is called Cleverbot and can be found at `http://www.cleverbot.com`, where you can interact with it through a web interface. These bots primarily speak English, but Cleverbot especially has been known to impress by answering in different languages.

Since we are all about the command line on the Pi, we'll be interacting with Cleverbot through an **Application Programming Interface (API)** module written in Python by Pierre-David Bélanger. Let's download it to the Profanity `plugins` directory with the following command:

```
pi@raspberrypi ~ $ wget
https://raw.githubusercontent.com/pierredavidbelanger/chatter-bot-api/maste
r/python/chatterbotapi.py -P ~/.local/share/profanity/plugins
```

Now we create our plugin by opening up an empty Python file for editing in the Profanity `plugins` directory:

```
pi@raspberrypi ~ $ nano ~/.local/share/profanity/plugins/agentbot.py
```

This is our plugin code:

```python
import prof
from chatterbotapi import ChatterBotFactory, ChatterBotType
factory = ChatterBotFactory()
bot = factory.create(ChatterBotType.CLEVERBOT)
# bot = factory.create(ChatterBotType.JABBERWACKY)
# bot = factory.create(ChatterBotType.PANDORABOTS, 'b0dafd24ee35a477')
bot_session = {}
bot_state = False

def prof_post_chat_message_display(jid, message):
  if bot_state:
    if jid not in bot_session:
      bot_session[jid] = bot.create_session()
      prof.cons_show("New AgentBot session created:          " +
str(bot_session[jid]))
    response = bot_session[jid].think(message)
    prof.send_line("/msg " + jid + " " + response)

def _cmd_agentbot(state):
  global bot_state

  if state == "enable":
    prof.cons_show("AgentBot Activated")
```

```
    bot_state = True
  elif state == "disable":
    prof.cons_show("AgentBot Stopped")
    bot_state = False
  else:
    if bot_state:
      prof.cons_show("AgentBot is running - current sessions:")
      prof.cons_show(str(bot_session))
    else:
      prof.cons_show("AgentBot is stopped - Type /agentbot enable to
activate.")

def prof_init(version, status):
  prof.register_command("/agentbot", 0, 1, "/agentbot [enable|disable]",
"AgentBot", "AgentBot", _cmd_agentbot)
```

 It's important to note, when working with Python code, that Python uses whitespace to delimit program blocks, so make sure to preserve the indentation levels in the code.

Save the file and exit from `nano`.

Let's take a closer look at the code:

- `import prof`: Every Profanity plugin must import this module.
- `from chatterbotapi`: We import the functions and variables we need from the `chatterbotapi.py` module.
- `bot = factory.create`: Here, we tell `chatterbotapi` to create a new `CLEVERBOT` for us and store it in a variable named `bot`. Uncommenting one of the other two `bot` = lines allows you to switch between the three different bot-types—Cleverbot, Jabberwacky, and Pandorabot.
- `bot_session = {}`: This empty dictionary will be used to keep track of which chat session belongs to which of your friends.
- `bot_state = False`: This Boolean is used to toggle the bot on or off.
- `def prof_post_chat_message_display(jid, message)`: Here comes the most important function of our plugin. Every time a new chat message is received and displayed by Profanity, we do the following:

  Check if `jid` (the unique identifier of your friend) has already started a chat session with the bot, and if not, create one now.

Take the message received from your friend, send it to the bot using the `.think` method and store the response from the bot in the variable named `response`.

Send the response back to your friend using the versatile `send_line` function, which can be used to trigger any command in Profanity.

- `def _cmd_agentbot(state):` Here we define the Profanity command `/agentbot`, which is used to `enable`, `disable`, or `query` the current status if issued without arguments.
- `def prof_init(version, status):` When our plugin loads, we use the `register_command` function to register our `/agentbot` command. The arguments are as follows:
  - The crucial command as typed in Profanity
  - Minimum command arguments. In this case we want to be able to type `/agentbot` without arguments to request status, so
  - Maximum command arguments. We also want to be able to specify `enable` or `disable`, so that's 1 argument
  - Usage information (currently unused)
  - Short help text (currently unused)
  - Long help text (currently unused)
  - Name of function to call when command is issued

# Awakening the bot

Now, all that is left for us to do is to tell Profanity to load the plugin. Open up the Profanity configuration file for editing (note it that may be empty if it's not been updated previously)

```
pi@raspberrypi ~ $ nano ~/.config/profanity/profrc
```

Now add these two lines:

```
[plugins]
load=agentbot.py
```

That's all we need. Fire up Profanity and verify with the `/plugins` command that our `agentbot.py` plugin was loaded successfully. If Profanity says that no plugins are installed, most likely, your plugin contains an error and needs to be corrected. Use the following command to check your plugin for Python syntax errors:

```
pi@raspberrypi ~ $ python -m py_compile
~/.local/share/profanity/plugins/agentbot.py
```

Now activate the bot with `/agentbot enable` and send a message to a friend or wait for them to message you. Either way, hilarity ensues.

You now have good building blocks to create your own custom bot. By inspecting the incoming messages for certain words, you could easily create a utility bot that will e-mail files from your Pi, tell you the weather, and so on.

# Keeping your conversations secret with encryption

Profanity has another cool feature that sets it apart from the native chat, Google Chat, namely **Off-the-Record Messaging (OTR)**. This encryption protocol allows you to send secret messages to your friends that even Google itself wouldn't be able to decipher.

OTR support and plugins are available for many instant messaging applications, so it is by no means a requirement for your friends to run Profanity on a Raspberry Pi. Take a look at `http://en.wikipedia.org/wiki/Off-the-Record_Messaging` for a partial list of client software. The following are the steps to send secret messages:

1. The first thing we're going to do is generate your private key for the chat service over which you'd like to send encrypted messages, as each service requires its own key. You can think of the private key as something that will unlock your secret conversations.

   Connect to your chat service of choice, then type the following command (this may take a good few minutes to run):

```
> /otr gen
```

2. Now we can try to initiate an encrypted OTR conversation with this command:

> `/otr start "Your Friend"`

> If your friend's client supports OTR, it should automatically detect that you want to establish a secure channel and enable encryption.

> You should now see that the encryption indicator in the blue top bar next to your friend's name has changed from **[unencrypted]** to **[OTR][untrusted]**.

> Your conversation is now encrypted until either you or your friend ends the OTR session with the `/otr end` command.

3. However, how do you know that your friend is indeed your friend and not a sneaky agent simply logged in to your friend's account? That's where the authentication feature of OTR comes in handy.

> There are three methods available in Profanity to help you verify that your friend is really who you think they are:

> Fingerprint verification: This is the classic method that all OTR-capable clients should support. An OTR fingerprint is like an identification string that is unique to your private key.

> Type the following command to view your OTR fingerprint:

> `/otr myfp`

> Now your friend does the same on their end. Then you two need to find a way to communicate each other's fingerprints outside of the chat. You could scribble them down and meet up for coffee, or, if you're not quite as paranoid, call up your friend and exchange the last four characters of your fingerprints.

> To see if your friend's fingerprint checks out, type the following command while in the OTR chat window:

> `/otr theirfp`

> If it matches what your friend told you, you would use the following command to flag your friend as trusted:

> `/otr trust`

You should now see that the encryption indicator on the blue top bar next to your friend's name has changed from **[untrusted]** to **[trusted]**.

Question and answer: This method allows you to verify the identity of your friend by asking a question and receiving the expected answer. For example:

```
> /otr question "Which berry is essential
to me?" raspberry
```

Your friend will be presented with the question in quotes. If your friend issues the following command:

```
> /otr answer raspberry
```

You should see that the encryption indicator on the blue top bar next to your friend's name has changed from **[untrusted]** to **[trusted]**.

Shared secret: This method allows you to verify the identity of your friend with a password that you two have agreed upon outside of chat. For example:

```
> /otr secret squirrel
```

Your friend will be prompted to provide a secret using the same command, and if it matches you should see that the encryption indicator on the blue top bar next to your friend's name has changed from **[untrusted]** to **[trusted]**.

4. Once you've established an encrypted, trusted conversation with your friend, you may want to ensure that any future conversations with that friend are always OTR enabled. We do this by changing the OTR policy with the following command:

```
/otr policy always "Your Friend"
```

# Summary

We started this chapter by focusing on the general airspace surrounding the Wi-Fi network in our home. Using the Kismet application, we learned how to obtain information about the access point itself and any associated Wi-Fi adapters, as well as how to protect your network from sneaky rogue access points.

Shifting the focus to the insides of our network, we used the Nmap software to quickly map out all the running computers on our network, and we also looked at the more advanced features of Nmap that can be used to produce a detailed HTML report about each connected machine.

We then moved on to the fascinating topics of network sniffing, ARP poisoning, and man-in-the-middle attacks, with the frightfully effective Ettercap application. We saw how to use Ettercap to spy on network traffic and web browsers, how to manipulate HTML code in transit to display unexpected images, and how to drop packets to keep your network guests from hogging all the juicy bandwidth.

Thankfully, there are ways to protect oneself from Ettercap's mischief, and we discussed how encryption completely changes the game when it comes to network sniffing. We also looked at static ARP entries as a viable protection against ARP poisoning attacks.

You got an introduction to network traffic analysis using Wireshark, where you learned about the standard pcap log format and how to open up packet dumps from Ettercap and Kismet over the network through SSH.

Then we took a look at dynamic DNS, port forwarding, and SSH tunneling, which help us locate and connect to our Pi over the Internet and even tunnel traffic through it.

We concluded the chapter with some refreshing Profanity, a versatile instant messaging client that allows you to send encrypted messages to your friends or to keep them occupied with a chat bot while you pop out for a quick errand.

In the upcoming chapter, we're sending the Pi outside the house while staying in touch and receiving GPS and Twitter updates.

# 5

# Taking Your Pi Off-Road

We're now going to unleash the Raspberry Pi from the wall socket and send it out into the world equipped with a few add-on peripherals for stealthy reconnaissance missions. We'll make sure your Pi stays protected and that you'll be able to stay in touch with the Pi throughout its mission, by doing the following in this chapter:

- Creating a point-to-point network connection between the Pi and another PC
- Turning your Pi into a Wi-Fi router which can be connected to the Internet using the Ethernet connector, or by using a 3G or 4G modem dongle
- Making yourself anonymous on the Internet by turning your Pi into an onion router
- Tracking where your Pi is using a GPS receiver
- Keeping your data secret and erasing it if it falls into the wrong hands
- Jamming radio signals and taking over the airways using a Pi Zero

## Keeping the Pi dry and running with housing and batteries

When sending your Pi away on outdoor missions, the two main concerns that need to be addressed are the supply of power and protection against moisture. A **lithium polymer** battery pack is a good choice for powering the Pi off-road. They are usually marketed as portable smartphone chargers, but as long as yours operates at 5V, and provides one or more USB ports with around 1000mA of output (or 2000mA for the Pi 3), it should keep your Pi happy and running, usually for five to ten hours. If you need a USB hub for your peripherals, make sure it can be powered by one of the USB ports on the battery pack, and not from one on the Pi.

The iMuto X4 type shown below (usually used as a phone charger) is one I use when I make my Pi portable and will power a Pi 3 for around 12 hours, depending on what else I have plugged in. It also has a separate output that can be used to power a separate USB hub if required:

iMuto X4 Power Bank will happily power your Pi for many hours

When it comes to housing your spy kit, there are no rules except—moisture will spoil your fun. A plastic food container with a tight lid is a good start for housing. It'll have to be transparent plastic if you plan to include a webcam with the kit, obviously. You might also want to line the insides with something soft, such as bubble wrap, to make the ride less bumpy for the components.

The Pi board itself will be the most fragile, and should not be put in the container unprotected—it can also be damaged by static discharge from the body or by the board simply being rubbed on plastic, hence why the wearable Pi in previous chapters was placed in an anti-static bag:

Tontec® Raspberry Pi Zero Enclosure available on Amazon

Your Raspberry Pi dealer will usually carry several enclosures for the Pi, but even the simple box in which your Pi was shipped will do.

If avoiding detection is a concern, try to think of a container that would blend into the surroundings in which you plan to put your kit. For example, an empty pizza box on top of a garbage bin wouldn't raise many eyebrows—just put the components inside a re-sealable bag in the pizza box to protect it.

In fact, if you make your kit look like trash, people are less likely to want to pick it up and take a closer look. Simply putting your container inside an old plastic bag will lend it a little trashy camouflage.

Finally, always think about any negative impact your kit could have on the environment. An abandoned battery pack left outside in the sun could potentially lead to a fire or explosion. Keep a watchful eye on your kit from a distance at all times and remember to bring it back inside after a mission.

# Setting up point-to-point networking

When you take your headless Pi outside into the real world, chances are you'll want to communicate with it from a netbook or laptop from time to time. Since you won't be bringing your router or access point along, we need a way to make a direct **point-to-point connection** between your Pi and the other computer.

# Creating a direct wired connection

As there won't be a DHCP server to hand out IP addresses to our two network devices, what we want to do is assign **static IP addresses** on both the Pi and the laptop. We can pick any two addresses from the private IPv4 address space we saw in the *Mapping out your network with Nmap* section in `Chapter 4, Wi-Fi Pranks – Exploring Your Network`. In the following example, we'll use 192.168.0.199 for the Pi and 192.168.0.200 for the laptop. These are the steps to create a direct-wired connection on Raspbian Jessie:

1. Type in the following command on the Pi to open up the DHCP client configuration:

   `pi@raspberrypi ~ $ sudo nano /etc/dhcpcd.conf`

2. Add the following lines to the end of the file (this assumes your normal router is 192.168.0.1 on your network):

   ```
   interface eth0
   static ip_address=192.168.0.199/24
   static routers=192.168.0.1 static
   domain_name_servers=192.168.0.1
   ```

3. Press *Ctrl* + *X* to exit and select **Y** when prompted to save the modified buffer, then press the *Enter* key to confirm the filename to write to. You can now reboot the Pi and shift the focus to your laptop:

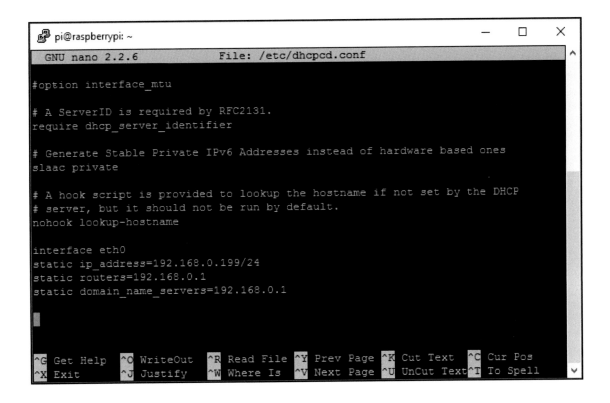

Adding a static IP address to a wired connection on the Raspberry Pi

 If your direct-wired connection seems unstable or outright refuses to work, your laptop might require a special crossover cable made specifically for direct connections between two computers. You can read more about it at `http://wikipedia.org/wiki/Ethernet_crossover_ cable`.

# Static IP assignment in Windows

Let's set up the other end of the direct wired connection:

1. From the Start menu, open **Control Panel** and search for `adapter` using the search box.
2. In the results, under **Network and Sharing Center**, click on **View network connections**.

3. Select your Ethernet connection (usually called **Local Area Connection**), right-click, and select **Properties**.

4. Select **Internet Protocol Version 4 (TCP/IPv4)** from the list and click on the **Properties** button.

5. Check the **Use the following IP address** checkbox, fill in 192.168.0.200 for the **IP address** and 255.255.255.0 for the **Subnet mask**, then click on the **OK** button:

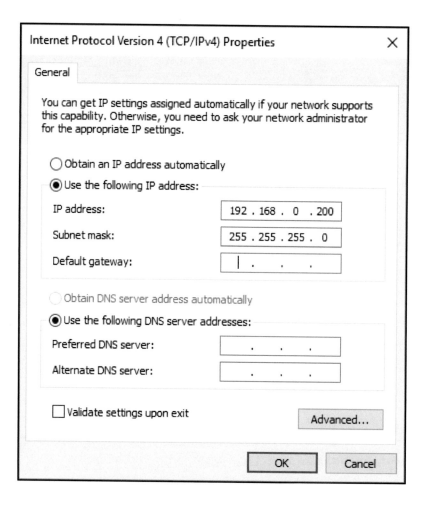

Adding a static IP address to a wired connection in Windows

# Static IP assignment in Mac OS X

Let's set up the other end of the direct wired connection:

1. From the **Apple** drop-down menu, open **System Preferences...** and click on the **Network** icon.
2. Select **Ethernet** in the list on the left-hand side, then, in the panel on the right-hand side, select **Manually** from the **Configure IPv4** drop-down menu.
3. Now fill in `192.168.0.200` for **IP Address** and `255.255.255.0` for **Subnet Mask**, then click on the **Apply** button.

# Static IP assignment in Linux

If your Linux distribution is based on Debian, you should be able to assign static addressing using the same method as we used for the Raspberry Pi. However, you can try the following command sequence to assign a static IP address to a running system:

```
$ sudo ip addr add 192.168.0.200/24 dev eth0
$ sudo ip route del default
```

# Turning the Pi into a Wi-Fi hotspot

Let's say you're out in the field with a couple of fellow agents and you want to quickly put up a network for your computers, maybe even share an Internet connection together; your Pi equipped with a Wi-Fi dongle (or with just a Pi 3 with the built-in Wi-Fi) can easily be made into a makeshift access point.

Before setting up your **wireless hotspot**, ensure you have set up a static IP on your Pi, as per the previous section, then follow these steps to set up your hotspot:

1. First install the required software with the following command:

```
pi@raspberrypi ~ $ sudo apt-get install hostapd bridge-
utils
```

2. Next we need to prevent Raspbian from interfering with the Wi-Fi interface. Open up `/etc/network/interfaces` for editing:

```
pi@raspberrypi ~ $ sudo nano /etc/network/interfaces
```

3. Find the block that starts with **allow-hotplug wlan0** and put a # character in front of each line, like we've done here:

```
#allow-hotplug wlan0
#iface wlan0 inet manual
#wpa-conf /etc/wpa_supplicant/wpa_supplicant.conf
#iface default inet dhcp
```

4. Optionally, if you would like to share a wired Internet connection with the wireless clients, add the following three lines to create a bridge between the Ethernet and Wi-Fi interfaces:

```
auto br0
iface br0 inet dhcp
bridge_ports eth0 wlan0
```

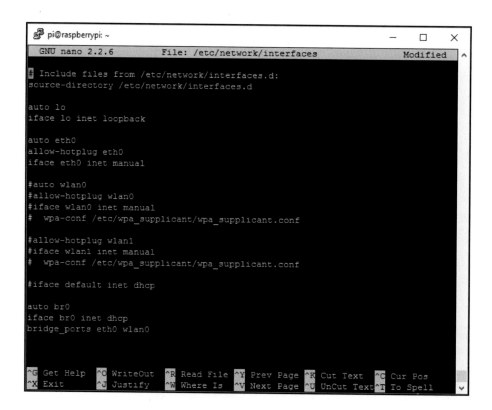

Adding a bridged Wi-Fi interface on the Raspberry Pi

5. Save and exit `nano`, then reboot your Pi.

6. Next we need to create a configuration file for `hostapd`. In `nano`, open/create the configuration file:

**pi@raspberrypi ~ $ sudo nano /etc/hostapd/hostapd.conf**

7. Add the following configuration options:

```
interface=wlan0
bridge=br0
driver=nl80211
country_code=UK
ssid=AGENT-PI
hw_mode=g
channel=6
auth_algs=1
wpa=2
wpa_passphrase=SecretAgent
wpa_key_mgmt=WPA-PSK
#Wireless N Settings
ieee80211n=1
wmm_enabled=1
```

8. Let's take a look at some of the options:
   - `interface=wlan0`: This is the wireless interface you are using for the access point.
   - `bridge=br0`: Allows `hostapd` to share the wired Internet connection by creating a bridge between the Ethernet and Wi-Fi interfaces. You can comment this out if you didn't create the bridge earlier.
   - `ssid`: Change this line to choose a name for your access point.
   - `auth_algs=1`: Supports WPA2 encryption that we're going to enable on our network.
   - `wpa=2`: Enable WPA2 encryption.
   - `wpa_passphrase`: The password (8 characters minimum) required to join your Wi-Fi network:

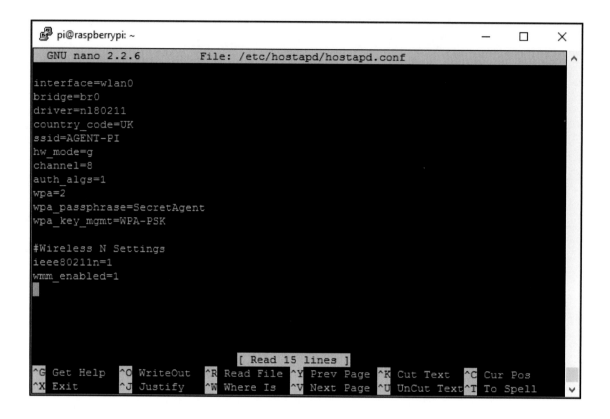

```
GNU nano 2.2.6          File: /etc/hostapd/hostapd.conf

interface=wlan0
bridge=br0
driver=nl80211
country_code=UK
ssid=AGENT-PI
hw_mode=g
channel=8
auth_algs=1
wpa=2
wpa_passphrase=SecretAgent
wpa_key_mgmt=WPA-PSK

#Wireless N Settings
ieee80211n=1
wmm_enabled=1

                    [ Read 15 lines ]
^G Get Help  ^O WriteOut  ^R Read File ^Y Prev Page ^K Cut Text   ^C Cur Pos
^X Exit      ^J Justify   ^W Where Is  ^V Next Page ^U UnCut Text ^T To Spell
```

9. Now we can try out our new access point, first running it in the foreground:

```
pi@raspberrypi ~ $ sudo hostapd -d
/etc/hostapd/hostapd.conf
```

10. You should now be able to find and connect to your Pi access point from other computers. Type *Ctrl* + *C* to quit hostapd.

Attention Edimax EW-7811Un Wi-Fi dongle users

This popular tiny USB dongle, and possibly others like it based on the Realtek RTL8188CUS chipset, needs a special version of hostapd to work. Simply download and replace your installed hostapd binary using the following command:

**pi@raspberrypi ~ $ sudo wget http://files.raspiplace.com/hostapd-rt -O /usr/sbin/hostapd**

11. To make your Pi run `hostapd` automatically in the background on boot, we need to make a slight adjustment to a configuration file:

```
pi@raspberrypi ~ $ sudo nano /etc/default/hostapd
```

12. Uncomment the line beginning with `DAEMON_CONF=""` and change it to point to your `hostapd` configuration file:

```
DAEMON_CONF="/etc/hostapd/hostapd.conf"
```

Then save and exit `nano`. Your Pi will now become an access point on boot.

# Connecting the Pi to the mobile Internet

If you're out in the field and need an Internet connection, then you could connect a USB 3G or 4G **modem dongle** to your Pi to obtain Internet access over the **cellular data network**. There are millions of dongles out there, but there are two main ways they are seen by the Pi-either as a serial modem device or as a virtual network interface.

The easiest ones to work with are those that present themselves as virtual network interfaces, since they require less configuration to get going, and that's the type we will use for this project.

Serial modem types, while working very well—and to an extent having greater flexibility, such as supporting the AT command set—need the addition of a point-to-point protocol (ppp) daemon and dialler software such as `wvdial` in order to make a connection to the Internet.

Huawei brand modems are readily available, and some older models can be bought cheaply on eBay and Amazon. Their HiLink range are the ones to look out for as these are the types that present themselves as a virtual network interface. These devices even have their own mini web server to allow access to a status page and configuration page using a web browser. In this project, I have used the Huawei E3372 4G/LTE modem:

Huawei E3372 4G/LTE modem works as a virtual network device

One limitation of the HiLink virtual network interface, however, is that its IP address is fixed at something like 192.168.1.1 or 192.168.8.1. This won't be a problem for our Pi, however, as we can set any of the other network devices on our Pi to a different subnet (for example, 192.168.0.x).

**A note about power:** USB modems can be quite power hungry and will often not work when plugged directly into the USB ports of earlier models of the Raspberry Pi. However, later models from the Model B+ onwards have more currently availability on the USB ports and you should have no problems with these boards.

# Multiple personalities

Huawei dongles, in particular, tend to be multi-personality USB devices. This means that when they are plugged into your Pi, they tend to show themselves to the Linux system as a read-only CD-ROM device—normally because they come pre-installed with driver software, or contain an SD-card reader. Because of this, we need our Raspberry Pi to persuade the device to switch to the modem mode so we can access it. This is known as **USB modeswitching**.

Plug your HiLink device into your Raspberry Pi and check its reported personality by entering the command:

```
pi@raspberrypi ~ $ lsusb
```

From the following screenshot, you'll see that it's reporting a device personality of **12d1:1f01**. This means that it's being presented as a CD-ROM device, and not the network adapter device required:

Huawei modem showing as the CD-ROM mode personality

# Switching modes

To help us with this, we're going to install the **sg3-utils** package, which includes the **usb-modeswitch** package as well. So let's do it:

```
pi@raspberrypi ~ $ sudo apt-get install sg3-utils
```

Once installed, reboot your Pi with your modem dongle still connected. After you log in again, run the lsusb command again to see if the personality has automatically changed on boot-up by presenting itself with the ID 12d1:14dc.

If it hasn't, then you'll need to force the switch using the sg_raw command—part of **sg3-utils**:

```
pi@raspberrypi ~ $ sudo /usr/bin/sg_raw /dev/sr0 11 06
20 00 00 00 00 00 01 00
```

You should then see the response **SCSI Status: Good**. Check with lsusb again and you should see something like the following screen:

```
pi@raspberrypi:~ $ sudo /usr/bin/sg_raw /dev/sr0 11 06 20 00 00 00 00 00 01 00
SCSI Status: Good

pi@raspberrypi:~ $ lsusb
Bus 001 Device 005: ID 12d1:14dc Huawei Technologies Co., Ltd.
Bus 001 Device 003: ID 0424:ec00 Standard Microsystems Corp. SMSC9512/9514 Fast
Ethernet Adapter
Bus 001 Device 002: ID 0424:9514 Standard Microsystems Corp.
Bus 001 Device 001: ID 1d6b:0002 Linux Foundation 2.0 root hub
pi@raspberrypi:~ $
```

Modem device mode-switched using the sg_raw command

Now run ifconfig to see if the network port eth1 has been created and given you an IP address:

```
eth1 Link encap:Ethernet HWaddr 0c:5b:8f:27:9a:64
  inet addr:192.168.8.100 Bcast:192.168.8.255
  Mask:255.255.255.0
  inet6 addr: fe80::584f:751f:bb3e:e26b/64 Scope:Link
  UP BROADCAST RUNNING MULTICAST MTU:1500 Metric:1
  RX packets:333 errors:0 dropped:0 overruns:0 frame:0
  TX packets:42 errors:0 dropped:0 overruns:0 carrier:0
  collisions:0 txqueuelen:1000
  RX bytes:157792 (154.0 KiB) TX bytes:8660 (8.4 KiB)
```

For my device, it's assigned the IP address 192.168.8.100 for the eth1 interface. This means that the modem's address is 192.168.8.1. Ping this address to see if you get a response from the modem.

If you don't have a network gateway connected to the normal Ethernet port on your Pi, then the `eth1` modem device will be defined as that default gateway. So, if you have a SIM card inserted into your dongle, and it has connected to the cellular network, your Pi will be connected to the Internet as if it was connected to your home network with a cable.

## Automatic mode-switching

Rather than having to go through all this mode-switching rigmarole each time we want to use our modem, we can create a device rule that will automatically run the `sg_raw` command whenever the USB modem is plugged in and detected. To do this, use Nano to create a new rules file:

```
pi@raspberrypi ~ $ sudo nano /etc/udev/rules.d/10-HuaweiModem.rules
```

Add the following rule to the file:

```
SUBSYSTEMS=="usb", ATTRS{modalias}=="usb:v12D1p1F01*", SYMLINK+="hwcdrom",
RUN+="/usr/bin/sg_raw /dev/hwcdrom 11 06 20 00 00 00 00 00 01 00"
```

Save the file and exit `nano`.

What this will do is tell the operating system that whenever a USB device with the personality ID 12d1:1f01 is plugged in, it will run the `sg_raw` command to perform the mode-switch.

 This procedure works for many devices, but you may need the personality IDs and `sg_raw` code may differ on other devices. In these cases, Google will be your friend by searching `usb modeswitch <personality>`, for example **usb modeswitch 12d1:1f01** to find potential solutions.

# Be anonymous on the Internet

Any secret agent needs to be stealthy and, well, secret—and that includes their Internet activity. If you suspect that you are being tracked by the authorities, or even advertisers, then you need to make your Internet traffic **anonymous** while online.

# Know your onions

In order to become anonymous on the Internet, we need to set up a Tor router. Tor (which stands for **The Onion Router**) facilitates anonymity by routing your traffic through a large worldwide network of relays that anonymize and obfuscate your location and web activity, making surveillance and analysis incredibly difficult. For more information about the Tor project see https://www.torproject.org.

The way it works is that we're going to use the Raspberry Pi as a wireless hotspot as we did earlier, but this time we're going to isolate the Wi-Fi network from the wired network and add some routing. The wired Ethernet will be connected to our Internet router on our home LAN. The Tor software will listen for traffic on the Wireless side and anonymize it via the Tor network.

# Setting up the Wi-Fi access point

Use the same procedure as in the preceding section, *Turning the Pi into a Wi-Fi hotspot*—with a couple of changes, which we'll apply later.

Once you've done that, this time we will set up our static IP for the Raspberry Pi Wireless device on a different subnet:

1. Type in the following command on the Pi to open up the DHCP client configuration:

   ```
   pi@raspberrypi ~ $ sudo nano /etc/dhcpcd.conf
   ```

2. Add the following lines to the end of the file:

   ```
   interface wlan0
   static ip_address=192.168.10.1/24
   static routers=192.168.10.1 static
   domain_name_servers=192.168.10.1
   ```

3. Press *Ctrl + X* to exit and select **Y,** when prompted, to save the modified buffer, then press the *Enter* key to confirm the filename to write to.

4. Remove or comment out the line bridge=br0 in /etc/hostapd/hostapd.conf

5. Remove or comment out the references to the `br0` interface in `/etc/network/interfaces`, as we're going to set up routing tables:

```
#auto br0
#iface br0 inet dhcp
#bridge_ports eth0 wlan0
```

# Installing and setting up a DHCP server

Since our network clients will be isolated from our main network, and there could be a few of them, we don't want the bother of having to set up static IP addresses on each device that wants to connect. So, we will install a **DHCP server** on our Raspberry Pi, whose job it is to serve IP addresses on the wireless network. We're going to use `Dnsmasq`, which is a DNS and DHCP server combined:

1. Install `dnsmasq`:

   **pi@raspberrypi ~ $ sudo apt-get install dnsmasq**

2. It will automatically start after being installed, so let's stop it for the time being while we set it up:

   **pi@raspberrypi ~ $ sudo service dnsmasq stop**

3. Rename the default `dnsmasq` configuration file, as it contains a long blurb of commented out options with descriptions (a good read if you're interested first though):

   **pi@raspberrypi ~ $ sudo mv /etc/dnsmasq.conf /etc/dnsmasq.conf.orig**

4. We're going to create more succinct configuration files with the options we need:

   **pi@raspberrypi ~ $ sudo nano /etc/dnsmasq.conf**

5. In the configuration file, add the following entries:

```
server = 8.8.8.8
server = 8.8.4.4
local = /local/
dhcp-authoritative
dhcp-option = option:router,192.168.10.1
#Wireless clients
interface = wlan0
dhcp-range =
wlan0,192.168.10.10,192.168.10.99,255.255.255.0,3h
```

6. Press *Ctrl* + *X* to exit and select **Y,** when prompted, to save the modified buffer, then press the Enter key to confirm the filename to write to.

# Set up the routing tables

Now we're going to set up the **routing tables** and **NAT** (network address translation), which will allow multiple devices connected to the wireless access point to be able to route through the Pi's single IP address on the Ethernet port:

1. Open the file /etc/sysctl.conf:

```
pi@raspberrypi ~ $ sudo nano /etc/sysctl.conf
```

2. Uncomment the line containing net.ipv4.ip_forward=1.
3. Exit nano and save the file.
4. Enable forwarding with the following command:

```
pi@raspberrypi ~ $ sudo sh -c "echo 1 >
/proc/sys/net/ipv4/ip_forward"
Enter the following commands to set up the routing
tables: pi@raspberrypi ~ $ sudo iptables -F
pi@raspberrypi ~ $ sudo iptables -t nat -F
pi@raspberrypi ~ $ sudo iptables -t nat -A POSTROUTING
-o eth0 -j MASQUERADE
pi@raspberrypi ~ $ sudo iptables -A FORWARD -i eth0
-o wlan0 -m state --state RELATED,ESTABLISHED -j ACCEPT
pi@raspberrypi ~ $ sudo iptables -A FORWARD -i wlan0
-o eth0 -j ACCEPT
```

5. In order to preserve these rules after a reboot, enter the following command:

```
pi@raspberrypi ~ $ sudo sh -c "iptables-save >
/etc/iptables.ipv4.nat"
```

6. Open up /etc/network/interfaces in Nano and add the following line at the end so that the rules are reloaded at boot time:

```
up iptables-restore < /etc/iptables.ipv4.nat
```

7. Now reboot your Pi using:

```
pi@raspberrypi ~ $ sudo shutdown -r now
```

We should now have a fully routing wireless access point, but before we set up Tor on our new router, let's test that it's functioning correctly as it is:

1. Plug the Ethernet port into your main network/Internet router.
2. With your PC or mobile device, connect to the wireless access point name you set up on your Pi.
3. Once connected, you should be able to access the Internet and browse the web.
4. If that's successful then your access point and DNS/DHCP servers are running correctly on the Pi.

# Installing and setting up Tor

Now it's time to install and set up Tor to turn our Pi into an anonymous router:

1. Install the Tor package:

```
pi@raspberrypi ~ $ sudo apt-get install tor
```

2. Once it's installed, we'll configure it to anonymize traffic on the wireless access point. Open the file `/etc/tor/torrc` with Nano and add the following entries before saving it:

```
VirtualAddrNetwork 10.192.0.0/10
AutomapHostsSuffixes .onion,.exit
AutomapHostsOnResolve 1
Transport 9040
TransListenAddress 192.168.10.1
DNSListenAddress 192.168.10.1
DNSPort 53
Log notice file /var/log/tor/notices.log
```

3. We'll now flush, then modify, the IP tables to exclude SSH from being routed through the Tor router and enable DNS lookups, but to ensure normal Internet traffic is redirected through it:

```
pi@raspberrypi ~ $ sudo iptables -F
pi@raspberrypi ~ $ sudo iptables -t nat -F
pi@raspberrypi ~ $ sudo iptables -t nat -A PREROUTING
-i wlan0 -p tcp --dport 22 -j REDIRECT --to-ports 22
pi@raspberrypi ~ $ sudo iptables -t nat -A PREROUTING
-i wlan0 -p udp --dport 53 -j REDIRECT --to-ports 53
pi@raspberrypi ~ $ sudo iptables -t nat -A PREROUTING
-i wlan0 -p tcp --syn -j REDIRECT --to-ports 9040
```

4. Save the rules with:

```
pi@raspberrypi ~ $ sudo sh -c "iptables-save >
/etc/iptables.ipv4.nat"
```

5. Start the Tor service:

```
pi@raspberrypi ~ $ sudo service tor start
```

6. Enable the Tor service at startup:

```
pi@raspberrypi ~ $ sudo update-rc.d tor enable
```

7. Reboot the Pi with:

```
pi@raspberrypi ~ $ sudo shutdown -r now
```

## Test your anonymity

Now that your Raspberry Pi has restarted and booted as a wireless access point, it's time to check our anonymity. Connect to the SSID you set for the access point and check if you have Internet access.

Once you have access then take a trip to `https://check.torproject.org` and check whether the IP address it is indicating you are from is actually different, your real IP address. If so, then you're now anonymous on the Internet.

> For this example, you've made quite a few changes to your system's configuration. Before you continue, you might want to start afresh with a new SD card image, or you can clear down the settings:
>
> Disable the Tor service with:
>
> **pi@raspberrypi ~ $ sudo update-rc.d tor disable**
>
> Reset the iptables with:
>
> **pi@raspberrypi ~ $ sudo iptables -F  pi@raspberrypi ~ $ sudo iptables -t nat -F  pi@raspberrypi ~ $ sudo sh -c "iptables-save > /etc/iptables.ipv4.nat"**
>
> Comment out the following line in `/etc/network/interfaces`:
>
> **#up iptables-restore < /etc/iptables.ipv4.nat**
>
> And then reboot your Pi.
>
> Disable the Access Point service with:
>
> **pi@raspberrypi ~ $ sudo update-rc.d hostapd disable**

# Tracking the Pi's whereabouts using GPS

Go right ahead and connect your GPS gadget to the USB port of your Raspberry Pi. I'm using a U-blox7 device, which supports both the well-known American-owned GPS system, as well as the lesser known Russian-own, GLOSNASS system, which it will use in conjunction with GPS to improve accuracy.

Many GPS modules designed for boards such as the Raspberry Pi or Arduino often come with a serial interface, which connects to the UART pins on the Raspberry Pi's GPIO connector, and work in the same way as USB dongles.

However, the Raspberry Pi Model 3 has changed the way these UART pins work, as the UART is now linked to the onboard Bluetooth system, and so devices designed to connect to those pins won't work anymore without a lot of work re-configuring the Pi's firmware. Therefore, stick to using the USB-based versions to save yourself a whole load of hassle.

U-blox7 GPS dongle is widely available from Amazon for about £15 and is supported by Linux

To see if your device is seen by the Raspberry Pi, after it's been plugged in, type the following command to list the USB devices the operating system can see:

```
pi@raspberrypi ~ $ lsusb
```

```
pi@raspberrypi:~ $ lsusb
Bus 001 Device 004: ID 1546:01a7 U-Blox AG
Bus 001 Device 003: ID 0424:ec00 Standard Microsystems Corp. SMSC9512/9514 Fast Etherne
t Adapter
Bus 001 Device 002: ID 0424:9514 Standard Microsystems Corp.
Bus 001 Device 001: ID 1d6b:0002 Linux Foundation 2.0 root hub
pi@raspberrypi:~ $
```

U-blox GPS device recognized by the Pi

Most GPS units appear to Linux as serial ports with device names starting with *tty* then are commonly followed by *ACM0* or *USB0*. Type in the following command and focus on the last line:

```
pi@raspberrypi ~ $ dmesg -T | grep tty
```

```
pi@raspberrypi: ~                                              —    □    ✕

pi@raspberrypi:~ $ dmesg -T | grep tty
[Sun May  8 19:21:06 2016] Kernel command line: 8250.nr_uarts=1 dma.dmachans=0x7f35 bcm
2708_fb.fbwidth=656 bcm2708_fb.fbheight=416 bcm2709.boardrev=0xa02082 bcm2709.serial=0x
b5a17e9f smsc95xx.macaddr=B8:27:EB:A1:7E:9F bcm2708_fb.fbswap=1 bcm2709.uart_clock=4800
0000 vc_mem.mem_base=0x3dc00000 vc_mem.mem_size=0x3f000000  dwc_otg.lpm_enable=0 consol
e=ttyS0,115200 console=tty1 root=/dev/mmcblk0p2 rootfstype=ext4 elevator=deadline fsck.
repair=yes rootwait
[Sun May  8 19:21:06 2016] console [tty1] enabled
[Sun May  8 19:21:06 2016] console [ttyS0] disabled
[Sun May  8 19:21:06 2016] 3f215040.uart: ttyS0 at MMIO 0x3f215040 (irq = 59, base_baud
 = 50000000) is a 16550
[Sun May  8 19:21:07 2016] console [ttyS0] enabled
[Sun May  8 19:21:09 2016] 3f201000.uart: ttyAMA0 at MMIO 0x3f201000 (irq = 87, base_ba
ud = 0) is a PL011 rev2
[Sun May  8 19:21:10 2016] systemd[1]: Expecting device dev-ttyS0.device...
[Sun May  8 19:21:11 2016] systemd[1]: Starting system-serial\x2dgetty.slice.
[Sun May  8 19:21:11 2016] systemd[1]: Created slice system-serial\x2dgetty.slice.
[Mon May  9 17:05:41 2016] cdc_acm 1-1.5:1.0: ttyACM0: USB ACM device
pi@raspberrypi:~ $
```

USB GPS receiver identifying as ttyACM0

The first couple of lines talk about the serial port built into the Pi (`ttyS0` on the Pi 3 or `ttyAMA0` in earlier models). On the last line, however, a USB device is identified, which is most likely our GPS unit and will be accessible as `/dev/ttyACM0`. We can confirm that it's a GPS by trying to read from it using the following command, where `[XXXX]` should be replaced by the name of your device:

```
pi@raspberrypi ~ $ cat /dev/tty[XXXX]
```

A GPS conforming to the NMEA standard will start flooding your screen with sentences beginning with a code such as **$GPGGA** followed by comma-separated data (see `http://aprs.gids.nl/nmea/` if you're curious about those messages). Even if your GPS outputs binary garbage, it'll probably work fine, so keep reading. Press Ctrl + C to stop the feed.

Once you've found the right device, it's important that you adjust the **baud rate** of your GPS port to the rate recommended in the manual for your GPS device. Use the following command to verify the current baud rate:

```
pi@raspberrypi ~ $ stty -F /dev/tty[XXXX] speed
```

If it differs from the recommended rate, use the following command to change it:

```
pi@raspberrypi ~ $ stty -F /dev/tty[XXXX] speed
[recommended speed]
```

Now we're all set to install some software to help us make sense of those cryptic NMEA strings:

```
pi@raspberrypi ~ $ sudo apt-get install gpsd
gpsd-clients
```

The `gpsd` package provides an interface daemon for GPS receivers, so that regular applications that want to work with GPS data don't have to know the details of how to talk to your particular brand of GPS. So, `gpsd` will be running in the background and relaying messages between your GPS and other applications through the `2947` TCP port.

Let's start `gpsd` using the following command:

```
pi@raspberrypi ~ $ sudo gpsd -n /dev/tty[XXXX]
```

Now we can try reading data from `gpsd` by using the basic GPS console client `cgps`:

```
pi@raspberrypi ~ $ cgps -s
```

```
┌ pi@raspberrypi: ~                                          —  □  ✕

lqqqqqqqqqqqqqqqqqqqqqqqqqqqqqqqqqqqqqqqqqqklqqqqqqqqqqqqqqqqqqqqqqqqqqqqqqqqqqqqq ^
x     Time:         2016-05-13T15:17:49.000Z   xxPRN:   Elev:   Azim:   SNR:   Used:
x     Latitude:       50.960933 N              xx  29     80      100     17       Y
x     Longitude:       1.422535 W              xx  31     64      272     30       Y
x     Altitude:      90.3 m                    xx  25     52      093     27       Y
x     Speed:         1.4 kph                   xx  26     26      284     33       Y
x     Heading:      174.9 deg (true)           xx   2     23      046     19       Y
x     Climb:         0.0 m/min                 xx  12     16      096     23       Y
x     Status:       3D FIX (11 secs)           xx  21     15      172     00       Y
x     Longitude Err:   +/- 9 m                 xx  14     14      222     00       N
x     Latitude Err:    +/- 16 m                xx  32     08      219     17       N
x     Altitude Err:    +/- 30 m                xx  23     05      339     19       N
x     Course Err:     n/a                      xx  47     00      000     00       N
x     Speed Err:      +/- 116 kph              xx
x     Time offset:    -155828.944              xx
x     Grid Square:    IO90gx                   xx
mqqqqqqqqqqqqqqqqqqqqqqqqqqqqqqqqqqqqqqqqqjmqqqqqqqqqqqqqqqqqqqqqqqqqqqqqqqqqqqq
```

cgps displaying GPS data obtained from seven satellites

You'll want to position your GPS receiver so that it has a clear view of the sky. If your **Status** continues to display **NO FIX**, try placing your GPS receiver on a windowsill.

The left-hand side frame contains the information that has been obtained from the list of satellites in the right-hand side frame. To quickly verify the coordinates on a map, simply paste the **Latitude** and **Longitude** strings into the search field at `http://maps.google.com`.

Press the *S* key to toggle the raw NMEA sentences that we've hidden by supplying the `-s` argument to `cgps`, or press the Q key to quit.

# Tracking the GPS position on Google Earth

So what can we do with this GPS data? We can either log the Pi's position at regular intervals to a waypoint database that can then be plotted onto a map, or we can update the position in real time on a remotely connected Google Earth session for that classic spy movie beaconing look.

## Preparing a GPS beacon on the Pi

To get the GPS data into a remote Google Earth session for live tracking, we must first massage the data into the **Keyhole Markup Language (KML)** format that Google Earth expects and then serve the data over an HTTP link so that Google Earth can request new GPS data at regular intervals.

First, we need to download a Python script called `gegpsd.py`, written by Stephen Youndt, with the following command:

```
pi@raspberrypi ~ $ wget http://files.raspiplace.com/agentpi/gegpsd.py
```

You can find out more information about this script on the Wiki at `http://tjworld.net/wiki/Linux/Ubuntu/GoogleEarthPlusRealTimeGPS`.

This script will continuously fetch data from `gpsd`, and write it in the KML format, to `/tmp/nmea.kml`. We'll also need an HTTP server to serve this file to Google Earth. Python comes with a simple HTTP server that we can use for this purpose. Start the Python script and HTTP server using the following command:

```
pi@raspberrypi ~ $ python ~/gegpsd.py & cd /tmp &&
python -m SimpleHTTPServer
```

The KML data should now be generated and available from `http://[IP address]:8000/nmea.kml`, where `[IP address]` is the address of your Raspberry Pi.

Let's move on to Google Earth.

# Setting up Google Earth

The setup procedure for Google Earth is very similar across all platforms:

1. Visit `http://www.google.com/earth/download/ge/agree.html` to download Google Earth for your platform.
2. Install and start Google Earth.

3. From the **Add** drop-down menu, select **Network Link**.
4. Put a name for your GPS link in the **Name** field and add the `http://[IP address]:8000/nmea.kml` KML data link to the **Link** field.
5. Go to the **Refresh** tab and change the **Time-Based Refresh** to **Periodically** in the drop-down menu.
6. (Optional) Tick the **Fly to View on Refresh** checkbox to have the view automatically centered on your GPS as it moves.
7. Now click on the **OK** button and you should see your GPS link as an entry under **My Places** in the sidebar on the left-hand side. Double-click on it to zoom in on your GPS location.

# Setting up a GPS waypoint logger

When you can't travel with your Pi, and you can't be within the Wi-Fi range to monitor its position in real time, you can still see where it has been by recording and analyzing **GPX files**—a standard file format for recording GPS waypoints, tracks, and routes. Use the following command to start logging:

```
pi@raspberrypi ~ $ gpxlogger -d -f /tmp/gpslog.gpx
```

The `-d` argument tells `gpxlogger` to run in the background and the `-f` argument specifies the log file. Before you open up the log file in Google Earth, it's important that the `gpxlogger` process has quit properly, otherwise you might end up with a broken log (usually, this can be fixed by adding a closing `</gpx>` tag to the end of the file). Kill the process using the following command:

```
pi@raspberrypi ~ $ killall gpxlogger
```

Next, start the simple Python HTTP server:

```
pi@raspberrypi ~ $ cd /tmp && python -m SimpleHTTPServer
```

Then download the log file to your computer through the following address:

`http://[IP address]:8000/gpslog.gpx`

Now in Google Earth, under the **File** drop-down menu, select **Open...** and point to your log file. Click on **OK** in the **GPS Data Import** dialog that follows, and you should see a post for your GPS device under **Temporary Places** in the sidebar to the left, and time controls that can be used to play back the travel route.

# Mapping GPS data from Kismet

If you run Kismet, which was discussed in the *Monitoring Wi-Fi airspace with Kismet* section of `Chapter 4`, *Wi-Fi Pranks – Exploring Your Network*, with GPS support, it will record geographic information about the access points to `~/kismetlogs/Kismet-[date].netxml`. To massage this data into the KML format that Google Earth expects, we need to install an additional utility called **GISKismet**.

1. It's written in Perl and requires a couple of modules to be installed first:

   ```
   pi@raspberrypi ~ $ sudo apt-get install
   libxml-libxml-perl libdbi-perl libdbd-sqlite3-perl
   ```

2. Now we need to download and install the GISKismet utility itself, with the following command sequence:

   ```
   pi@raspberrypi ~ $ wget
   http://files.raspiplace.com/agentpi/giskismet-
   svn30.tar.bz2
   pi@raspberrypi ~ $ tar xvf giskismet-svn30.tar.bz2
   pi@raspberrypi ~ $ cd giskismet
   pi@raspberrypi ~/giskismet $ perl Makefile.PL
   pi@raspberrypi ~/giskismet $ make
   pi@raspberrypi ~/giskismet $ sudo make install
   ```

3. Once installed, you may exit the source directory and delete it:

   ```
   pi@raspberrypi ~/giskismet $ cd .. && rm -r giskismet
   ```

4. Getting a KML file out of GISKismet is a two-step process; first we import the Kismet network data into a SQLite database, and then we select the information that we want to export to KML with a SQL query. This line will perform both steps with one command, but adjust `[date]` to the correct filename:

   ```
   pi@raspberrypi ~ $ giskismet -x kismetlogs/Kismet-
   [date].netxml -q "select * from wireless"
   -o /tmp/mywifi.kml
   ```

   The `-x` argument tells GISKismet to import the data from the specified `netxml` file to an SQLite database in the current directory called `wireless.dbl` by default. The `-q` argument specifies the SQL query that will be used to obtain data from the database, which will be written in KML format to the file we specify after the `-o` argument.

You can restrict which access points go into the database using Input Filters (type `giskismet` without arguments to see them), or filter the KML output through the SQL query, for example, `select * from wireless where Channel=1` would put only access points on channel one in the KML file.

5. Next, start the simple Python HTTP server:

```
pi@raspberrypi ~ $ cd /tmp && python -m SimpleHTTPServer
```

6. Now in Google Earth, add a new **Network Link** as in the previous section but adjust the address to `http://[IP address]:8000/mywifi.kml`. You should now see a list of all the access points in the sidebar to the left.

# Using GPS as a time source

As we've mentioned in previous chapters, the Raspberry Pi lacks a Real-Time Clock, and depends on other computers to relay the correct time through the network. While the Pi may not have network connectivity out in the field, a GPS can actually be used as an alternative time source. All we need to do is to tell `ntpd`, the **Network Time Protocol** daemon, to use the time information supplied by `gpsd` as a potential time source:

1. Type in the following command to open up the `ntpd` configuration file for editing:

```
pi@raspberrypi ~ $ sudo nano /etc/ntp.conf
```

2. Find the predefined block of `server` directives ending with `server 3.debian.pool.ntp.org iburst` and add the following statements beneath:

```
# GPS
server 127.127.28.0
fudge 127.127.28.0 time1 0.420 refid GPS
server 127.127.28.1 prefer
fudge 127.127.28.1 refid PPS
```

3. Now restart `ntpd` using the following command:

**pi@raspberrypi ~ $ sudo service ntp restart**

4. We can verify that the GPS is being used as a time source with the following command:

**pi@raspberrypi ~ $ ntpq -p**

You'll have two lines mentioning **GPS** and **PPS** in the **refid** column. The second line will show activity only if your GPS receiver supports the more accurate PPS pulse method.

If your `date` command reports a year of 1969 or 1970 (an unset clock), `ntpd` will refuse to set the correct time. This can happen when an unset clock date has been saved to `/etc/fake-hwclock.data`. You need to set a date manually using the following command, and then reboot your Pi:

**pi@raspberrypi ~ $ sudo date --set='Mon Jan 1 12:00:00 GMT 2016**

# Setting up GPS on boot

Out in the field, we obviously won't be there to start `gpsd` manually, so we need a way to make it run at boot time. The `gpsd` package does come with a few scripts for this purpose, but they're not the most reliable and will only auto-detect a handful of GPS models.

Instead, we'll add our own GPS setup routine to the `/etc/rc.local` script that we've used throughout this book:

1. Open it up for editing using the following command:

**pi@raspberrypi ~ $ sudo nano /etc/rc.local**

2. Anywhere before the last **exit 0** line, add the following script snippet, adjust the `GPSDEV` and `GPSBAUD` variables to match your GPS, and enable the optional `GPSBEACON` and `GPSLOGGER`, as follows:

```
# GPS startup routine
GPSDEV="/dev/ttyACM0"
GPSBAUD="38400"
GPSBEACON="y"
GPSLOGGER="y"
if [ -c "$GPSDEV" ]; then
```

```
stty -F $GPSDEV speed $GPSBAUD
gpsd -n $GPSDEV
if [ "$GPSBEACON" = "y" ]; then
  sleep 5
  sudo -u pi python /home/pi/gegpsd.py &
  cd /tmp && sudo -u pi python -m SimpleHTTPServer &
fi
if [ "$GPSLOGGER" = "y" ]; then
  sudo -u pi gpxlogger -d -f /tmp/gpslog.gpx
fi
fi
```

3. Now reboot the Pi with the GPS attached and verify with `cgps -s` that `gpsd` was started.

# Controlling the Pi with your smartphone

There is something oddly satisfying about controlling a small device remotely from another small device. To do this with a headless Pi and a smartphone, all we need is a Wi-Fi adapter on the Pi with SSH running and a remote control app for the phone that knows how to send commands through an SSH connection.

## Android (Raspi SSH)

Raspi SSH is a free remote control application available from the Google Play Store. It is a very simple application in appearance and functionality but works well enough:

1. Find and install Raspi SSH by Philipp Stoppel from the Google Play Store.
2. Fill in the **Connection details** for your Pi. You may be able to use `raspberrypi` as **Hostname** instead of the IP address if your home router supports it.

3. Start adding your own commands to the list or take a look at the table of common remote control commands later in this section for inspiration:

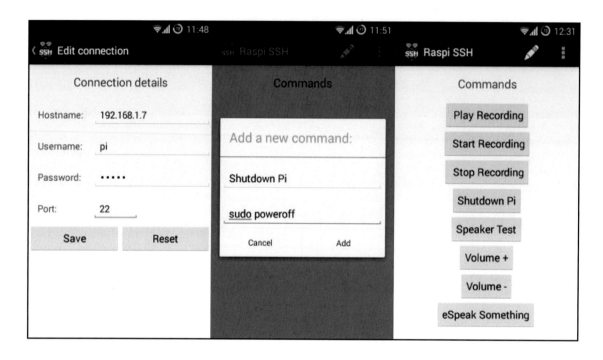

Controlling the Pi remotely with Raspi SSH on Android

# iPhone/iPad (SSH Remote)

SSH Remote is a free remote control application available through the iPhone App Store. It is a very simple application in appearance and functionality but works well enough.

1. Find and install SSH Remote by Robin Speerstra from the iPhone App Store.
2. Click the plus icon to add new SSH buttons. Fill in the login information for your Pi. You may be able to use `raspberrypi` as *IP* instead of the IP address if your home router supports it.
3. Start adding your own commands to the list or have a look at the table of common remote control commands later in this section for inspiration:

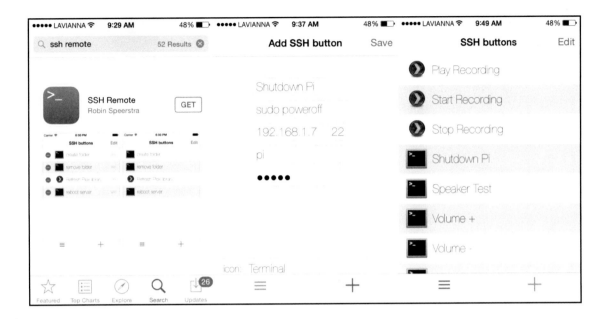

Controlling Pi remotely with SSH Remote on the iPhone

# Common remote control commands

Use this handy command reference table to quickly map out your Pi remote control:

| Button Name | Command |
|---|---|
| **Play Recording** | sox myrec.wav -d |
| Start Recording | sox -t alsa plughw:1 myrec.wav |
| Stop Rec/Play | killall sox |
| Volume Up | amixer set PCM 10dB+ |
| Volume Down | amixer set PCM 10dB- |
| Volume Mute | amixer set PCM toggle |
| Speaker Test | speaker-test -c2 -t wav -l1 |
| Set Analog Out | amixer cset numid=3 1 |
| Set HDMI Out | amixer cset numid=3 2 |

| Button Name | Command |
|---|---|
| eSpeak Something | espeak "Something!" |
| TV On | echo "on 0" \| cec-client -d 1 -s |
| TV Off | echo "standby 0" \| cec-client -d 1 -s |
| Reboot Pi | sudo reboot |
| Shutdown Pi | sudo poweroff |

# Receiving status updates from the Pi

When you send your Raspberry Pi out in the world on stealthy missions, you might not be able to stay connected to it at all times. However, as long as the Pi has Internet access via a Wi-Fi network or USB modem, you'll be able to communicate with it from anywhere in the world.

In this example, we'll be using **Twitter**, a popular social networking service for sharing short messages. We're going to make the Pi send regular tweets about the mission and its whereabouts. If you do not already have a Twitter account, or you'd like a separate account for the Pi, you'll need to sign up at https://twitter.com first. Follow these steps to get started with Twitter:

1. Before you post anything on Twitter, you should consider enabling tweet privacy. This means the messages won't be publicly visible and only selected people on Twitter will be able to read them.

   To enable tweet privacy, go to your account settings (https://twitter.com/settings/account) and check the **Protect my Tweets** checkbox under **Security and privacy**, then click on the **Save changes** button.

2. Next, install a console Twitter client using the following command:

```
pi@raspberrypi ~ $ sudo apt-get install ttytter
```

3. Now start the client and follow the onscreen instructions for the one-time setup procedure:

```
pi@raspberrypi ~ $ ttytter -ssl
```

4. Once you've entered your PIN and you are back at the prompt, you can run `ttytter -ssl` again to start the client in interactive mode, where anything you type that doesn't start with a slash will be tweeted to the world. Type `/help` to see a list of the possible commands and `/quit` to exit `ttytter`.

5. Let's try a simple status update first, with a few useful arguments added for good measure:

```
pi@raspberrypi ~ $ ttytter -ssl -status="Alive: $(date)
from $(curl -s ipogre.com)" -autosplit -hold
```

```
pi@raspberrypi ~ $ ttytter -ssl -status="Alive: $(date) from $(curl -s ipogre.com)" -autosplit -hold
-- using SSL for default URLs.
trying to find cURL ... /usr/bin/curl
test-login SUCCEEDED!
post attempt SUCCEEDED!

Tweets    Tweets & replies

Secret Agent @SecretAgent · 3m
Alive: Tue Nov 11 20:41:49 EST 2014 from
91.91.139.206
```

Raspberry Pi reporting its time and external IP address on Twitter

- The `-ssl` argument enables encryption when we're talking to Twitter and is now a requirement.
- The `-status` argument with the tweet enclosed in double quotes is the quickest way of sending a single message from the command line without entering interactive mode. In this message, we're using a feature of the shell called command substitution that allows the output of a command to be inserted back in place.

- -autosplit is used to automatically split messages that are longer than 140 characters into multiple tweets.
- -hold instructs ttytter to keep retrying to send the message in case there's a problem communicating with Twitter.

6. Chances are that you'll want to use those same three arguments with all future ttytter commands, therefore it makes sense to put them into a file called ~/.ttytterrc that will be interpreted by ttytter as a list of features to enable automatically on startup. Open it up for editing with the following command:

```
pi@raspberrypi ~ $ nano ~/.ttytterrc
```

7. Then put the features in, one per line, but in a slightly different form from what we saw earlier:

```
ssl=1
autosplit=1
hold=1
```

As an alternative to regular tweets, we can also send direct messages to a specific person using the following command, but replace [user] with the person's Twitter account name:

```
pi@raspberrypi ~ $ ttytter -runcommand="/dm [user]
My hovercraft is full of eels"
```

The -runcommand argument is used to launch, from the command line, any action that you could type while in interactive mode.

What if we need our Pi to report the contents of an important document or other lengthy output? How can we break the 140-character barrier? Simple: paste the document to a private **pastebin** and report the link on Twitter. Debian's Pastezone at http://paste.debian.net is a good candidate; it's easy to interact with and supports hidden pastes.

Download a utility Python script to interact with Debian's Pastezone, written by Michael Gebetsroither, with the following command:

```
pi@raspberrypi ~ $ sudo wget
http://files.raspistuff.com/agentpi/debpaste.py
-O /usr/bin/debpaste && sudo chmod +x /usr/bin/debpaste
```

We can now combine the `debpaste` and `ttytter` utilities in the following command line:

```
pi@raspberrypi ~ $ cat /boot/config.txt | debpaste
-n ScrtSqrl -e 24 -p add | grep -o
'http://paste.debian.net/hidden/.*' | ttytter -status=-
```

We start with piping the text file that is to be pasted to the `debpaste` utility. The `-n` argument is optional and sets the name to be associated with the paste. The `-e` argument sets the number of hours the paste will remain readable for before it is deleted. The `-p` flag is important and enables the hiding of your paste from public view. After the paste has been submitted, the `debpaste` utility outputs a bit of information about your entry.

Since we can't fit all of this information in a tweet, we use `grep` to fish out only the URL that we're interested in from that output. We then pipe the URL to `ttytter` and tell it to read the message to be posted from standard input by using the `-` character.

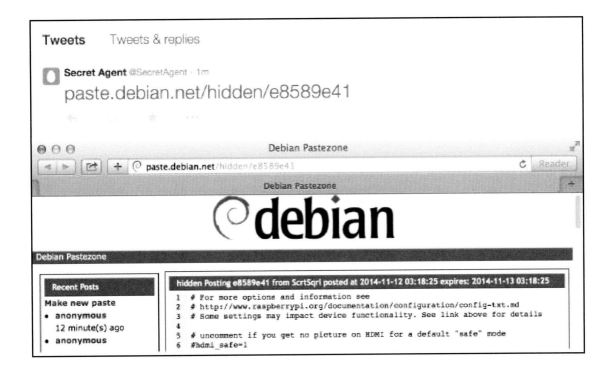

Raspberry Pi tweeting a link to a pasted document

# Tagging tweets with GPS coordinates

If you have a GPS connected to the Pi, we can tag each tweet with a geographical location. Follow these steps to get started:

1. First, you need to allow **geotagging** for your Twitter account. Go to your account settings and check the **Add a location to my Tweets** checkbox under **Security and privacy**, then click on the **Save changes** button.

2. Next, we need a way of obtaining the coordinates from `gpsd` and feeding them to `ttytter`. We'll need to create our own shell script for this purpose. Open up `~/passgps.sh` for editing with the following command:

   **pi@raspberrypi ~ $ nano ~/passgps.sh**

3. Add the following script snippet:

   ```
   #!/bin/bash

   LAT=""
   LONG=""

   gpspipe -d -w -o /tmp/gpsdump

   while ([ -z $LAT ] || [ -z $LONG ]) ; do
     if [ -f /tmp/gpsdump ] ; then
       LAT=$(cat /tmp/gpsdump | awk 'BEGIN{RS=","; FS=":"}
       /lat/ {save=$2} END {print save}')
       LONG=$(cat /tmp/gpsdump | awk 'BEGIN{RS=","; FS=":"}
       /lon/ {save=$2} END {print save}')
     fi
   done

   killall gpspipe
   rm /tmp/gpsdump

   echo "-lat=$LAT -long=$LONG"
   ```

Save and exit `nano`, then make the script executable with `chmod +x` `~/passgps.sh`.

The script launches a `gpspipe` session in the background, which will fill up `/tmp/gpsdump` with data obtained from `gpsd`. We then enter a while loop until we're able to filter out the latitude and longitude from `/tmp/gpsdump` by using an `awk` command and we put the coordinates into the `LAT` and `LONG` variables. Then we clean up a bit after our script and output the coordinates on a line suitable for `ttytter`.

4. Now, all we need to do is tweet something with `-location` added as an argument, to enable geotagging for this particular tweet, then let our script pass in the GPS coordinates. Just remember that you need to have `gpsd` running for our script to work:

```
pi@raspberrypi ~ $ ttytter -status="$(vcgencmd
measure_temp) today, feeling cozy" -location
$(~/passgps.sh)
```

Tweet tagged with location obtained from GPS

# Sending e-mail updates

With the right software, it's possible to compose e-mails, complete with attachments, directly from the command line. We'll be using some simple tools to add e-mail capabilities to your shell scripts.

**Important:**

It seems that the `voicecommand` package we installed back in `Chapter 2`, *Audio Antics*, sets up a Cron job, which tries to out an e-mail every minute. It's important that you remove the job file before going any further otherwise you are going to receive a non-delivery report in your mailbox every minute!!

pi@raspberrypi ~ $ sudo rm /etc/cron.d/gtextcommand

# Installing and setting up the SMTP client

```
pi@raspberrypi ~ $ sudo apt-get install ssmtp
```

You'll now need to set up the client to send e-mails through your e-mail account. In the following configuration file, I've assumed that you have a Gmail account. The settings may be different if you use another e-mail provider.

Open the **ssmtp** configuration file using **Nano**:

```
pi@raspberrypi ~ $ sudo nano /etc/ssmtp/ssmtp.conf
```

Replace the entries with the following configuration:

```
root=<your-username>@gmail.com
mailhub=smtp.gmail.com:587
rewriteDomain=gmail.com
AuthUser=<your-username>@gmail.com
AuthPass=<your-password>
FromLineOverride=YES
UseSTARTTLS=YES
```

Let's break down each option:

- `root`: This identifies what user account receives all mail for user ID under 1,000 on the local system. That basically means system accounts, such as the root user account. In other words, if your computer is trying to send your root account an e-mail message, it will send it to whatever e-mail address you specify here. This should normally be your primary e-mail account—probably the account for which you're configuring `ssmtp` to send e-mails.

- `mailhub`: This is the fully qualified hostname for the SMTP server you will be using, so that `ssmtp` knows where to send outgoing e-mails. This option may actually take the form `mailhub=mail.domain.com:587`, which sets the port number to use when contacting the SMTP server to 587. This allows unencrypted connections to use 25 (the default port number for SMTP traffic). Port 587 is the standard alternate port number for TLS-protected SMTP connections on Gmail.

- `rewriteDomain`: This tells `ssmtp` that your mail headers need to be edited to say that the domain name you use for your e-mail address will be listed as the source of your e-mail address. Failing to rewrite the source domain name in this manner may cause problems at the receiving end when your e-mail address arrives at its intended destination.

- `AuthUser`: This is the username used to log in to the remote SMTP server. In many cases, this is the part of the e-mail address that comes before the @ sign in your e-mail address, or could be the entire e-mail address.

- `AuthPass`: This is the authentication password used with the username above.

  > Because your e-mail password is stored in the file, you may want to make sure the `ssmtp.conf` file permissions are set to `640` using the `chmod` command. This ensures that the `ssmtp` and root accounts can access the file as needed, but no other accounts have access to the contents of the file.

  > You will also need to ensure that you create an SSMTP user (with a command like:

```
pi@raspberrypi ~ $ sudo pw useradd ssmtp -g nogroup
-h - -s /sbin/nologin -d /nonexistent -c "ssmtp
system user"
```

  > And set ownership of `ssmtp.conf` to that user:

```
pi@raspberrypi ~ $ sudo chown ssmtp ssmtp.conf
```

- `FromLineOverride=YES`: The From: header in an e-mail handled by `ssmtp` can be overwritten. Setting this to YES just uses the From: value provided by the program that sent the e-mail to `ssmtp` to be forwarded to the SMTP server in the first place.
- `UseTLS=YES`: This is the configuration line that tells `ssmtp` to encrypt its connection to the SMTP server, protecting your authentication username and password, as well as the rest of the communications.

**ssmtp** can be used on its own, but can be a bit of a faff to automatically send e-mails (by default, you manually type the e-mail in with the command line, or create a text file), so we're also going to install the mailutils package:

```
pi@raspberrypi ~ $ sudo apt-get install mailutils
```

Once it's installed, we can use the **mail** command to send emails more easily. Send a test email through the (G)mail account setup above using the following command to make sure your settings are working:

```
pi@raspberrypi ~ $ echo "Test Email" | mail -s
"Test Pi-Mail" me@mydomain.com
```

In the preceding example, we are simply sending an e-mail with the body text **Test Email** to the recipient me@domain.com with the subject Test Pi-Email.

All being well, you should receive the test e-mail in your mailbox within a few seconds or so.

# Sending attachments

Now that we can send basic e-mails from our Pi, let's try sending the WAV file we recorded earlier. But first, we need to install yet another package to help us with this:

```
pi@raspberrypi ~ $ sudo apt-get install mpack
```

Once that's installed, we'll use Gmail to send a message with a WAV file attachment:

```
pi@raspberrypi ~ $ sudo mpack -s "Pi Report"
~/myrecording.wav fellow.peer@agenthq.com
```

If the e-mail delivery fails, it's likely that you've received an e-mail in your Gmail inbox with the subject sign-in attempt blocked. To allow `ssmtp` to send mail, you will need to enable "less secure apps" by visiting the link in that e-mail. Alternatively, you can find it under the security settings of your Gmail account.

# Scheduling regular updates

While we've done plenty of command scheduling with `at` in this book, it will only run a command once. If we need a command to be run regularly at certain times, **Cron** is better for the job and is already installed. To add a new task to run, we need to add it to our scheduling table, or `crontab`, with the following command:

```
pi@raspberrypi ~ $ crontab -e
```

If you are prompted to choose your text editor because it's the first time you've opened `crontab`, then select number 2 for `nano`.

Add your task to the bottom of the file on a blank line according to the following form:

```
Minute | Hour | Day of month | Month | Day of week | Command to execute
```

For example, to tweet a status update every hour:

```
0 * * * * ttytter -status="Alive: $(date)"
```

To tweet a status update every 10 minutes:

```
*/10 * * * * ttytter -status="Alive: $(date)"
```

You can also use one of the special predefined values among `@hourly`, `@daily`, `@weekly`, `@monthly`, `@yearly`, or `@reboot` to have a command run at startup.

Once you're happy with your line, save and exit `nano` to have your new `crontab` installed. To view your `crontab`, use this command:

```
pi@raspberrypi ~ $ crontab -l
```

# Accessing your files from anywhere with Dropbox

Dropbox is a popular file hosting service with client software available for a wide range of devices. In essence, Dropbox allows you to store files in a special folder on one computer and have the files appear automatically on any other device with Dropbox installed. Files may also be accessed and modified through a regular web browser.

Unfortunately, the company behind Dropbox does not yet offer client software for the Raspberry Pi. Instead, we'll be using a bash script called **Dropbox Uploader** that works just as well, and is in some ways even more flexible than the native client:

1. Start by signing up for a Dropbox account if you haven't already got one:
   `http://www.dropbox.com`

     It's free with a storage limit of 2 GB.

2. Grab the latest Dropbox Uploader script from the developer's GitHub repository and put it in a convenient location:

```
pi@raspberrypi ~ $ sudo wget
https://raw.githubusercontent.com/
andreafabrizi/Dropbox-
Uploader/master/dropbox_uploader.sh
```

3. Next we need to give the script executable permission:

```
pi@raspberrypi ~ $ sudo chmod +x dropbox_uploader.sh
```

4. Now we need to jump through a few hoops to allow Dropbox Uploader to access your Dropbox account. Start the script and follow the onscreen instructions:

```
pi@raspberrypi ~ $ ./dropbox_uploader.sh
```

5. The first thing the instructions tell you to do is to log in to your Dropbox account and create a new App. You can access this directly at `https://www.dropbox.com/developers/apps/create`. The App creation screen should be set up as follows for Dropbox Uploader:

Create a new app on the Dropbox Platform

1. Choose an API

Dropbox API

For apps that need to access files in
Dropbox. Learn more

Dropbox Business API

For apps that need access to Dropbox
Business team info. Learn more

2. Choose the type of access you need

Learn more about access types

App folder – Access to a single folder created specifically for your app.

Full Dropbox – Access to all files and folders in a user's Dropbox.

3. Name your app

AgentBox

☑ I agree to Dropbox API Terms and Conditions

Create app

Creating an application configuration for Dropbox Uploader

6.  Once the initial setup is done, your application settings are stored in a hidden text
    file called `~/.dropbox_uploader` that could be copied to other computers.

Now we can type `dropbox_uploader.sh` without arguments to get a list of all possible commands.

Let's create a sub-folder in our Dropbox account to hold our agent-specific stuff:

```
pi@raspberrypi ~ $ ./dropbox_uploader.sh mkdir
agentstuff
```

We could, for example, store all the evidence from *Detecting an intruder and setting off an alarm* in `Chapter 3`, *Webcam and Video Wizardry* in our `agentstuff` folder:

```
pi@raspberrypi ~ $ ./dropbox_uploader.sh
-p upload ~/evidence/* agentstuff
```

The `-p` flag gives you a handy progress indicator for each file transfer.

Now let's say you add additional files to your `agentstuff` folder from another computer, and would like to keep a synchronized copy on your Pi:

```
pi@raspberrypi ~ $ ./dropbox_uploader.sh
-p -s download agentstuff
```

The previous command will create a mirror copy of the `agentstuff` folder, but will skip files that may already exist. The `-s` flag makes the command more suitable to be run repeatedly, as part of a backup script or a cron job like in the following example:

```
0 * * * * dropbox -s download agentstuff /home/pi/agentstuff
```

The previous `crontab` entry will make sure your `agentstuff` folder is kept up to date once every hour. See *Scheduling regular updates* earlier in this chapter for more details on Cron.

# Keeping your data secret with encryption

In this section, we'll create a file container, you can think of it as a vault, and we encrypt whatever is put inside. As long as the vault is unlocked, files can be added to or deleted from it just like any regular filesystem, but once we lock it, no one will be able to peek inside or guess what's in the vault.

This technique will give you an encrypted vault mounted under a directory. You can then add files to it as you wish, and once locked, you can copy it and open it up in Windows.

We'll be using a tool called **cryptsetup** that will help us create and manage the encrypted containers:

```
pi@raspberrypi ~ $ sudo apt-get install cryptsetup
```

1. First, we need to create an empty file to hold our vault. Here you'll have to decide how much storage space to allocate to your vault. Once created, you won't be able to increase the size, so think about what kind of files you plan to store and their average size. Use the following command, but replace [size] with the number of megabytes you'd like to allocate:

```
pi@raspberrypi ~ $ dd if=/dev/zero of=~/myvault.vol
bs=1M count=[size]
```

2. Next, we'll create an encrypted filesystem inside the myvault.vol file compatible with a platform-independent standard called **Linux Unified Key Setup (LUKS)**. We'll specify -t vfat to get a FAT32 filesystem that can be accessed under Windows. If you don't intend to move the container, you may prefer ext4:

```
pi@raspberrypi ~ $ sudo luksformat -t vfat ~/myvault.vol
```

> Since formatting something will overwrite whatever was there before, even though it's just a single file in this case, you'll be prompted with a warning and will have to type **YES** in all caps to initiate the process. Next, you'll be asked (three times) for a password that will be required to unlock your vault. You can safely ignore the warning from mkfs.vfat about drive geometry.

3. If you're curious about the encryption in use on your vault, you can type the following command to get a detailed report:

```
pi@raspberrypi ~ $ sudo cryptsetup luksDump
~/myvault.vol
```

> You'll see that cryptsetup uses AES encryption by default and that the LUKS format actually allows multiple passwords to unlock your vault as displayed by the **Key Slots**. Type cryptsetup --help to get a list of possible actions that can be performed on your vault.

4. Now that the vault has been created, let's see how we would use it. First we need to unlock it with the following command:

```
pi@raspberrypi ~ $ sudo cryptsetup luksOpen
~/myvault.vol myvault
```

> Once you've entered the correct password, your vault will be made available in `/dev/mapper` under the name we've specified at the end of the line, `/dev/mapper/myvault` in this case. You can now use this device as if it was a regular attached hard disk.

5. The next step is to mount the vault under a directory in `/home/pi` for easy access. Let's create the directory first:

```
pi@raspberrypi ~ $ mkdir ~/vault
```

6. Now we can mount the vault using the following command:

```
pi@raspberrypi ~ $ sudo mount -o uid=1000,gid=1000
/dev/mapper/myvault ~/vault
```

> The user ID/group ID arguments that we specify here are specifically for the FAT32 filesystem. It ensures that the `pi` user (which has an uid/gid of `1000`) will be able to write to the `~/vault` directory. With an `ext4` filesystem, these extra flags are not necessary because the permissions of the directory itself determine access.

That's all there is to it. You can now start filling up the `~/vault` directory. Use `df -h ~/vault` to keep an eye on the space available in the vault.

To safely close the vault, you need to unmount it first with the following command:

```
pi@raspberrypi ~ $ sudo umount ~/vault
```

Now, most importantly, remember to lock your vault:

```
pi@raspberrypi ~ $ sudo cryptsetup luksClose myvault
```

To make the daily locking/unlocking routine a little less tedious, you can define these aliases:

```
alias vaulton='sudo cryptsetup luksOpen ~/myvault.vol myvault && sudo mount
-o uid=1000,gid=1000 /dev/mapper/myvault ~/vault'
alias vaultoff='sudo umount ~/vault && sudo cryptsetup luksClose myvault'
```

To access your vault from Windows, try FreeOTFE Explorer. It's a portable application and very easy to use. Download it here: `https://sourceforge.net/projects/freeotfe.m irror`

Install the application, copy your vault file from the Pi withWinSCP or Dropbox, and unlock it in FreeOTFE Explorer using your passphrase:

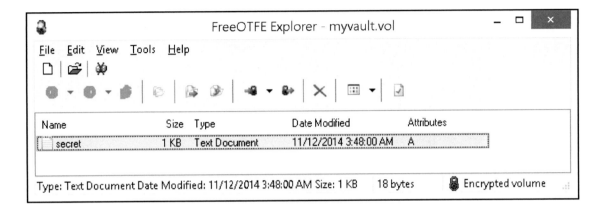

Accessing an encrypted file container with FreeOTFE Explorer

# Erasing the Pi should it fall into the wrong hands

No secret agent device worth its name would be complete without a self-destruct mechanism. While we can't quite make the Pi disappear in a puff of smoke, we can rig a sneaky booby trap that will eliminate all traces of our secret agent setup if the Pi were to get caught behind enemy lines.

First we are going to encrypt our entire home directory. Since we've been doing all of our pranks and projects inside the `pi` user's home directory, if someone were to read the SD card on another computer, they wouldn't be able to get any valuable data from the card except for a pretty standard Raspbian installation.

Then we'll add an optional wipe trigger-mechanism, which can be initiated either locally from a USB keyboard, or remotely via SSH, that will erase our encrypted home directory and replace it with an empty, innocent-looking, and original home directory.

# Encrypting your home with eCryptfs

eCryptfs is a stacked cryptographic file system. Unlike the cryptsetup/LUKS encryption system that we saw in the previous section, it is layered on top of an existing file system and encrypts/decrypts individual files on the fly (as they are read and written).

**Note:** For this exercise to work successfully, you need to be logged directly into the Pi's Terminal as the root user and not over a SSH session:

1. Let's install the necessary tools:

```
root@raspberrypi ~ # apt-get install ecryptfs-utils
lsof cryptsetup
```

2. Next, we need to load the `ecryptfs` kernel module:

```
root@raspberrypi ~ # modprobe ecryptfs
```

3. To help us migrate to an encrypted home directory, `ecryptfs` provides a handy script that will make some initial safety checks and then guide us through the whole process. The script will ensure that no running process is reading or writing files to our home directory. Now we can try running the `ecryptfs` home directory migration script:

```
root@raspberrypi / # ecryptfs-migrate-home -u pi
```

   If it finds any files being accessed in `/home/pi`, it will print the process that is holding the file open together with its process ID (PID). You'll have to shut down the offending application nicely, or kill it using the `kill [pid]` command.

4. With the initial checks out of the way, the migration script will now ask for your **login passphrase**. This is your regular login password for the `pi` user.

   The script will now rename your current home directory, create an encrypted home directory, and copy all the contents back, encrypting everything as it goes.

```
pi@raspberrypi / $ sudo ecryptfs-migrate-home -u pi
INFO:  Checking disk space, this may take a few moments.  Please be patient.
INFO:  Checking for open files in /home/pi
INFO:  The following files are in use:

    COMMAND  PID USER   FD   TYPE DEVICE SIZE/OFF   NODE NAME
    tmux    4059  pi  cwd    DIR  179,2     4096 262429 /home/pi
    bash    4060  pi  cwd    DIR  179,2     4096 262429 /home/pi

ERROR:  Cannot proceed.
pi@raspberrypi / $ tmux attach
[exited]
pi@raspberrypi / $ sudo ecryptfs-migrate-home -u pi
INFO:  Checking disk space, this may take a few moments.  Please be patient.
INFO:  Checking for open files in /home/pi
Enter your login passphrase [pi]:

************************************************************************
YOU SHOULD RECORD YOUR MOUNT PASSPHRASE AND STORE IT IN A SAFE LOCATION.
  ecryptfs-unwrap-passphrase ~/.ecryptfs/wrapped-passphrase
THIS WILL BE REQUIRED IF YOU NEED TO RECOVER YOUR DATA AT A LATER TIME.
************************************************************************


Done configuring.

chown: cannot access '/dev/shm/.ecryptfs-pi': No such file or directory
INFO:  Encrypted home has been set up, encrypting files now...this may take a while.
sending incremental file list
./
.bash_logout
         220 100%    0.00kB/s    0:00:00 (xfer#1, to-check=3/5)
.bashrc
        3243 100%  633.40kB/s    0:00:00 (xfer#2, to-check=2/5)
.profile
         675 100%   43.95kB/s    0:00:00 (xfer#3, to-check=1/5)
pistore.desktop -> /usr/share/indiecity/pistore/pistore.desktop

sent 4431 bytes  received 75 bytes  9012.00 bytes/sec
total size is 4182  speedup is 0.93


========================================================================
Some Important Notes!

  1. The file encryption appears to have completed successfully, however,
     pi MUST LOGIN IMMEDIATELY, _BEFORE_THE_NEXT_REBOOT_,
     TO COMPLETE THE MIGRATION!!!

  2. If pi can log in and read and write their files, then the migration is complete,
     and you should remove /home/pi.c1U0KkNX.
     Otherwise, restore /home/pi.c1U0KkNX back to /home/pi.

  3. pi should also run 'ecryptfs-unwrap-passphrase' and record
     their randomly generated mount passphrase as soon as possible.

  4. To ensure the integrity of all encrypted data on this system, you
     should also encrypted swap space with 'ecryptfs-setup-swap'.
========================================================================
```

Migration to encrypted home directory with eCryptfs

Once the migration script has finished, we're going to follow the advice it gave us very closely.

5. Log out now and log back in as the `pi` user. You'll notice that the time it takes to log in has increased dramatically because of the automatic `ecryptfs` mounting that's going on in the background.

6. Once you're logged in, type `ls` to verify that your home directory looks roughly intact. Then type `mount` to verify that an `ecryptfs` file system is really mounted over `/home/pi`, like in the following screenshot:

```
pi@raspberrypi ~ $ mount
/home/pi/.Private on /home/pi type ecryptfs (rw,nosuid,nodev,relatime,ecryptfs_fnek_sig=1c015f2ff90
34631,ecryptfs_sig=04404d0ca6fa5cb5,ecryptfs_cipher=aes,ecryptfs_key_bytes=16,ecryptfs_unlink_sigs)
```

Encrypted file system mounted on top of home directory

7. If everything seems fine, you should now delete the unencrypted backup copy of your home directory that the migration script made previously. The name of this directory was randomly generated and is called `/home/pi.[XXXXXXXX]`. Type `ls /home` to find the name of yours, then issue the following command:

```
pi@raspberrypi ~ $ sudo rm -rf /home/pi.[XXXXXXXX]
```

8. (Optional) Type the following command to reveal your recovery mount password:

```
pi@raspberrypi ~ $ ecryptfs-unwrap-passphrase
```

This randomly generated passphrase can be used to recover your data from another computer.

9. Finally, we're going to encrypt the swap file on our system. A swap file/partition is a reserved area on the SD card that can be used by the kernel to move data in and out of memory. On Raspbian, this 100Mb file is called `/var/swap` and is very rarely used. But just to make absolutely sure our encrypted home directory data doesn't leak into the swap file, we can run the following command:

```
pi@raspberrypi ~ $ sudo ecryptfs-setup-swap
```

# Rigging the self-destruct mechanism

Even though your home directory is much more secure now that it's encrypted, there are still situations where one might want to abort a mission and pull the plug on the important data. For instance, let's say you're continuously recording inside a `tmux` session; your data remains mounted and unencrypted until the `pi` user logs out.

We will construct a booby trap hooked into the Raspbian login system. There will be two versions of the trigger mechanism:

- A special login name of your choice is used as a trigger word. As soon as you try to log in as this user, directly on the console with a keyboard or remotely over SSH, the encrypted `pi` home directory is wiped clean and recreated.
- A certain number of failed login attempts as the `pi` user will be used as a trigger signal to wipe the encrypted home directory and recreate it.

The beauty of having both versions is that the special login name can be triggered by you from a distance, and the failed login attempt could be triggered by a foe trying to gain access to the Pi.

1. The Raspbian login system uses **Pluggable Authentication Module (PAM)** to authenticate users. That's where we need to put our hook for the booby trap. Open up the common authentication configuration file for editing with the following command:

   **pi@raspberrypi ~ $ sudo nano /etc/pam.d/common-auth**

2. Find the line that contains **success=1** and change it to **success=2**.

   > This directive specifies how many rules to skip if the user login is successful. We change it to 2 because we're going to add a new rule next.

   > Create a new line under the one we just changed and put the following:

   ```
   auth optional pam_exec.so /home/slatfatf.sh
   ```

   > This rule means that when a user login fails, a script that we'll write, called `/home/slatfatf.sh`, will be run. You're free to name the script whatever you want and place it in any location (except the `pi` home directory).

3. Now create another new line at the bottom of the file and put the following:

```
auth optional pam_exec.so /bin/rm -f /home/slatfatf.count
```

This rule will reset the bad login counter whenever `pi` logs in successfully:

```
  GNU nano 2.2.6             File: /etc/pam.d/common-auth                    Modified

# /etc/pam.d/common-auth - authentication settings common to all services
#
# This file is included from other service-specific PAM config files,
# and should contain a list of the authentication modules that define
# the central authentication scheme for use on the system
# (e.g., /etc/shadow, LDAP, Kerberos, etc.).  The default is to use the
# traditional Unix authentication mechanisms.
#
# As of pam 1.0.1-6, this file is managed by pam-auth-update by default.
# To take advantage of this, it is recommended that you configure any
# local modules either before or after the default block, and use
# pam-auth-update to manage selection of other modules.  See
# pam-auth-update(8) for details.

# here are the per-package modules (the "Primary" block)
auth    [success=2 default=ignore]      pam_unix.so nullok_secure
auth    optional                        pam_exec.so /home/slatfatf.sh
# here's the fallback if no module succeeds
auth    requisite                       pam_deny.so
# prime the stack with a positive return value if there isn't one already;
# this avoids us returning an error just because nothing sets a success code
# since the modules above will each just jump around
auth    required                        pam_permit.so
# and here are more per-package modules (the "Additional" block)
auth    optional                        pam_ecryptfs.so unwrap
auth    optional                        pam_exec.so /bin/rm -f /home/slatfatf.count
# end of pam-auth-update config

^G Get Help   ^O WriteOut   ^R Read File   ^Y Prev Page   ^K Cut Text    ^C Cur Pos
^X Exit       ^J Justify    ^W Where Is    ^V Next Page   ^U UnCut Text  ^T To Spell
```

PAM configuration altered to execute custom script on failure

4. Now all we need is the script to run on login failures. Open it up for editing:

```
pi@raspberrypi ~ $ sudo nano /home/slatfatf.sh
#!/bin/bash
TRIGGER_USER="phoenix"
MAXFAIL=3
COUNTFILE=/home/slatfatf.count
```

```
self_destruct() {
  pkill -KILL -u pi
  umount /home/pi
  rm -rf /home/pi
  mkhomedir_helper pi
  rm -rf /home/.ecryptfs
  rm -f $COUNTFILE
  # rm -f /home/slatfatf.sh
}

if [ $PAM_USER == $TRIGGER_USER ]; then
  # self_destruct
  exit
fi

if [ $PAM_USER == "pi" ]; then
  if [ -f $COUNTFILE ]; then
    FAILCOUNT=$(cat $COUNTFILE)
    ((FAILCOUNT++))
    if [ $FAILCOUNT -ge $MAXFAIL ]; then
      # self_destruct
      exit
    else
      echo $FAILCOUNT > $COUNTFILE
    fi
  else
    echo "1" > $COUNTFILE
  fi
fi
```

 There are three comments in the previous script that work as safety pins to prevent you from accidentally deleting your home directory or the script itself. Remove them once you understand how the script works.

- The TRIGGER_USER variable holds the username that will trigger an immediate wipe of the home directory. Note that this should not be a real user account on the system.
- The MAXFAIL variable sets the number of failed login attempts in a row by the pi user that triggers a wipe of the home directory.
- The COUNTFILE variable holds the path to a text file that will be used to keep track of the number of failed login attempts by the pi user.

- The `self_destruct` function is where all the action is. It deletes and recreates the `pi` user's home directory and erases a few traces of eCryptfs.
- The `PAM_USER` variable is passed to our script from the `pam_exec.so` module that started our script. It contains the name that was entered at the login prompt and failed to authenticate.
- If the user that failed to log in was our `TRIGGER_USER`, then start the `self_destruct` sequence.
- If the user that failed to log in was `pi`, see whether the number in `FAILCOUNT` is greater, or equal to `MAXFAIL` and if so, start the `self_destruct` sequence.

5. The last step is to make the script executable with the following command:

```
pi@raspberrypi ~ $ sudo chmod +x /home/slatfatf.sh
```

> To verify that your trigger mechanism is set up correctly, you can make a faiied login attempt with the `pi` user to see that the `/home/slatfatf.count` file is created.

# Jam the airwaves with a Pi Zero

Our final project in this chapter is the ultimate in mischievous mayhem. We're going to use our Pi Zero to take over the airwaves by transmitting whatever audio we choose to a standard **FM radio** by using a rather nifty piece of software called **PiFm**. PiFm was originally written by Oliver Mattos and Oskar Weigl, and updated by a guy called Ryan Grassel.

The Pi Zero is perfect for this, because of its small size, and can be integrated with our wearable audio recorder built in `Chapter 2`, *Audio Antics*, so you can interfere with FM radio reception out in the field.

 **Very important:** The laws for broadcasting FM signals—even over a short distance—vary from country to country. Ensure you check your local regulations before attempting this project.

In order to get range out of your **radio jammer** you'll need to solder a 20cm piece of wire to pin 4 of your Pi Zero's GPIO connector to act as an antenna. This should give a surprising range—perhaps up to 20 or 30 meters.

**Compatibility Note:** Owing to the way this software works, it's dependent on the operating clock speed of your Raspberry Pi. Having tested this, PiFm currently doesn't work on the Pi Model 2 or Pi Model 3 because they operate at a higher operating speed than it was originally designed for. Therefore, this project will only work with the Pi Zero and also earlier models such as the Model 1 B+ and B.

# Installing PiFm

Let's get the code and compile it:

1. Download the source code from the Git repository:

```
pi@raspberrypi ~ $ sudo git clone https://github.com/rm-hull/pifm
```

2. Change directories to pifm:

```
pi@raspberrypi ~ $ cd pifm
```

3. Compile the PiFm application with:

```
pi@raspberrypi ~ $ sudo make
```

# Broadcasting to the airwaves

Copy across a few of your favorite MP3 files to the Pi and put them in the default /home/pi/Music directory.

PiFm currently works only with 16-bit 22050 Hzfiles in the WAV format. But this is OK, as we can use the **SoX** sound exchange processor we installed in *Chapter 2, Audio Antics,* to take your MP3 file and convert it into the required WAV file on-the-fly and direct it to **PiFm** using the following command:

```
@raspberrypi ~ $ sox -t mp3 /home/pi/Music/somesong.mp3
-t wav -r 22050 -c 1 - | sudo /home/pi/pifm/pifm - 88.5
```

If you want to stash your mp3 files in a different directory, simply change the directory path that's underlined in the command above.

The above command works by converting the MP3 file into a WAV file using SoX, changing its audio sampling rate to 22050 Hz (-r 22050), and down-mixing the track to a single mono channel (-c 1). The converted track is then sent to the standard output, denoted by the hyphen sign (-) and is then piped (|) into the input of the pifm command.

**Caution:** Commands and filenames are case sensitive in Linux, so make sure you duplicate the exact capitalization of the previous commands (for example, the /Music folder name).

Now we have our favorite tune broadcasting, grab a radio and tune your dial to 88.5 MHz to listen to the audio output of your Pi Zero.

You can also do other clever things such as broadcasting your voice by piping the output of the arecord command, as we did in Chapter 2, *Audio Antics*, to send to an audio device, or by using SoX to access a live Internet stream and broadcasting that over FM.

# Summary

We kicked off our final chapter with a few words of advice about taking your Pi outside the house. You learned that a battery pack is a good source of power for the Pi and that you can be very creative with your housing as long as the container is resistant to moisture.

As you wouldn't bring a router or access point with you outside, we looked at how to connect a laptop directly to the Pi using either a wired connection with static IP addressing or an ad-hoc Wi-Fi network. Should you need to connect more than two computers, you also have the option of turning the Pi into a Wi-Fi access point with optional Internet sharing, including connecting to the mobile Internet using a USB modem dongle. Concluding our look at Internet connectivity, we became anonymous on the Internet by connecting to the Tor network.

We then expanded our outdoor adventure with a GPS receiver and saw how to track the Pi's position in real time on Google Earth. You also learned how to log waypoints along the route, so that the journey can be retraced on Google Earth at a later time, and how to massage GPS data collected from Kismet into an access point map. Finally, we explored the GPS as an alternative time source for the Pi and how all the GPS features we've covered could be started at boot time with a simple script.

We moved over to our smartphone for a spell and saw how an Android or iPhone app could be used to construct a custom remote control by sending commands over SSH to the Pi at the touch of a button.

Proving that machines can also be social, we let the Pi post status updates on Twitter on a regular basis with an optional link to a longer document and GPS coordinates. We could also let it send e-mails to inform us about important updates at regular intervals using the Cron scheduler.

Sharing files between the Pi, and all your other devices, was made a little easier using the Dropbox online file hosting service, where a common folder can be kept synchronized and up to date among all computers.

We took a closer look at data encryption and how we could create a vault to hold selected sensitive data. We then expanded upon the idea to encrypt our home directory and saw how to implement an optional self-destruct mechanism that would wipe the home directory clean in case of tampering.

Finally, we looked at how to create the ultimate mayhem by using our Pi as an FM transmitter and jammer, and taking over the airwaves using a clever piece of software and a short piece of wire.

In our next and final chapter we're going to protect our territory from enemy spies and unwanted intrusions using a variety of sensors and gadgets.

# 6
# Detecting and Protecting Against Your Enemies

In our final masterclass, we're going to look at ways to detect infiltrations and protect ourselves against other would-be spies. To help us do this, we will be plugging sensors and other gadgets into our Raspberry Pi so we can be alerted when people stray into our territories.

The Raspberry Pi has lots of ways of connecting things to it, such as plugging things into the USB ports, connecting devices to the onboard camera and display ports, and to the various interfaces that make up the **GPIO (General Purpos Input/Output)** connector. As part of our detection and protection regime, we'll be focusing mainly on connecting things to the GPIO connector.

During this chapter we will:

- Explore the GPIO and how to connect things safely to it
- Build a laser trip wire to protect corridors and entrances
- Protect areas of space using a passive infrared detector
- Send messages to our phone using SMS rather than e-mail
- Gain access to certain files on your Pi using your mobile phone as an access control device
- Send secret encoded messages to your fellow agents using an LED display
- Use the Pi Zero as a portable hardware random number generator to improve encryption on other PCs and servers.

# Say hello to the GPIO

The GPIO connector is the large group of pins on the edge of your Raspberry Pi board. On earlier models, there were 26 pins that made up this connector. Since the Model B+ there are now 40 pins, although the first 26 pins are identical to the previous models, and it's these 26 pins we'll be working with. You won't need to worry about the rest of the pins.

Essentially, the GPIO connector provides access to:

- Power supplies
- Digital I/O pins
- I²C bus
- SPI bus
- UART Serial bus

Some of the pins on the GPIO have more than one purpose, depending on how they are programmed. The following diagram is a reference guide to all of the pins on the GPIO. The GPIO numbers on the yellow labels relate directly to those on the Broadcom chip, and are numbers generally used within the scripts:

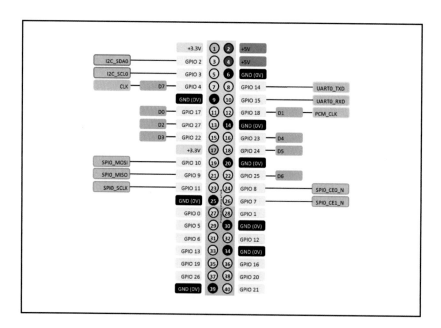

GPIO connector pin-out

# Power connections

The GPIO connector also provides access to the onboard power supplies. The +5V connection (pins 2 and 4) is essentially the +5V input from the external power supply connected to the micro-USB power port. This can be used to power small external circuits if necessary, although it is recommended that an additional external +5V supply is used, if significant current is required.

The +3.3V supply (pins 1 and 17) is the output from the onboard 3.3V regulator, and provides a small amount of current up to 50mA. If you need to draw more than 50mA for your external circuits then you should use an external power supply.

IMPORTANT: The I/O pins on the Raspberry Pi operate at 3.3V levels. Connecting voltages higher than this to the pins could irreversibly damage your Pi. If you follow the instructions in this book, then everything should be fine, but randomly connecting things to your Pi that use lots of power will break it!

Shameless plug alert: If you're interest in building more sophisticated security systems, or want to learn more about using the Pi's various interfaces, then my previous book, *Building a Home Security System with Raspberry Pi*, published by *Packt Publishing*, will show you how:

```
https://www.packtpub.com/hardware-and-creative/building-home-security-s
ystem-raspberry-pi
```

So, now we know a little bit more about the Raspberry Pi's GPIO connector, let's get on and play with it. You won't need to do any soldering, but you will need to connect things to the GPIO connector with bits of jumper wire.

# Building a laser trip wire

You may have seen Wallace and Gromit's short film, *The Wrong Trousers,* where the penguin uses a contraption to control Wallace in his sleep, making him break into a museum to steal the big shiny diamond. The diamond is surrounded by laser beams, but when one of the beams is broken, the alarms go off and the diamond is protected with a cage!

In this project, I'm going to show you how to set up a laser beam and have our Raspberry Pi alert us when the beam is broken— aka a laser trip wire. For this, we're going to need to use a Waveshare Laser Sensor module (`www.waveshare.com`), which is readily available to buy on Amazon for around £10 / $15.

The module comes complete with jumper wires, that allow us to easily connect it to the GPIO connector in the Pi:

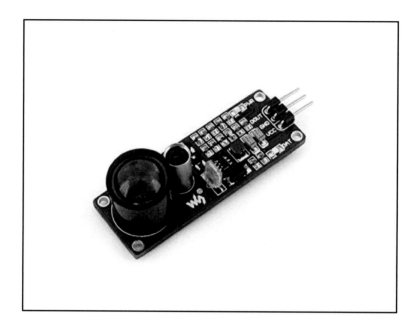

The Waveshare laser sensor module contains both the transmitter and receiver

# How it works

The module contains both a laser transmitter and receiver. The laser beam is transmitted from the gold tube on the module at a particular modulating frequency. The beam will then be reflected off a surface, such as a wall or skirting board, and be picked up by the light sensor lens at the top of the module.

The receiver will only detect light that is modulated at the same frequency as the laser beam, and so does not get affected by visible light. This particular module works best when the reflective surface is between 80 and 120 cm away from the laser transmitter.

When the beam is interrupted and prevented from reflecting back to the receiver, this is detected and the data pin will be triggered. A script monitoring the data pin on the Pi will then do something when it detects this trigger.

Important: Don't ever look directly into the laser beam as it will hurt your eyes, and may irreversibly damage them. Make sure the unit is facing away from you when you wire it up.

# Wiring it up

This particular device runs from a power supply of between 2.5V and 5.0V. Since our GPIO inputs require 3.3V maximum when a high level is input, we will use the 3.3V supply from our Raspberry Pi to power the device:

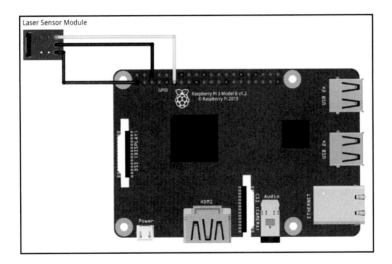

Wiring diagram for the laser sensor module

1. Connect the included 3-hole connector to the three pins at the bottom of the laser module, with the red wire on the left (the pin marked **VCC**).
2. Referring to the earlier GPIO pin-out diagram, connect the yellow wire to pin 11 of the GPIO connector (labeled **D0/GPIO 17**).
3. Connect the black wire to pin 6 of the GPIO connector (labeled **GND/0V**).
4. Connect the red wire to pin 1 of the GPIO connector (3.3V). The module should now come alive.
5. The red LED on the left of the module will come on if the beam is interrupted.

This is what it should look like in reallife:

The laser module connected to the Raspberry Pi

# Writing the detection script

Now that we have connected the laser sensor module to our Raspberry Pi, we need to write a little script that will detect when the beam has been broken.

In this project, we've connected our sensor output to **D0,** which is **GPIO17** (refer to the earlier GPIO pin-out diagram). We need to create file access for the pin by entering the following command:

```
pi@raspberrypi ~ $ sudo echo 17 > /sys/class/gpio/export
```

And now, set its direction to *in*:

```
pi@raspberrypi ~ $ sudo echo in > sys/class/gpio/gpio17/direction
```

We're now ready to read its value, and we can do this with the following command:

```
pi@raspberrypi ~ $ sudo cat /sys/class/gpio/gpio17/value
```

You'll notice that it will have returned 1 (digital high state) if the beam reflection is detected, or a (digital low state) if the beam is interrupted.

We can create a script to poll for the beam state:

```bash
#!/bin/bash
sudo echo 17 > /sys/class/gpio/export
sudo echo in > /sys/class/gpio/gpio17/direction

# loop forever
while true
do
  # read the beam state
  BEAM=$(sudo cat /sys/class/gpio/gpio17/value)

  if [ $BEAM == 1 ]; then
    #beam not blocked
    echo "OK"

  else
    #beam was broken
    echo "ALERT"
  fi
done
```

Code listing for beam-sensor.sh

When you run the script, you should see **OK** scroll up the screen. Now interrupt the beam using your hand and you should see **ALERT** scroll up the console screen until you remove your hand.

Don't forget that once we've finished with the GPIO port, it's tidy to remove its file access:

```
pi@raspberrypi ~ $ sudo echo 17 > /sys/class/gpio/unexport
```

We've now seen how to easily read a GPIO input; the same wiring principle and script can be used to read other sensors, such as motion detectors or anything else that has an on and off state, and act upon their status.

# Protecting an entire area

Our laser trip wire is great for being able to detect when someone walks through a doorway or down a corridor, but what if we wanted to know if people are in a particular area or a whole room?

Well, we can with a basic motion sensor, otherwise known as a passive infrared (PIR) detector. These detectors come in a variety of types, and you may have seen them lurking in the corners of rooms, but fundamentally, they all work the same way, by detecting the presence of body heat in relation to the background temperature, within a certain area, and so are commonly used to trigger alarm systems when somebody (or something such as a pet cat) has entered a room.

For the covert surveillance of our private zone, we're going to use a small Parallax PIR Sensor, available from many online Pi-friendly stores such as **ModMyPi**, Robot Shop, or Adafruit for less than £10 / $15. This little device will detect the presence of enemies within a 10 meter range of it. If you can't obtain one of these types then there are other types that will work just as well, but the wiring might be different to that explained in this project:

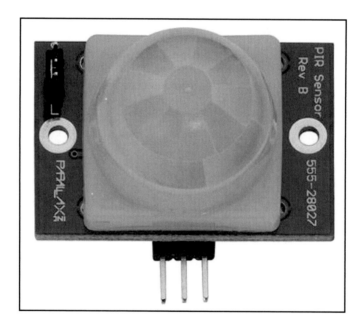

Parallax passive infrared motion sensor

# Wiring it up

As with our laser sensor module, this device also just needs three wires to connect it to the Raspberry Pi. However, they are connected differently on the sensor, as shown below:

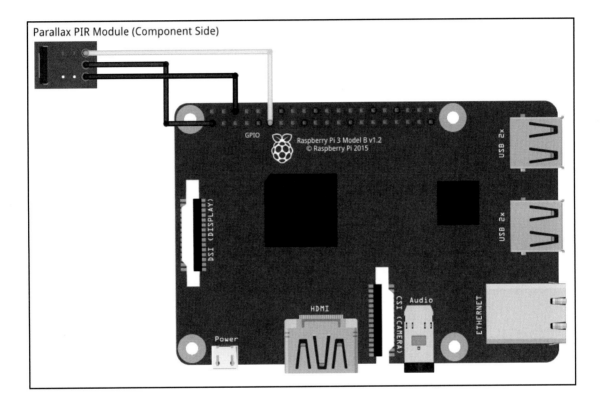

Wiring diagram for the Parallax PIR motion sensor module

1. Referring to the earlier GPIO pin-out diagram, connect the yellow wire to pin 11 of the GPIO connector (labelled **D0 /GPIO 17**), with the other end connecting to the OUT pin on the PIR module.
2. Connect the black wire to pin 6 of the GPIO connector (labelled **GND / 0V**), with the other end connecting to the GND pin on the PIR module.
3. Connect the red wire to pin 1 of the GPIO connector (3.3V), with the other end connecting to the VCC pin on the module. The module should now come alive, and you'll notice the light switching on and off as it detects your movement around it.

This is what it should look like for real:

PIR motion sensor connected to Raspberry Pi

# Implementing the detection script

The detection script for the PIR motion sensor is similar to the one we created for the laser sensor module in the previous section.

Once again, we've connected our sensor output to **D0,** which is **GPIO17** (refer to the earlier GPIO pin-out diagram). We create file access for the pin by entering the following command:

```
pi@raspberrypi ~ $ sudo echo 17 > /sys/class/gpio/export
```

We then set its direction to in:

```
pi@raspberrypi ~ $ sudo echo in >/sys/class/gpio/gpio17/direction
```

We're now ready to read its value, and we can do this with the following command:

```
pi@raspberrypi ~ $ sudo cat /sys/class/gpio/gpio17/value
```

You'll notice that this time, the PIR module will have returned 1 (digital high state) if the motion is detected, or a (digital low state) if there is no motion detected.

We can modify our previous script to poll for the motion-detected state:

```
#!/bin/bash
sudo echo 17 > /sys/class/gpio/export
sudo echo in > /sys/class/gpio/gpio17/direction

# loop forever
while true
do
  # read the beam state
  BEAM=$(sudo cat /sys/class/gpio/gpio17/value)

  if [ $BEAM == 0 ]; then
    #no motion detected
    echo "OK"

  else
    #motion was detected
    echo "INTRUDER!"
  fi
done
```

Code listing for motion-sensor.sh

When you run the script, you should see **OK** scroll up the screen if everything is nice and still. Now move in front of the PIR's detection area and you should see **INTRUDER!** scroll up the console screen until you are still again.

Again, don't forget that once we've finished with the GPIO port, we should remove its file access:

```
pi@raspberrypi ~ $ sudo echo 17 > /sys/class/gpio/unexport
```

# Sending alerts to your phone using SMS

We saw in Chapter 5, *Taking Your Pi Off-road*, how to send e-mails from the Raspberry Pi so that we can pick them up on our smartphone. But what if we're in an area where we can't get a good mobile Internet signal? All of our elaborate work to protect our things or get status updates from the field goes to waste because we don't get alerted in time.

SMS (**Simple Messaging Service**)—or text messaging—actually uses the mobile voice channel to deliver the message to your handset rather than the mobile Internet channel, so you're likely to receive your message in areas of poor reception and where there is no data service.

# SMS gateway

Fortunately, sending a text message from our Pi can be as easy as making a URL request to a server if we choose an SMS gateway provider with a good API, such as **BulkSMS**. You can sign up for a UK account at `http://www.bulksms.com/countries/u/united-king dom`, and just about any other country at `http://www.bulksms.com`. They have good documentation for their API which can be found at `http://developer.bulksms.com/ea pi/`.

# Sending messages through the API

Once you've opened an account, to send an SMS message from your Pi to a mobile phone through the BulkSMS API, you need to send an HTTP POST request containing several parameters. Fortunately, this is pretty straightforward using the `curl` command in conjunction with the `--data-urlencode` option, which POSTs the name-value pair to the base URL for the API.

So, to send an SMS with the text `Infiltration Alert!` to the mobile number `447700000000`, we would simply run the following command:

```
pi@raspberrypi ~ $ curl
http://www.bulksms.co.uk/eapi/submission/send_sms/2/2.0
--data-urlencode username="<your username>"
--data-urlencode password="<your password>"
--data-urlencode msisdn="447700000000"
--data-urlencode message="Infiltration Alert!"
--data-urlencode stop_dup_id="20160529192254"
```

All being well, within a few seconds, you should have the SMS message arrive on your phone.

Since it's just a simple piece of Bash script, you can easily slot this in the earlier sensor examples to text you when there is a security breach at HQ.

# Use your phone as an access control device

We saw in Chapter 4, *Wi-Fi Pranks-Exploring Your Network*, how we could use our Raspberry Pi to scan the wireless networks to see what devices are around. Most smartphones come with either Wi-Fi or Bluetooth, or both, on them nowadays, which transmits an identifier unique to that device.

We can take advantage of that by using our phone as an access control device, so our Pi can know when we're nearby and act accordingly. For example, let's say if each time you were near your Pi with your smartphone, it could automatically unlock the encrypted container you set up in Chapter 5, *Taking Our Pi Off-Road*, and then lock it again when we're not nearby. By constantly scanning for our phone's broadcast packets, we can do this.

## Probe Requests

When a smartphone is searching for nearby routers to connect to, it will periodically broadcast packets of data called Probe Requests. The Probe Requests contain the unique MAC address of the device and often the name of a network to which it has previously connected. Phones do this because by actively scanning for nearby routers, they can initiate a wireless connection faster than if they wait for the router to send out what's called a Beacon Frame. We can use this to see what devices are around by scanning for these Probe Requests.

## Scanning with tshark

To do all the hard work of the Wi-Fi scanning, we're going to use tshark, which is a command-line version of the Wireshark utility we used in Chapter 4, *Wi-Fi Pranks – Exploring Your Network*. Let's get started by installing it:

```
pi@raspberrypi ~ $ sudo apt-get install tshark
```

During the installation, you'll receive the following prompt. Select **Yes:**

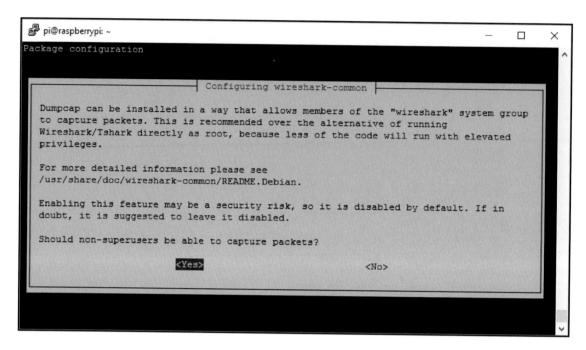

We now need to put our wireless device into monitor mode by running the following commands:

```
pi@raspberrypi ~ $ sudo ifconfig wlan0 down
pi@raspberrypi ~ $ sudo iwconfig wlan0 mode monitor
pi@raspberrypi ~ $ sudo ifconfig wlan0 up
```

As mentioned in Chapter 4, *Wi-Fi Pranks—Exploring Your Network*, the Wi-Fi chip built into the new Raspberry Pi 3 *does not* support monitor mode, therefore, you'll have plug in an external USB Wi-Fi dongle which does support monitor mode, such as the **Farnell element14 Wi-Pi** device. This will be seen by the Pi 3 as device wlan1 rather than wlan0.

Let's now test our Wi-Fi scanner by searching for devices for 30 seconds:

```
pi@raspberrypi ~ $ sudo tshark -i wlan0 -n -a duration:30
```

You should start seeing output on the console similar to the following screenshot:

```
pi@raspberrypi: ~                                                    —   ☐   ✕
pi@raspberrypi:~ $ sudo tshark -i wlan0 -n -a duration:30
tshark: Lua: Error during loading:
 [string "/usr/share/wireshark/init.lua"]:46: dofile has been disabled due to running Wiresha
rk as superuser. See http://wiki.wireshark.org/CaptureSetup/CapturePrivileges for help in run
ning Wireshark as an unprivileged user.
Running as user "root" and group "root". This could be dangerous.
Capturing on 'wlan0'
  1   0.000000 84:1b:5e:47.      . -> ff:ff:ff:ff:ff:ff 802.11 206 Beacon frame, SN=3399, FN=0,
 Flags=........, BI=200, SSID=CUBIK-WLAN
  2   0.396576 00:1f:3b:12:1..: -> ff:ff:ff:ff:ff:ff 802.11 88 Probe Request, SN=1133, FN=0,
 Flags=........, SSID=Broadcast
  3   0.426488 00:1f:3b:12:1..: / -> ff:ff:ff:ff:ff:ff 802.11 88 Probe Request, SN=1136, FN=0,
 Flags=........, SSID=Broadcast
  4   0.442669 00:1f:3b:12:.  .. -> ff:ff:ff:ff:ff:ff 802.11 101 Probe Request, SN=1137, FN=0
, Flags=........, SSID=CUBIK-WLAN-5G
  5   0.443505 00:1f:3b:12:.    -> ff:ff:ff:ff:ff:ff 802.11 88 Probe Request, SN=1138, FN=0,
 Flags=........, SSID=Broadcast
  6   0.459932 00:1f:3b:12:.   ⌐ -> ff:ff:ff:ff:ff:ff 802.11 88 Probe Request, SN=1139, FN=0,
 Flags=........, SSID=Broadcast
  7   0.631694 00:1f:3b:12:`   ` -> ff:ff:ff:ff:ff:ff 802.11 88 Probe Request, SN=1150, FN=0,
 Flags=........, SSID=Broadcast
  8   0.632652 00:1f:3b:12:.`  ./ -> ff:ff:ff:ff:ff:ff 802.11 101 Probe Request, SN=1151, FN=0
, Flags=........, SSID=CUBIK-WLAN-5G
  9   0.633495 00:1f:3b:12:.`    -> ff:ff:ff:ff:ff:ff 802.11 88 Probe Request, SN=1152, FN=0,
 Flags=........, SSID=Broadcast
 10   9.537858 d0:66:7b:02:.     -> ff:ff:ff:ff:ff:ff 802.11 161 Probe Request, SN=202, FN=0,
 Flags=........, SSID=BTHub5-PR6X
 11  10.158993 60:f1:89:85:ſ     -> 01:00:5e:00:^: · 802.11 175 Data, SN=3514, FN=0, Flags=.
p....F.
 12  25.329652 d0:66:7b:02:      ` -> ff:ff:ff:ff:ff:ff 802.11 161 Probe Request, SN=237, FN=0,
 Flags=........, SSID=BTHub5-PR6X
12 packets captured
pi@raspberrypi:~ $
```

Output from the tshark wlan scan

Note that you can ignore the error about Lua.

Now that we know our Wi-Fi scanner is picking up devices in the area, we can get it to detect our actual device; but first, we need to know what the MAC address of our device is. On an Android 6.x smartphone you can find this in **Settings** | **AboutDevice** | **Status**:

Wi-Fi MAC address shown in Android smartphone settings

As you can see from the preceding image, we will be looking for MAC address `60:F1:89:85:5B:EC`.

By applying a filter to the `tshark` command with the `-f` parameter, we can tell it to just output information about the MAC address we're interested. In this case:

```
pi@raspberrypi ~ $ sudo tshark -i wlan0 -n -a duration:30 -f
"ether host 60:f1:89:85:5b:ec"
```

You should then see outputs only for the specified MAC address. If you don't get any output, then you may not have run the scanner for long enough. You can change this with the `-a duration:` parameter. Also, sometimes the phone may not search for access points if it's busy doing something else or is in sleep mode—which is often the case when the phone is screen-locked.

By outputting the results to a file, we can then interrogate the file for our device's ID:

```
pi@raspberrypi ~ $ sudo tshark -i wlan0 -n -a duration:30 -f
"ether host 60:f1:89:85:5b:ec" > wifiscan.txt
```

Now we need to `grep` the generated file to see if our device was detected:

```
pi@raspberrypi ~ $ grep -qi '60:f1:89:85:5b:ec' wifiscan.txt && echo $?
```

If the device's MAC address was found, then the command will return:

Let's put this together in a simple shell script that will detect when our device is detected, which you can enhance to make it perform whatever task you want. In this script, we're also going to return the number of times it was detected in the period using grep's -c parameter:

```bash
#!/bin/bash
MAC="60:f1:89:85:5b:ec" #MAC address to find
FILEPATH="/home/pi/wifiscan.txt"
WIFI="wlan0"
#set up wifi device for monitoring
sudo ifconfig $WIFI down
sudo iwconfig $WIFI mode monitor
sudo ifconfig $WIFI up
while true
do
  #scan wifi probe requests
  echo "Scanning..."
  sudo tshark -i $WIFI -n -a duration:15 -f "ether host $MAC" >
$FILEPATH
  #get number of times found - case insensitive
  FOUND=$(grep -ci $MAC $FILEPATH)
  echo "Result: $FOUND"
  if [ $FOUND -gt 0 ]; then
    #device found
    echo "DEVICE FOUND"
  else
    #device not found
    echo "DEVICE NOT FOUND"
  fi
done
```

wifi-scan.sh

Then make the script executable with the following:

```
pi@raspberrypi ~ $ chmod +x wifi-scan.sh
```

Run the script with this:

```
pi@raspberrypi ~ $ ./wifi-scan.sh
```

You should then see something like the following screenshot:

```
pi@raspberrypi: ~                                              —    □    ✕

pi@raspberrypi:~ $ sudo ./wifi-scan.sh
Scanning...
tshark: Lua: Error during loading:
 [string "/usr/share/wireshark/init.lua"]:46: dofile has been disabled due to ru
nning Wireshark as superuser. See http://wiki.wireshark.org/CaptureSetup/Capture
Privileges for help in running Wireshark as an unprivileged user.
Running as user "root" and group "root". This could be dangerous.
Capturing on 'wlan1'
7
Result: 7
DEVICE FOUND
```

You now have a script that can do something you want when it detects your device over Wi-Fi.

# Displaying secret codes and messages

Let's say that you need to leave your fellow agents a message in a particular location, but you don't want anyone else to know what it contains. You could write the encoded message on a piece of paper so it could be decoded by hand, but it would be much more convenient to show the encoded message electronically on a display, so it can easily be changed—even from a remote location.

For this project, we're going to use Ciseco's Pi-Lite board, which sits on top of the Raspberry Pi, plugged into the GPIO connector. It features a matrix of 126 LEDs combined with a small microcontroller enabling the device to be easily programmed using the Pi's serial port:

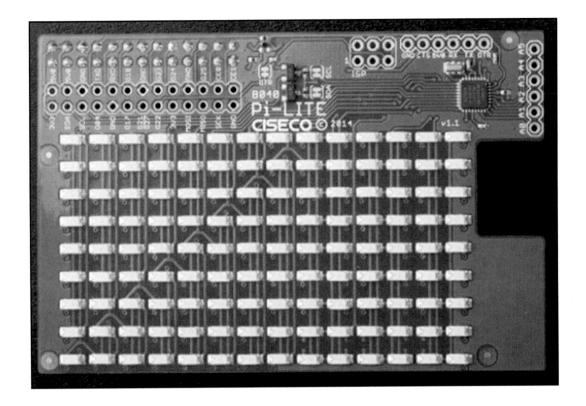

Ciseco Pi-Lite board contains 126 LEDs

# Enabling the serial port

Before we can access the serial port we need to enable it for our own use on the Pi, as by default, it's used for the terminal console. Fortunately, this is now straightforward on the latest Raspbian releases:

1. Launch the Raspberry Pi configuration tool with the following command:

   ```
   pi@raspberrypi ~ $ sudo raspi-config
   ```

2. Select option 9-Advanced Options.
3. In the next screen, select option A7 Serial.
4. Select No to disable the console serial port.
5. Reboot your Pi to apply the settings.

# Connecting the Pi-Lite

Make sure your Pi is switched off and connect the Pi-Lite to the GPIO connector. Note that the connector only has 26 pins, as it will work on older Pis that didn't feature the 40-pin GPIO port, so just plug it into the first 26 pins if yours has 40 pins.

When you power up your Pi, the Pi-Lite LEDs will display a start-up sequence, and finish by displaying the words **Pi Lite**.

The Pi-Lite is a serial device and should show up as /dev/ttyAMA0. To start playing with our display, we use the Minicom utility to send messages to it.

If you don't already have minicom installed, then run the following command:

```
pi@raspberrypi ~ $ sudo apt-get install minicom
```

Launch Minicom with the following:

```
pi@raspberrypi ~ $ minicom -b 9600 -o -D /dev/ttyAMA0
```

Once in the Minicom terminal, we can enter command mode by typing $$$ followed by *Enter*. You should then see the response OK. We then need to send our command within a few seconds. Command mode is used to set things like the scroll speed, or switching on and off individual pixels. The full list of commands can be found at: http://openmicros.org /index.php/articles/94-ciseco-product-documentation/raspberry-pi/280-b0 40-pi-lite-beginners-guide#examples.

If you just start typing into the terminal window, you'll see whatever you type scroll across the Pi-Lite display. This is how we're going so show our secret messages—by writing to the serial port.

# Encoding our messages

We want to make our message encoder flexible enough that we can change it to suit the secret language we use to communicate with our fellow agents. In this example, we are going to use Morse Code notation as our communication method.

Morse Code, created by Samuel Morse, was designed to transmit a string of letters across telegraph wires to form words and sentences, with frequently used letters having short codes and less frequently used letters having longer codes. Each letter's code is a sequence of dots and dashes, which could be heard audibly and decoded at the other end.

In our project, we're going to represent these dots and dashes visually in order to transmit our message.

# Writing the encoder script

First we need to write a script that will take our sentence or string of letters and convert them to an encoded output. The script below will allow you to change the code represented by each letter to something different if you decide to use a different encryption method.

In nano, enter the following Bash script and save it as text-encoder.sh:

```
#!/bin/bash
#read the input parameter
sText=$1

#replace all spaces with an underscore
sText=$(echo ${sText//' '/_})

#get the string length
nLen=$(echo ${#sText})

#add each character to an array
aText=()
for i in $(seq 0 $(($nLen - 1)))
do
    aText+=(${sText:$i:1})
done

#build the character encoder
#spaces are encoded as ~
declare -A asEncode
asEncode=([_]='~'          \
        [A]='.-'          \
        [B]='-...'        \
        [C]='-.-.'        \
        [D]='-..'         \
        [E]='.'           \
        [F]='..-.'        \
        [G]='--.'         \
        [H]='....'        \
        [I]='..'          \
        [J]='.---'        \
        [K]='-.-'         \
        [L]='.-..'        \
        [M]='--'          \
        [N]='-.'          \
```

```
[O]='---'        \
[P]='.--.'       \
[Q]='--.-'       \
[R]='.-.'        \
[S]='...'        \
[T]='-'          \
[U]='..-'        \
[V]='...-'       \
[W]='.--'        \
[X]='-..-'       \
[Y]='-.--'       \
[Z]='--..'       \
[a]='.-'         \
[b]='-...'       \
[c]='-.-.'       \
[d]='-..'        \
[e]='.'          \
[f]='..-.'       \
[g]='--.'        \
[h]='....'       \
[i]='..'         \
[j]='.---'       \
[k]='-.-'        \
[l]='.-..'       \
[m]='--'         \
[n]='-.'         \
[o]='---'        \
[p]='.--.'       \
[q]='--.-'       \
[r]='.-.'        \
[s]='...'        \
[t]='-'          \
[u]='..-'        \
[v]='...-'       \
[w]='.--'        \
[x]='-..-'       \
[y]='-.--'       \
[z]='--..'       \
[0]='-----'      \
[1]='.----'      \
[2]='..---'      \
[3]='...--'      \
[4]='....-'      \
[5]='.....'      \
[6]='-....'      \
[7]='--...'      \
[8]='---..'      \
[9]='----.'      \
```

```
    [.]='.-.-.-' \
    [,]='--..--' \
    [:]='---...' \
    [?]='..--..' \
    [-]='-....-' \
    [/]='-..-.' \
    [=]='-...-' \
    ["'"]='.----.')

#encode the text for outputing
sOutput=""
for i in $(seq 0 $((`echo ${#aText[@]}`-1)))
do
    sOutput=$(echo $sOutput ${asEncode[`echo ${aText[$i]}`]})
done
#restore spaces and output encoded text
echo $sOutput | tr '~' ' '
```

text-encoder.sh

Next we need to give the script execute permissions:

```
pi@raspberrypi ~ $ chmod +x text-encoder.sh
```

We can test our script by giving it some text and display the encoded output:

```
pi@raspberrypi ~ $ ./text-encoder.sh "Hello"
```

Which should give the following Morse Code response:

```
.... . .-.. .-.. ---
```

Here's what it looks like in the terminal window:

If you want to explore more encryption techniques, which can be used to replace the letters in the above script, then visit Tyler Akins' Cypher Tools site at `http://rumkin.com/tools/cipher`, which is a great resource for many types of encoding.

# Sending our text to the display

Now that we can generate our secret messages, we need to be able to send them to the Pi-Lite display:

First set up the serial port for the right data rate supported by the display:

```
pi@raspberrypi ~ $ sudo stty -F /dev/ttyAMA0 9600
```

Now send some encoded text to the display via the serial port:

```
pi@raspberrypi ~ $ ./text-encoder.sh "The lagoon is green today" >
/dev/ttyAMA0
```

Obviously, this will just display the message once, but ideally, we need to just run it continuously, unattended. So, let's write a simple script that will loop endlessly, ready for when our fellow agents turn up to pick up the message:

```
#!/bin/bash

sEnc=$(./text-encoder.sh "The breeze is blowing east")
echo $sEnc
sudo stty -F /dev/ttyAMA0 9600
while true; do
  echo -e -n "#START# " >/dev/ttyAMA0
  echo -e -n $sEnc > /dev/ttyAMA0
  echo -e -n "#END# " > /dev/ttyAMA0
  sleep 30
done
```

Pi-Lite display showing our Morse Code message

 As an alternative to the Pi-Lite device, you could also try Pimoroni's smaller Scroll pHAT device, which also fits nicely on a Pi Zero. You need to talk to it through the I2C interface, so changes to the previous code examples will be required (`https://shop.pimoroni.com/products/scroll-phat`).

# Better security with a true random number generator

We looked at encryption in the section *Keeping your conversations secret with encryption* in `Chapter 4`, *Wi-Fi Pranks – Exploring Your Network;* however, the key to secure cryptography is **entropy**—a high-quality source of randomness.

Most random numbers used in computer programs are **pseudo-random**, which means they are generated in a predictable manner using mathematics. In many circumstances this is fine, but for strong cryptography, this is may not be suitable, even with a good random seed, so we need a **True Random Number Generator (TRNG)**.

Usually, this requires expensive hardware, or weird physical events such as noise analysis to generate random number using a high level of entropy. But did you know that your Raspberry Pi—including the Pi Zero—also contains a hardware-based TRNG?

# Kernel entropy pool

In the Linux environment, the root of all randomness is something called the **kernel entropy pool**. This is a 4,096-bit secret number stored in the kernel's memory. The kernel needs to be able to fill that memory from a source with 4,096 bits of entropy—and the challenge is finding all of the randomness for this.

When random numbers are generated from the pool, the pool's entropy is reduced, and as the pool's entropy reduces as random numbers are handed out, the pool must be replenished. One of the uses for our TRNG is to replenish a server's entropy pool, or indeed the Pi's own pool, with a good source.

# Setting up our hardware RNG

Whilst we can use any model of Pi for this, the Pi Zero makes it more interesting because we can make a pocket-sized low-cost TRNG that we can take anywhere out in the field and connect to a PC or server, which needs high-quality randomness.

## Enabling the hardware RNG in Raspbian Wheezy

The Pi's built-in random number generator is disabled by default, so we have to enable it in the modules file. Open the file with nano, as follows:

```
pi@raspberrypi ~ $ sudo nano /etc/modules
```

At the end of the file, add the following line:

```
bcm2708-rng
```

We'll now enable the module immediately with having to reboot with:

```
pi@raspberrypi ~ $ sudo modprobe bcm2708-rng
```

## Enabling the hardware RNG in Raspbian Jessie

The Pi's built-in random number generator is disabled by default, so we have to enable it using a device tree parameter in the config.txt file. Open the file with nano, as follows:

```
pi@raspberrypi ~ $ sudo nano /boot/config.txt
```

At the end of the file, add the following line:

```
dtparam=random=on
```

Then reboot your Pi.

## Testing the hardware RNG

We can test that the hardware RNG (HWRNG) module is enabled properly by using the following command.

```
pi@raspberrypi ~ $ sudo dd if=/dev/hwrng count=1 iflag=fullblock
```

You should then see random data being displayed on the console, followed by some statistics, such as:

```
1+0 records in
1+0 records out
512 bytes (512 B) copied, 0.00471074 s, 109 kB/s
```

We now have a hardware-based true random number generator built into our Pi.

## Using the HWRNG for our entropy pool

Now that we have a HWRNG, we can use this to replenish the entropy pool on our Pi with a much higher grade of randomness.

So that we can use the random data generated, we need to install the rng-tools package:

```
pi@raspberrypi ~ $ sudo apt-get install rng-tools
```

Use the following to enable it to start on reboot:

```
pi@raspberrypi ~ $ sudo systemctl enable rng-tools
```

That's it! The entropy on your Pi is now of a much higher quality. You can check the level of entropy in the pool from time to time, and obtain some stats using the following commands.

To see the current level of entropy:

```
pi@raspberrypi ~ $ cat /proc/sys/kernel/random/entropy_avail
```

To see the maximum pool size:

```
pi@raspberrypi ~ $ cat /proc/sys/kernel/random/poolsize
```

To get some stats:

```
pi@raspberrypi ~ $ sudo systemctl -l status rng-tools
```

Status output from the hardware random number generator

# Exporting the HWRNG data to another Linux server

We can transfer the random number data generated by our system to another server by linking our Pi to the other server using a serial connection. If you want to use the Pi Zero as your ultra-low-cost source of random data, then you will need to add a header to the GPIO area on the board, or solder wires directly to the UART pins on the board.

At the other end, we need a small device that will plug into a USB port, and give us a 3.3V TTL serial port to connect to (sometimes referred to FTDI connectors after the chip manufacture that mainly features on these boards). These can be picked up online for just a few dollars. Note that it must be a device that is 3.3V TTL and *not* 5V TTL:

USB to TTL serial/UART converter

## Connecting the UART pins

Following are the steps to connect the UART pins:

1. Connect the Pi's RX pin (pin 10 of the GPIO connector) to the TX pin of the USB-to-Serial module.
2. Connect the Pi's TX pin (pin 8 of the GPIO connector) to the RX pin of the USB-to-Serial module.
3. Connect GND/0V pin on the Pi (pin 6) to the GND pin on the USB-to-Serial module.

Refer to the wiring diagram below and to the GPIO pin-out diagram earlier in this chapter if you need more clarity:

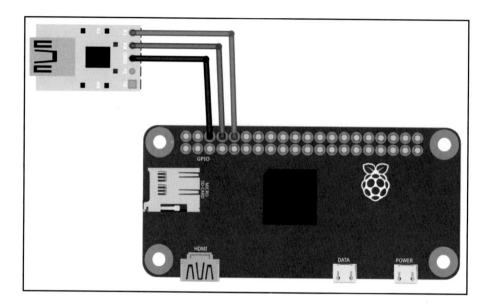

Typical wiring for the USB-to-Serial converter module Learn to solder!

 If you've never soldered before and want a good guide, then head over to Sparkfun's tutorial at `https://learn.sparkfun.com/tutorials/how-to-solder---through-hole-soldering`.

If you haven't already done so, then you'll need to enable the serial port on the Pi as we did earlier in this chapter, in the section *Displaying secret codes and messages*.

# Transferring entropy to the serial port

Now that we have our serial port wired up, we can configure the port, then continuously write out the hardware random number data to the port with the following commands:

Configure the serial port:

```
pi@raspberrypi ~ $ sudo stty -F /dev/ttyAMA0 -echo raw 115200
```

Write the data continuously to the port using the dd command:

```
pi@raspberrypi ~ $ dd if=/dev/hwrng of=/dev/ttyAMA0 &
```

You can add these commands into your /etc/rc.local file if you want them to always run at boot time.

# Receiving entropy on the server

With the USB-to-Serial converter connected to your server, it should present you with a device such as /dev/ttyUSB0 or /dev/ttyACM0 — this is the serial device that will receive the entropy data. You can check this with the following:

```
$ ls /dev/tty*
```

On the server, configure the serial port (assuming it's /dev/ttyUSB0):

```
$ stty -F /dev/ttyUSB0 -echo raw 115200
```

We can now copy data in from the serial port using the following:

```
$ sudo dd if=/dev/ttyUSB0 count=1 iflag=fullblock
```

All being well, you should see random data, as you did when you ran this command locally on the Pi. If not, then check your wiring between the Pi and server on the serial connection.

Now we need to install the rng-tools package on the server:

```
$ sudo apt-get install rng-tools
```

We can now add the following lines to our /etc/rc.local file on the server, which, after it's been rebooted, will cause the rngd service to automatically replenish the entropy pool with data from our Pi when it falls below 3584:

```
stty -F /dev/ttyUSB0 -echo raw 115200 rngd -b -r /dev/ttyUSB0 -W 3584 &
```

**USB-powered Pi Zero**: The Pi Zero consumes very little power, so if you want your Pi Zero permanently connected to the server's USB port, you may be able to power it from the USB's supply. If your USB-to-Serial module provides a +5V output, then you can back-power the Pi Zero by connecting the +5V of the USB module to Pin 2 (+5V) of the GPIO connector. Take extra care when doing this, however, to prevent damaging your little Pi!

# Summary

We kicked off our final chapter with a guide to the Raspberry Pi's GPIO connector and how to safely connect peripherals to it. We followed that up by connecting a laser sensor module to our Pi to create a rather cool laser trip wire that could alert you when the laser beam is broken.

Following along the same theme, we also connected a passive infrared motion detector to our Raspberry Pi, which observed an area of space and detected when our space had been infiltrated.

Because we may not always have an Internet connection to our smartphone when out in the field, we extended our methods of being remotely alerted to include SMS, using a few simple lines of script which connected to the API of an SMS gateway service.

Moving away from protecting our space to protecting our digital assets, we looked at a way for our Pi to know when we're in the vicinity, with a script that scanned for the Wi-Fi address of our personal phone, which if found, could then do something, such as unlocking our encrypted data vault—or indeed, anything else we'd like to control with our proximity.

So that we can send secret messages to our fellow agents, with the potential to update the message from anywhere if we have remote access to our Pi, we devised a script that would encode a string of text using a method of our choosing (in this case Morse Code), and show that on a LED display board.

For the final topic of this final chapter, we looked at something a little bit more esoteric, turning a Raspberry Pi Zero into a portable true hardware random number generator that could be plugged into another device in order to give it high levels of entropy to increase the effectiveness of cryptography and other systems that rely on randomness.

# Graduation

Our secret agent training has come to an end, but surely it is only the beginning of your mischievous adventures. At this point, you probably have plenty of crazy ideas for pranks and projects of your own. Rest assured, they can all be accomplished with the right tools and an inquisitive spirit, in most cases, right from the command line.

Now, take the techniques you've learned and build upon them, teach your fellow pranksters what you know along the way, then show the world what you've come up with on the Raspberry Pi forums!

# Index

network
  mapping out, with Nmap 157, 159, 160
  protecting, against Ettercap 170, 171, 172
  visitors, knocking off 169
night vision 139
Nmap
  used, for mapping network 157, 158, 159, 160
NMEA standard 224
NoIR camera module 139
NOOBS 33
nslookup utility 178

# O

Off-the-Record Messaging (OTR)
  about 197
  reference 197
OGG file
  used, for recording audio 51, 52
one-line sampler command 103

# P

packet dump
  analyzing, with Wireshark 172
Parallax (PIR) module
  connecting, to Raspberry Pi 269
  detection script, implementing 270, 271
passive infrared (PIR) detector 268
pastebin 236
pcap 172
PCMA 96
PCMU 96
phone
  using, as access control device 273
Pi Hut
  reference 17
Pi-Lite display
  text, displaying to 284
Pi-Lite
  connecting, to GPIO connector 280
PiFm
  about 256
  installing 257
Pimoroni
  reference 17
playback scare

scheduling 142, 144
Pluggable Authentication Module (PAM) 253
point-to-point networking
  setting up 204
port forwarding rule
  adding 180, 181
  adding, via UPnP 181, 182
port forwarding
  about 179, 180
  security 183, 184
  verifying 182
port tunneling
  in Linux 189
  in MacOS X 189
  in Windows 185, 186
Probe Requests 273
Profanity package
  downloading 191
  installing 191
Profanity
  about 190
  basics 193
  connecting, to Google chat 192
  connecting, to XMPP servers 193
Pscp packages
  reference 61
pseudo-random 285
PulseAudio
  installing 68
PuTTY
  about 28
  reference 28

# R

radio jammer 256
Raspberry Pi 3
  about 8, 15
  board layout 18
  connectors 18
Raspberry Pi camera module
  about 106
  connecting 107
  setting up 109, 110, 112, 113
Raspberry Pi Foundation
  reference 16

# S